FROM M.DIV. TO REV.

FROM M.DIV. TO REV.

Making an Effective Transition from Seminary into Pastoral Ministry

by J.E. Eubanks, Jr.

www.doulosresources.org

From M.Div. to Rev.: Making an Effective Transition from Seminary into Pastoral Ministry

Published by:

Doulos Resources, 195 Mack Edwards Drive, Oakland, TN 38060; PHONE: (901) 451-0356; WEBSITE: www.doulosresources.org.

☺ Copyright 2011 by J. E. Eubanks, Jr. Some rights reserved. This work is licensed under the Creative Commons Attribution-NonCommercial-NoDerivs License. To view a copy of this license, (a) visit www.creativecommons.org; or, (b) send a letter to Creative Commons, 171 2nd Street, Suite 300, San Francisco, California, 94105, USA.

Please address all questions about rights and reproduction to Doulos Resources, 195 Mack Edwards Drive, Oakland, TN 38060; PHONE: (901) 451-0356; E-MAIL: info@doulosresources.org.

Scripture taken from the Holy Bible, NEW INTERNATIONAL VERSION®. Copyright © 1973, 1978, 1984 International Bible Society. All rights reserved throughout the world. Used by permission of International Bible Society.

NEW INTERNATIONAL VERSION® and NIV® are registered trademarks of International Bible Society. Use of either trademark for the offering of goods or services requires the prior written consent of International Bible Society.

Published 2011

Printed in the United States of America by Ingram/Lightning Source

ISBN 978-0-9828715-0-8

Library of Congress Control Number: 2010935150

Cover image by Vasko Miokovic; used with permission. For more information, visit www.thephoto.ca or www.istockphoto.com.

Cover design by Doulos Resources, 2011.

To Marcie

You have walked through so much of this with me, from the first uneasy steps of candidacy through the several calls to ministry, and through the beginning of a project that gave way to many hours of writing to become this book. May it be, at very least, a testimony to your faithful love, care, and companionship.

I love you with all of my heart.

Table of Contents

Introductory Thoughts

Introduction 3
Backgrounds— How This Book Came To Be 5

Part 1: Starting Points

Before Candidacy 13
A Spiritual Season 25
Attitude Adjustments 39
Factors For Effective Placement 49
If You Build It, They Will Come 63

Part 2: From Knowing To Doing

On Early Birds And Worms 77
Paperwork Shuffle 95
Phone Tag 117
No Vacation 125
Who? Where? Why? 135

Part 3: Transition Steps

Beyond Minimum Wage 151
A Sea Of Cardboard 173
Not Done Yet 181
Benediction 193

Appendices / Back Matter

Appendix A: Recommended Reading 195
Appendix B: Questions & Answers 199
Appendix C: Survey Instrument 209
Appendix D: Summary Of Survey Results 215
Acknowledgements 219
About The Author 221
About Doulos Resources 223

INTRODUCTORY THOUGHTS

Introduction

"They didn't teach me about that in seminary!"

Perhaps you've heard such a comment from recent graduates from your school. I certainly did while I was in seminary. Often it followed a former classmate's story of being blind-sided by this struggle or that problem. Sometimes it was even said about mundane, everyday concerns, like worship leadership, visitation, or the transition from seminary into ministry. Usually the comment was made half-jokingly, but there was a hint of resentment, nevertheless.

Of course, seminaries cannot teach us everything we will need to know for ministry. If they were even to attempt to do so, the degree would require so many credits that no one would enroll! The professors know this, and work hard to reduce the problem as much as possible. The wise seminarian will be aware of this, as well, and will take measures to prevent it from catching up to him more than it has to.

While entire books could be filled with details about what they *aren't* teaching you in seminary, I want to focus on one particular area that may be a weakness in the curriculum: the process of ministry candidacy, placement, and transition. I was fortunate; there was an elective class on that subject at my seminary (with surprisingly low enrollment). You may not be so blessed, or you may not be able to take the class for one reason or another. (Or perhaps you are reading this book as a part of that class!)

For whatever reason you are reading this book, I congratulate you: you have already demonstrated that you will likely fair better than many of your classmates in the placement process. By simply taking the step of picking up a book on this subject, you have categorized yourself as a seminarian who cares about his own placement enough to put some effort into it; believe it or not, some of your fellow students do not possess the same level of concern.

My interest in seeing seminarians and others well-placed in ministry began with my own placement— actually, my second placement—**before** I was even in seminary. I didn't really know what I was doing, but I found myself working with an elaborate system of exchanging information and building relationships, some of which would end abruptly while others would lead to deeper interest. While at the time I felt I had navigated the waters successfully, time would teach me that I had not been careful enough in some ways.

After enrolling in seminary, my interest increased when I took the class on the process of candidacy and transition into ministry. Some of my friends had already graduated, and while some were placed well, others struggled with their placement. I had also heard some shocking statistics about how few in ministry make it past the five-year mark, and I didn't want to be another casualty in just a few years.[1] It occurred to me as I worked through the assignments for that class that what I was doing

---

[1] I'll touch on some of these statistics in future chapters.

would largely determine whether I would thrive or struggle upon leaving seminary. As you can imagine, my level of investment skyrocketed!

The following summer, that interest turned to passion when, working with my seminary and through an independent study course, I undertook a research project that included a survey of all Master of Divinity graduates from my seminary over the previous six years— more than 300 graduates. I wanted to learn about how they went through the candidacy and placement process, and figure out what worked and what didn't. Most importantly, I wanted to know what truly effective placement looked like, and what factors led to effective placement. (I'll describe my research in detail in the next chapter.)

Since then, I've learned a lot about candidacy, placement, and transition. I've learned it through research and studying research; through books and articles on transition; and through interviews with others, some following up on my research. I've also made another transition myself, this time completing the "from M.Div. to Rev." cycle: I accepted a call to full-time, ordained pastoral ministry in 2007. You can be sure that I learned a lot about candidacy and transition from that.

In fact, that is the main reason I would urge you to read this book. It isn't because it is well-researched, backed by good statistics, or ground-breaking in its ideas (though I hope and believe it is all of those things to some degree). It isn't because I have developed an elaborate set of guidelines and principles for cracking the code to effective pastoral placement (I myself am skeptical of such concepts). It is because, by God's grace and through the experiences He has given me, I have unearthed some helpful ideas that have been a guide to me, and to many others, who have employed them in our candidacy and transition processes. We set before us the aim, not merely of placement, nor even simply of timely placement, but of effective placement. In God's gracious provision, He has provided that for me and others. What you will find on the following pages is a collection of ideas that, also by His grace, will help you along the way to your effective placement, as well.

Backgrounds—
How This Book Came to Be

It may be helpful to recount my own candidating history. Although, at the time of this writing, I am currently serving my first pastoral call after seminary, I have a fair amount of experience with candidacy and placement. To be specific, I've actually held five different paid ministry positions, and I went through some form of candidacy with four of those. (There was a fifth time when I went through candidacy but eventually returned to school.) If you will indulge me, I'll summarize my candidacy and placement experiences to establish some of the context for this book.

Beginnings in Ministry

While I was in college, I volunteered with Young Life; this was a great experience, and at times I was greatly encouraged at how God used that ministry, and me through it. A year into my ministry with Young Life, I got to know a student (Iain) whose father was/is a pastor. Over time, I got close with Iain and with his family, and his father (Richard) and I began to go hunting together.

One day we were making plans by phone for another duck hunt, and Richard mentioned that the man who was serving their small church as Youth Minister was leaving, and if I knew anyone who might be interested in a part-time youth ministry position, he would appreciate a recommendation. As we talked, Richard asked me: would I be interested in that position? I was astounded, and flattered; I had longed for such a position for what seemed like several years. I said I would pray about it, and we agreed to meet for lunch the following week to discuss it.

Lunch went well; Richard gave me a brief history of the church, another brief history of the youth ministry, and told me exactly what he wanted. Was I interested? Yes— but wasn't there more to it than that? Didn't I need to be interviewed by someone— the elders, the parents, the youth ministry committee? There was no youth ministry committee; Richard was as representative of the parents as anyone, as he had two kids in the group (and one about to enter it); and the elders would likely agree with Richard's decision, but I would meet with them the following Sunday.

Sunday came, and I met the elders along with Richard in his study at the church property. They heard my testimony, my account of my sense of calling to the ministry, and asked about my experience (which was all volunteer experience at that point). I left the room, and a few minutes later they came out and welcomed me to the staff! I later found out that they were in agreement almost as soon as I had left the room, and the remaining minutes were passed in prayer.

So there I was, a 22-year-old college student with no substantial church ministry experience[2] and no training at all, and I was about to start a youth ministry— from scratch, as far as I knew. The candidacy process, in this case, was the easiest part of the whole experience. In one form or another, I remained on that staff for four years— way beyond the average for a typical Youth Minister.

My Introduction to Real Ministry Candidacy

In my fourth year there, shortly after Marcie and I were married, I had a strange sense of restlessness: I had this feeling that God was stirring my heart up to prepare me for a change— and I was confident that this change would take me away from my (then) current ministry to something else. Uncertain of what to do about it, I decided I would put my name and resume[3] out there and see if God would make it clearer through the candidacy process where I was supposed to go.

As I look back now, I have to say that this was when I was truly introduced to the candidacy process. Everything before then was of no significance in terms of candidating experience.

My options were, admittedly, limited. I was fairly young— 25 at the time— without even a college degree, let alone a seminary degree. My experience was only in youth ministry. This was fine, however, because I planned to remain in youth ministry. I completed my denomination's Youth Ministry Data Form[4] and submitted it to the denominational Christian Education office, which handles that sort of thing. I also called a friend of mine who had gone to work for the a sister denomination as their coordinator of Christian Education and Youth Ministry. Both offices were more than happy to circulate my information.

We began to hear from a few churches here and there, mostly basic inquiries for more information— sometimes with an list of questions, sometimes with a form to fill out, sometimes just asking for some occasion to speak by phone. The first church we heard from was in Florida. After an hour-long phone interview, they invited us to visit for a weekend. We went, and found that these visits were non-stop 48-hour interviews. We were picked up (late in the evening) from the airport by the senior pastor, who asked us questions for the entire 45-minute drive to where we were staying. We were welcomed by our hosts with another 15 or 20 minutes of introductions and questions before being allowed to get to bed. Breakfast the next morning was the same, with questions left and right, before the elder drove us to the church for an official interview with the search committee (that lasted nearly two hours). That was followed by lunch, after which the associate pastor and his wife took us to a Sunday School class picnic at the lake, which lasted most of the afternoon. After supper with

---

2   I had volunteered as a leader at the church I grew up in for about a year and a half; I had also done a summer internship at that church. That, plus my Young Life years, were the sum total of my ministry experience at that point.

3   A quick word about wording here: technically, the "proper" rendering of the word is "résumé" -- but this is sometimes seen as obtuse over-correctness. "Resumé" isn't correct in either way (accented or not). Throughout the rest of the book, I'll use the most common form, "resume" (without the accents).

4   In my denomination, the Youth Ministry Data Form is a specialized version of the denominational Ministry Data Form, which I will discuss in detail in a later chapter. This form is what the denominational offices use to help with placement.

the associate pastor, we got back to the elder's house in time to get to bed at a reasonable hour. I had been asked to teach Sunday School the next morning, followed by attending worship, then lunch with two parents who drove us around and gave a tour of the town for the rest of the afternoon. We had just enough time to pack before returning to the church for the evening youth group meeting, of which we were just observers. Then off to the airport.

We heard from that church late the next week... it wasn't going to work out. More packets mailed out, more phone calls, phone interviews, e-mails, etc. produced some interest, little clarity, and a few serious queries for further information. I figured out that I knew what I wanted to do— what I felt called to do— more than most of the other guys out there; at least, I articulated it more completely. The result was that the documents I presented simultaneously drew more interested and did a lot of the "weeding" for me— I got a fair amount of response simply because I had a lot to say, but most of the churches I sent information to were able to determine I wasn't for them strictly based on what I sent.

Pressing On...

After the trip to Florida, my next trip was a whirlwind out to Texas. I went by myself, because they indicated this was just an exploring visit, not so much an advanced interview (they would bring me back for that, if need be). I left my house around 5am on a Tuesday, flew to Texas, went full-throttle for about 40 hours, and flew back the next evening (touchdown right at midnight). This trip, in addition to being the single-most exhausting candidacy experience I've ever had, was a big lesson for me in humility: it seemed like everything I said was followed by the insertion of my foot into my mouth. In retrospect, I am not surprised in the least that I never heard from them again.

But for a few more phone interviews (which developed into nothing), the opportunities dried up as we moved into the fall. This was providential, however, as it forced us into the best decision we could have made: focus on finishing my undergraduate degree. I had been sputtering along, at this point barely into my "Junior year," and at that pace I would not have finished until late 2003 (12 years after beginning)! Instead of changing ministries, the best transition to make was to change focus and return to school full-time. I quit work altogether, took 53 credit-hours in one calendar year, and graduated from the University of South Carolina in December 1999.

Of course, while I was finishing school we began to consider what opportunities awaited us after my graduation. This actually began as early as April of '99, because some possibilities landed in our laps. One of the churches, being in a fairly nearby city, brought me up for a Sunday morning worship time, followed by lunch and then an extensive interview. It didn't work out, but it got the ball rolling on our candidacy process.

I spotted another church's ad in the back of a Christian magazine. It turned out that I knew the pastor of this one, although briefly. We exchanged philosophies of ministry, and both he and I were astonished at how similar they were. For a while, it looked like this was going to be a lock— in April, 8 months before I was available— but it fell through near the end, because of some concerns on the part of their Session that related to past staffing issues.

After that, we didn't really continue the search until mid-summer, but at that point it took off. Around July, we suddenly had three churches we were talking to at once, and two scheduled trips with the invitation for a third. We had a trip to Virginia scheduled for one weekend, a trip to Michigan scheduled for two weeks later, and tentative plans to travel to another town in Virginia after the Michigan trip.

Honestly, as we were driving to the first interview, we were more inclined toward the Michigan church than any other. However, once we got to Virginia, we began to get more interested in what was happening there, so that on the way home we were asking, "Are we missing something here? It seems too good..."

We took the job in Virginia only days before our plane was to leave for Michigan; the folks in Michigan wanted it that way, and we were thankful they were willing to wait for the Lord as we sought His will. We quickly called things off with the third church as well.

We only stayed in Virginia for 18 months; in retrospect, God used that time greatly to prepare us for future ministry, but some of the difficulties faced there also represent the beginning of an understanding of how vital effective placement truly was and is. From Virginia we moved to St. Louis to begin seminary. We toyed with the idea of candidating again as we were preparing to leave Virginia, but decided that God was clearly taking us to seminary, so nothing really developed from that.

R-E-S-P-E-C-T

As I moved through seminary, I began to rethink my sense of calling— that is, what I believed it meant for me to be called to what I was. I no longer felt I was cut out for a life-long ministry to students as a Youth Minister; God seemed to be moving me in a different direction. I'll go into greater detail about this in a later chapter, but for now it will be enough to say that God was leading me into pastoral ministry as a solo pastor. When I began exploring candidacy toward the end of my seminary career, I found that candidacy was quite different in this domain of pastoral ministry.

For example, I received a number of letters during my candidacy, explaining the circumstances surrounding the search at a given church. These letters represent a stark contrast to previous experiences. In each, there was a tone of respect and an attitude of consideration that I had not often seen before in the candidacy process. It was prominent enough to cause both Marcie and me to comment on the difference between a search for an ordained— or ordainable— pastor (perhaps especially a solo pastor) and a search for a non-ordained youth minister.

In the past, the "norm" had been the utter antithesis of this. We might hear from a church we were candidating with, or we might not— and this was not relative to their expressed interest in us. We had a church call us for a second phone interview after not hearing from them for several months. One church owed us money for plane tickets to come to the interview, and they conveniently "forgot" that they had not paid us— right around the same time that they decided they weren't going to hire me; it took a phone call from me to finally get a check in the mail. And right after an in-person interview, a pastor at one church actually looked me in the eye and told me he would call me in a few days; I never heard from him again.

But this round proved to be quite different. Whether it is the position I was applying for (solo pastor vs. youth minister), the status of my qualifications (finishing an

Backgrounds— How This Book Came To Be

M.Div. and ordainable vs. having only a B.A. and not ordainable), or life-stage I was in (33 at graduation, married with chidren vs. being in my 20s and recently married), something changed— and I don't think it was simply the fact that I was working with different churches.

Starting The Research

The first signs of this change were one part of many factors that led me to begin the research I did in 2004. I had seen a number of my classmates graduate with greater or lesser degrees of confidence about the call they had accepted. I had enough experience in the candidacy process to know that it was difficult— but I didn't understand what kept one classmate from finding placement while another saw quick success. And it seemed like almost everyone was wondering how to do this effectively.

Beyond that, I was beginning to hear reports of statistics that showed many pastors leaving the ministry after just a few years, and of others placing for only a year or two before moving on to another ministry, only to move again shortly thereafter. I began to ask questions about the candidacy and placement process:

- Why were so many students having difficulty finding placement?
- What caused others to find placement so easily?
- What was behind the difficulties that placed pastors seemed to be experiencing?
- Could there be a connection between the candidacy and placement process and a stable, effective ministry?

I didn't have anyone in particular to ask these questions of; I was just asking them to myself. Then I thought: what if I could ask those who had made a transition recently? Could that reveal some answers? I decided I would try to do a survey of recent seminary graduates, asking them some of the questions I was asking myself.

To begin, I thought about what the ideal was. It seemed to me that the goal of candidacy and placement was to find a good ministry call, with the work going into both candidacy and placement being as effective as possible. I determined what I believed an "effective placement" would look like, and I began to share this model with friends, the faculty at my seminary, and with pastors I knew. Many had helpful input, and before long I had what appeared to be a good model.[5]

Along the way I formed some hypotheses about what it would take to achieve such an effective placement— I had some ideas, based on my own experiences and those of my friends and classmates, of how someone could pursue an effective placement intentionally. So I wrote a four-page survey that, I hoped, would test my hypotheses and reveal where I was right. I also hoped it would fill in the gaps, suggesting ways to achieve effective placement that I had missed.[6]

My hypotheses and survey were based on a few presuppositions: I was assuming that there was a spiritual dimension to the transition process, and that seminarians were taking that part seriously. In other words, I was assuming that they were prayerful about their own candidacy and placement, and that they (and the churches and ministries they were candidating with) were relying on the Holy Spirit to guide and

---

[5] I describe this model in Chapter Four: Factors for Effective Placement.

[6] A copy of the survey instrument, as well as a brief tabulation of the results, can be found in the Appendices.

drive the process.[7] I also assumed that they had a valid and tested call to ministry, and that they and others had confirmed that the ministry was the direction that the Lord was leading them. And I assumed that they were concerned about their own placement— that they were putting at least some effort into finding out what the Lord had next for them. These assumptions led to my focus on the "nuts and bolts" of the process: what did they do, when did they do it, how did they do it, and with whom did they do it.

Thanks to the help of many, I eventually surveyed over 600 seminary graduates, and I had a response rate of over 60%: almost 400 graduates responded to my survey. There were those who went into church and parachurch ministries; campus ministers, church planters, and pastors; solo pastors, senior pastors, associate/assistant pastors, and youth workers. In short, my survey returned a solid sample of a broad range of ministry directions, all coming straight out of seminary.

Many of my hypotheses were confirmed and advanced to greater levels. I also learned a number of things I never could have guessed. From my research, I developed the principles found in this book: something of a "blueprint" for effective placement. These principles opened the door for me to participate in preparing students at my seminary to transition well— and many of these students have reported that the principles I developed were keys to their own effective placement. Today, I regularly have seminary students and ordained pastors who contact me and seek my assistance in navigating the transition process, and these principles continue to bear much fruit.

I benefited from them, too. After completing my research, I put my own principles to work and saw the Lord bless my efforts. As you'll see throughout the rest of the book, God used each of the principles to effect the steps that led me to the church that I now serve, and it has all of the markers of an effective placement for me.

My goal for every student to be well-placed after seminary, ministering with confidence in an effective placement where they can grow, thrive, and serve others as they grow. I hope this book will serve in some small way to accomplish that goal.

---

[7] I later realized that this particular presupposition was inaccurate; to compensate for it, I have included a chapter in this book entitled "A Spiritual Season" in which I offer some advice and guidance on how to better approach the process with spiritual discipline.

PART 1: STARTING POINTS

Before Candidacy

If you're approaching your final year of seminary, what should you be doing to prepare for the time between now and graduation? What can you do now, more than a year from graduation, to ensure that the stage is set for an effective candidacy?

Six things:
- Grasp your calling
- Get the experience
- Gather the tools
- Know the hurdles
- Keep it humble
- Tag your mentors.

Grasp Your Calling

The starting point is a sense of calling. Has God called you— and is He calling you— to serve Him in vocational pastoral ministry?

Not everyone is called to be a pastor. Not everyone is called to serve in vocational ministry. Not even every student enrolled in seminary is. I would wager that you know at least a few classmates who are wrestling with exactly this. A number of my classmates did.

One fellow student had an experience that I've since learned is, unfortunately, far too common. My classmate (I'll call him "Steve" since there were about 10 Steves in my Beginning Greek class— even though this guy wasn't one of them!) had become a Christian late in high school, and had become active in a campus ministry while in college. The leaders of Steve's college ministry had done Steve a great disservice: through their words, actions, and examples, they had given Steve the distinct impression that real Christians— those who were serious about their faith— went into full-time vocational ministry. In fact, there was a hierarchy; serious Christians went into a vocational ministry like campus work or youth ministry; as they matured, they were expected to aspire to be an ordained pastor— and eventually a senior pastor (and of course, the size of the church they served was a valid metric of how mature they were); and the really hard-core, sold-out Christians eventually became long-term overseas missionaries.

Steve came to seminary with this mindset fully ingrained into his head. Steve was a good student and a smart guy, so he didn't have difficulty with the academic side. Steve's passion for ministry training, on the other hand, waned quickly: most of the first-year seminarians had a zeal about preparing for ministry that Steve lacked. By the spring semester, Steve had begun to seriously doubt whether he was called to ministry.

Fortunately for Steve, the professors at our seminary didn't share the mindset that Steve's college ministry leaders had. They encouraged Steve to explore God's calling for him— at least, whether God was calling Steve into vocational ministry. They gave him permission to have a sense of calling to something else without feeling like an inferior Christian. One of our professors helped each Master of Divinity student work through a process he called, "Discovering Your Divine Design,"[1] wherein he counseled them in discerning how God had gifted and shaped them for service in ministry and in other ways. By the end of his first year, Steve had decided to leave seminary and work in the field of Accounting (where he had gotten his undergraduate training). Steve went on to serve as a ruling elder in his local church, and continues to thrive in his non-ministry vocation— exactly where God intended him to be, as far as any of us can tell!

Steve's problem was that he didn't have a true calling to ministry. This manifested in two ways: first, he had been given an improper "outward" calling to ministry, by leaders who told him he was a lesser Christian if he didn't pursue a career in full-time ministry. Secondly, he lacked an inward calling to ministry, and the incongruence of the two left him in a state of confusion.

Early in my adult life, a wise pastor helped me to discern my own ministry calling. He talked me through three distinct parts of a true calling to vocational ministry:

- The Inward Calling
- The Scriptural Calling
- The Outward Calling

The inward calling to ministry is, in most cases, the easiest one to discern: your heart cries out to minister to others. Maybe you find yourself counseling others through their spiritual struggles. Perhaps you willingly take up leadership or service tasks in your church that others aren't able or willing to handle. It could be that you surprised yourself the first time you had a teaching or speaking opportunity, and now you can't do it enough. Charles H. Spurgeon suggested that the way to discern whether you possessed an inward calling to ministry is to ask, "Can I honestly see myself doing anything else with my life?" If the answer is, "Yes" then go and pursue that career instead![2] There are dozens, if not hundreds, of ways to sense an inward calling to ministry. I know that many seminarians do sense an inward calling to ministry; I trust that, and consider that to be a foundational aspect of a calling to ministry— but it is vital to keep in mind that it is one aspect of a few.

Second to the inward calling is a "scriptural" call to ministry. We must ask ourselves, what does the Bible teach about those who are called to ministry? One way to proceed with considering whether you should continue to pursue a pastoral call might be to dig deeply into a study of the Word. Do a survey of those who served as leaders throughout the Scriptures, and consider whether there are normative factors in their calling. Dig into Paul's teachings on gifts, and look at what gifts he teaches are crucial for leadership and servanthood in the pastoral office. Do some serious exegetical work in the pastoral epistles and construct a biblical portrait of the elder/overseer. Study the writings of Peter, James, and John on those who lead the church.

---

1 The title of this process is actually borrowed from the sub-title of a book by Aubrey Malphurs: *Maximizing Your Effectiveness: How to Discover and Develop Your Divine Design* (Grand Rapids, MI: Baker Book House, 2003), which is a great work on the same subject. If you are questioning your sense of calling, you'll find this and other books on the topic (many of which are listed in an appendix) helpful guides in discerning where God may be leading you.

2 See C.H. Spurgeon, *Lectures to My Students* (London: Purnell and Sons, 1958), p. 26.

There is more study to do here than most will have time to complete between now and when the Lord places them! I would strongly suggest spending devotional time in this sort of study— so that regularly, in your time in the Word, you are more deeply affirmed from Scripture of your call to ministry. Incidentally, if God is **not** calling you into vocational ministry, such a study should reveal that— or at least suggest that— to your heart, as well.

Finally, is there an external call to ministry? You should ask, "Who first encouraged me to attend seminary, and why? How was I affirmed in my call to ministry by seminary professors and classmates? What do those whom I served, and those whom I served under, during field education and/or internships have to say about affirming my call to ministry? Am I involved in leadership in the church now— and if so, what do those whom I serve under say about a call into ministry?"

Between now and when you first were led to begin seminary study, there should be many people (dozens? more than that?) who have first-hand experience with your efforts in ministry, and who can speak honestly and informedly to whether they see God calling you into ministry. You must find these people, and ask them. You must invite them to be frank, even blunt with you. If they have any love for the church and for you, they will tell you whether they see God calling you into vocational ministry.

Get The Experience

The next thing you *MUST* do is get the experience.

By now, you've probably figured out that you're not going to learn everything you need to know for ministry in the classroom; there are plenty of essential ministry skills that can only be gained in the doing. You've heard this before— but what are these elusive skills and experiences?

- **Preaching experience.** Unless you think you'll be fine (you won't) with just a handful of sermons under your belt— the ones you preached in class— you should find some opportunities to preach before you start candidacy.
- **Teaching time.** In your first year of ministry, many of you will spend more time teaching than you will preaching; logging time here can be easier to come by, but shouldn't be taken for granted.
- **Familiarity with leadership.** It's highly possible that you have never been singularly in charge of an event, an ongoing activity, or a group of people. Yet these circumstances will occur all the time in ministry, and you need to be ready. Often even a short stint leading a team (planning a church-wide retreat, for example) can render valuable leadership experience.
- **Comfort with counseling.** Unless you specialize in this, you won't necessarily spend a lot of time in formal, structured counseling; nevertheless, you WILL see a lot of time where your people ask you sincere, important questions over the fellowship hall table, or stop you after the Bible study to tell you something intimate and vulnerable. I've actually been surprised by how much counseling I do in my pastoral ministry— especially pre-marital and couples counseling. Getting more comfortable with this now (under the supervision of others) will take some of the edge off when you're on your own.

- **An initiation to visitation.** It's almost impossible to overstate how much visitation most pastors do— and how foreign and awkward it can be until you've gotten the hang of it. Asking your pastor or a leader in the church (like an elder) if you may tag along while he visits will give you both exposure and a model.

There are others that will also be prominent: small group leadership, organizing and leading meetings, developing reports and budgets, leading in worship.

Where do you gain these vital experiences?

Look at what you already do. Maybe there are opportunities for some of these in the job(s) you already have; some, more than others, of course. Ask to be given more leadership, and you might find a number of necessary experiences coming your way.

Look (and ask) around your seminary. Most seminaries have plenty of leadership opportunities that current students could fulfill, and they know of a lot more. Helping to lead a community Bible study, giving prospective students a tour of campus or hosting them in a class, or leading worship for chapel may be readily available to you. Your seminary will certainly know of nearby preaching opportunities, too.

Talk to your pastor(s). Finding out what needs there are in your local congregation may be the easiest way to find all of these experiences. Teaching Sunday School is not the only path of service in the local church (though it is a good one!). Ask to sit in on meetings, come along to visit a home-bound member, or lead worship. Be willing to serve.

Find local ministries to serve. There are many church-affiliated and parachurch ministries that need volunteers, and some may also be hiring interns or part-time staff. Here you may get experience with administrative leadership that might elude you elsewhere— and you'll likely have ample opportunities for teaching and counseling, as well.

Serve as a student pastor. For the ultimate orientation to pastoral ministry, there may be a church nearby that needs a part-time or interim pastor. Here you'll see it all— but you will likely find them quite forgiving of your inexperience, as well.

Getting some exposure— even a little— to each of these areas of experience will serve you well in ministry, and it will give you a great way to process what you're learning in the classroom. If you aren't already, start with getting the experience.

Gather The Tools

The third thing you can do to prepare for an effective season of candidacy is to assess the tools you'll need for ministry.

You're already gathering some of these tools as a part of seminary education: the know-how to do many of the tasks that will be before you is key, of course, but even more important is having a catalog and library of information to go to when you need answers. The truth is, most seminary graduates don't so much remember a lot of what they were taught as they remember which class they learned a specific idea in, and we go to the materials from that class to get the particulars for the moment. Thus, taking good notes and becoming familiar with the textbooks for the classes you're taking is important— not just for now while you're earning the grades, but for later when you'll need to reference that material again.

Furthermore, there are other resources you'll encounter during your time in seminary. I once quipped to a classmate that, "Seminary is 50% bibliography," and that has held true for me. The book recommendations that your professors make in an aside in class, the titles written by guest lecturers and chapel speakers, the articles you reference for exegetical papers— all are invaluable to your future ministry. A member of my congregation visited my study at one point and commented about the number of books I have. This particular member works in a fairly mechanical service industry, so it only took him a moment to make a connection: "These are your tools, aren't they? You've got about as many tools in your toolbox as I do."

On a more mundane level, as yourself: what other things will I need for ministry? And by "things" I mean the physical, tangible tools that you will use as a pastor or minister. Depending on factors such as what demographic you anticipate ministering to, what role you will have, etc., you may identify any of the following (or other similar things):

- **Musical equipment.** Do you play guitar or another instrument as a part of your ministry? If so, do you have the equipment you would need if you were to begin work in that area of ministry today? Maybe you need to upgrade your instrument, or fortify your equipment list with amplification, microphones, a more capable mixing board or effects unit, etc.
- **Computer hardware and software.** Most of us use a computer to some degree, yet there are still a lot of guys who do seminary in a very low-tech way. (If this is true for you, it may be that you don't need a computer for ministry, either.) Do you have a computer that will serve your needs in ministry? Does it have the software installed that you will need to serve your people? Many classmates of mine assumed that their churches would buy them a new computer when they accepted a position— and some did, for sure, but others couldn't afford one right away. Consider whether you need to upgrade your hardware or software (or acquire new hardware and software) in preparation for your new ministry.
- **Clothing.** I think this is one of the most overlooked areas for seminarians. Take a look in your closet; now, picture your pastor or the kind of ministry worker you sense a call to become, and think of the circumstances that they might find themselves in. Could you dress for all of those occasions with what you already have? Could you lead worship on Sunday morning, or teach a Wednesday evening study, or attend a Session meeting in the context you'll minister? Would you be appropriately dressed for the funerals you will attend, the visitation you'll perform, or the day-to-day events and activities? I'm convinced that any American pastor needs to have a suit, a sportcoat or blazer, a few ties and dress shirts, and pants and shoes to match— no matter how casual you anticipate your circumstances will be. One graduate I interviewed served at a church that is rarely more formal than flip-flops and shorts, but he admitted he was surprised at how frequently his suit came out.
- **Special pastor stuff.** Does your ecclesiastical tradition use vestments such as a pulpit robe or alb, stoles, or clerical collars? Are there other accoutrements that your pastor regularly utilizes? You may not even be aware of

these— or if you are, you might not realize just how many things you will need. Begin to ask questions of the pastors and/or ministry leaders in your church and denomination about what sorts of vestments and other tools you might be gathering. You may want your own pulpit Bible, a nice copy of your denomination's hymnal, or a bound copy of your denomination's book of order. You won't know what these are until you ask.[3]

Okay— so one take-away here is that you probably need to spend a lot of money to get all of these tools together! But if you're like most seminarians, this is one of the most financially-strapped seasons of your life. How can you possibly get all of the things you need?

I have a few suggestions here. There are other creative ways to do it, but these have worked for my friends and me:

Books: look for used book sales at libraries and at your seminary; often you'll find titles for free or very inexpensively. You might also utilize used book services online or second-hand bookstores locally.

Clothes: I don't know what it's like in your family, but my mother still loves to give me clothes for Christmas or my birthday. If you have a family member who gives clothes, ask them if you might make specific requests (you might tell them that it will serve your future ministry— they may like knowing they are helping you gather your tools). There are good second-hand clothing stores in many towns and cities, too— or check with your seminary to see if they have a clothing exchange.

Equipment (computer and other): 90% of the musical gear that I've owned has been second-hand, and a number of computers have been, too. There are many sources for used and refurbished equipment, both online and locally. For musical equipment, you might also check with some of the larger retailers (again, both "brick-and-mortar" and online) for "scratch-and-dent sales". Many computer manufacturers offer refurbished, open-box specials, and clearance items (Apple does this, and so does Dell). These make great Christmas and birthday gifts, too— especially if you have a similarly-minded relative with whom you exchange gifts.

Pastor stuff: short of finding a retiring pastor who will give or sell you his stuff, finding real "bargains" on these won't be easy. I know a couple of guys with hand-me-down robes, which is a big money-saver; but finding someone who is BOTH your size and willing to part with his robe is difficult. Shopping online may turn up bargains (as compared to buying from a local retailer) on stuff like stoles and other ready-made vestments. For example, Murphy Robes offers a "factory outlet" section on their website.

All of the above: you've got a big milestone coming up, right? You'll be graduating from seminary! Some of your family or close friends may want to give you a nice graduation gift that will serve you in your ministry. (Many will do the same for ordination, by the way.) If you get nothing else from this, then I've given you something to think about when they ask what you might want for graduation/ordination presents.

---

[3] You'll find, also, that some of these are options for you in your tradition, even if some or most of the pastors you know don't embrace them. As a Presbyterian pastor, most of my peers prefer a tie in contexts when they are serving others pastorally; I began wearing a clerical collar not long after my ordination, and have found it to be a great and useful option for a variety of reasons. This point in your seminary study is a good time to begin to think about how you will conduct yourself, and why.

One more thing; some of this will be tax-deductible, especially if you buy it in the same year that you begin your ministry. Save your receipts and ask a tax professional which expenses will serve you an extra duty on April 15.

Know The Hurdles

What stands between you and your first pastorate or ministry? If you think it is only graduation and candidacy, you may be in for a big surprise.

If you're affiliated with a denomination or other ecclesiastical affiliation— or if you intend to serve in ministry in one— there are probably additional requirements beyond the simple academic exercises. Most denominations have some sort of formalized process for ordination wherein a pastoral candidate is examined and tested in his readiness for ministry. Some denominations do a better job of shepherding ministerial candidates through the preparation for this than others. There may also be requirements that your seminary has beyond classroom study, such as field education.

My advice: make sure you understand the process before you, and know what your part in all of it is. It may not be very involved — but it might be that you simply don't know how involved it really is!

For example: in my denomination (the Presbyterian Church in America), ministerial candidates must go through a series of steps in order to be "ordainable"— and in most cases the available ministry positions require (or at least prefer) ordainable candidates. Here's a summary of the steps between first sensing a call to ministry and final ordination in the PCA (as the saying goes, your mileage may vary):

1. **Becoming a "candidate for gospel ministry" under the care of your presbytery:** To do this, you must have met with the Session at your church and discussed your testimony of faith and sense of calling to the ministry. They must then write a letter to your presbytery (which is the regional affiliation of the churches and pastors in that geographic region) on your behalf, asking that you be placed "under care" of the presbytery as a "candidate for gospel ministry". The presbytery will also examine you (usually through a committee first) and hear your testimony of faith and of your call to ministry. Once you have been approved at this stage, you are officially under the care of a presbytery (which, in some presbyteries means almost nothing, unfortunately— but others do a very good job with it). According to the PCA's Book of Church Order (BCO), you must have been a member of your PCA church for at least six months before you may come under care of a presbytery, you must apply to come under care at least one month before the next meeting of presbytery, and you must be under care to become an Intern of presbytery.

2. **Becoming an "intern of presbytery":** The difference between a candidate and an intern is that, while a candidate is "under care" in the sense that the presbytery has assumed some level of responsibility for the development of the candidate for ministry, the intern is supervised in fulfilling specific tasks to gain experience for ministry. Every presbytery has a slightly different set of tasks and expectations, but all of them have the same goal: to give interns a comprehensive set of experiences that will expose them to all aspects of pastoral ministry. According to the PCA's BCO, an internship

must be at least one year long; most interns will find that it will be difficult to fulfill every requirement within a year, and would prefer more time. Your internship will be done in conjunction with your local church; your pastor (or possibly a ruling elder) will oversee and supervise this stage of your training.
3. **Candidacy:** Typically (and minimally— if you're looking for the least number of steps), the next step after completing your internship is to find a pastoral call. In the PCA, you cannot be ordained unless there is a specific local church who has called you to be a pastor. Thus, the next step is to find placement (and that's what most of this book is all about!).
4. **Ordination Trials:** After you have a call, the presbytery where the church that calls you is a member will begin the process of examining you for ordination. These will begin at a committee level, where you'll likely taken both written and oral exams on areas of knowledge including theology, Bible content, church history, PCA history, and the Book of Church Order. You'll also be required to preach before presbytery, and there will be oral exams before the entire presbytery as well. I won't spend a lot of time on these, though there's much to tell— I've blogged about them before. (And here, and here.)
5. **The ordination service:** After you're approved by your trials, the ordination service is the final step. A "commission" from presbytery (like a committee, but with acting authority) will fulfill this function, administering your vows, giving a charge to you and to the congregation, and laying hands on you to complete this momentous event. This event has a similar significance to a marriage, and will be a great time of celebration and worship.

So what? Why am I telling you all of this? Because it's important to know the hurdles.

A classmate of mine bumped up against this very problem about 4 months before graduation. I knew he was entering his last semester, and I asked him how his search was going. To my surprise, he reported that he had quit searching for now! It turns out that no one had ever told him about the required internship, and he knew that he was stuck until he completed that crucial step— yet he had not even become a candidate under care of his presbytery. He was forced to take an additional year AFTER seminary to work through the lingering steps to be ready for ordination, and he had to work hard to get it all done in a year.

Don't let this happen to you. Make sure that you know the required steps to obtain the credentials and approval you will need to fulfill your calling in ministry.

Keep It Humble

So you're getting a seminary degree... what does that mean to you?

For many (most?) of us, it was an accomplishment that we were/are pretty proud of. It means a lot of hard work: difficult study, learning new languages, writing papers, reading mountains of books. It also means building new friendships, getting to know some amazing professors and others, getting to study the Bible and other wonderful fields of study with intensity.

For some of us it also means working full-time or nearly so to support ourselves and our families as we accomplish all of the above.

Your seminary degree is a great achievement, and something you ought to take great pride in. But it is also something that you need to keep a healthy (read: humble) perspective about.

Frankly, many people in your future congregation won't care so much about your achievements in seminary— or if they do, it may be because they are intimidated by what you know that they don't. They won't have a clear understanding of how hard you worked, or how difficult it was for you to learn all that you have. At best, they will appreciate the fact that you know the answers to tough questions, and that you have gathered the tools you will need to minister the Word of God effectively.

You need to begin to cultivate now the attitude that will allow you to minister to them in the future.

When you complete your degree, you'll be awarded a "Master of Divinity" (or perhaps a "Master of Arts etc.") Degree— which is to say, you may feel compelled to consider yourself a master of these materials! But be careful: as you have probably become all too aware, you haven't mastered very much through the seminary process. If anything, seminary may (and probably should) have served to reveal to you how little you have mastered, and how much you have yet to learn.

A case in point: I didn't know of anyone in my preaching classes who earned an "A" on their sermons. I certainly didn't— and shouldn't have. Think of what such a message would communicate to a seminary student? For many of us (including me), these were among the first real sermons we had ever preached. Yet preaching is an artform that takes years of practice to master, and often hundreds of sermons to become adept at. One pastor I know suggested that it took a pastor his first 100 sermons or so just to find his own style and voice in preaching. Should a seminarian be given any inclination of mastery after having preached his third of fourth?[4]

Another factor to consider is that, despite your best efforts, you will likely have very little real-world experience applying the many things you have learned. You know lots of facts, and you know many good methods. But you don't yet know people— especially the people you will be called to serve and shepherd in the context of your first pastoral call.

Who will those people be? Some of them will be better-educated than you, academically. Others won't have anything approaching a graduate degree, yet they will have many years of life experience and knowledge in fields you may never have heard of. All (or nearly all) of them have some things you don't: they know who they are, who the people in their congregation are, what the dynamics of that congregation are, and what the community and culture that they live in are like.

A few years ago, the TV show *Ed* centered around the lives of a few old classmates in their home town. One of these, Mike, had completed medical school and returned home to work with the old, well-established Dr. Jerome, who had served that

---

[4] In his book *Outliers*, Malcolm Gladwell estimates that it requires about 10,000 hours of work in a field before someone becomes an expert. For preaching, this represents roughly 1000 sermons— in other words, 10 years or more of preaching— to be an expert at sermon preparation (and many more to be an expert in sermon delivery). This should give all of us a healthy perspective on our mastery and "expertise."

community as the only doctor for decades. Dr. Jerome was a real curmudgeon, and showed Mike almost no respect as a doctor— frustrating Mike almost to the point of quitting— until finally Mike learns that Dr. Jerome has been waiting for Mike to begin to respect and care about the people he cares for as much as he cares about the medicine itself. At that point (not until the third season, by the way) Dr. Jerome finally begins to treat Mike with the respect and authority that Mike deserves.

Ministry is very much like that: until we respect the people we serve (or will serve) in ministry as much as we respect the knowledge and office of ministry itself, we won't have their ear and our efforts will be like spinning our wheels in the snow: no traction.

You've done good work in your seminary degree; don't undervalue it. But don't assume that because you've earned a "Master of Divinity" that you're fully prepared for the humbling work of ministry.

A more reasonable title would be, not Master of Divinity, but Apprentice of Divinity. You've (almost) completed a huge step along the way toward gaining the knowledge and tools you will need for good ministry. Now it's time to begin shaping the heart of a pastor by seeking an appropriate level of humility.

Tag Your Mentors

The last thing you must do to prepare well for the transition while in seminary is to make a list: who will your mentors be in ministry?

You will inevitably face circumstances that you won't know how to handle, or will need some basic orientation for. Your first wedding or funeral; the first time you do a hospital visitation; the first Session meeting you moderate or Board meeting you oversee. You may not know how to lead worship effectively, or how to lead another through basic discipleship. There will be a thousand blind spots, things you didn't know that you didn't know— until you were in the midst of needing to know!

You will have questions. How do you start to counsel one of your parishioners? How do you stop counseling without leaving them feeling abandoned? Are you spending too much time (or too little) preparing your sermon or lessons, or too little time (or too much) meeting with your congregants? Which issues are worth fighting for? How do you repent well when you've sinned against one of your members? What do you do about the strange situation that you never saw coming? Are you pushing for change too fast?

Where will you turn for answers to your questions? Where will you go for advice about your blind spots? You will serve yourself well if you've thought through who you will call or meet with in these times of need.

There will inevitably be some that you can't list at this point. Perhaps you will work under a seasoned senior pastor, or there will be experienced elders and/or deacons in your congregation who can guide you in the moment. There will certainly be other pastors around— perhaps in your presbytery, or other like gathering— and some of these will present themselves as available for such advice. Maybe, as it was in my case, there will be willingness in the man who put you in contact with your new congregation, and he will offer his wisdom and experience when you need it.

But even these present gaps that need to be filled elsewhere. In the midst of a funeral, your elders and deacons won't be as available for guidance; they will assume that you know what to do— not just preaching the sermon, but ordering the service, guiding the family through their grief, leading the church in serving the bereaved. When you have conflict with your senior pastor, you will probably want to avoid talking to anyone close to the situation. There will be times when you need your mentors to know you, not just ministry in general.

Seek out, therefore, a few trusted mentors— men who know you, whose experience and wisdom in ministry is trustworthy, in whom you know you can safely place your confidence— and approach them. Simply ask them if they would mind if you called them from time to time when you need advice on pastoral ministry. I would be astonished if they refused.

It will be a lot easier knowing now than waiting until the first incident presents itself. Go ahead: get out a sheet of paper and make a list (maybe five names?) and begin asking these friends for their willingness. When you call them on the way to the hospital or as you wait for your first counseling appointment, you'll be so glad you did this now.

A Spiritual Season

Your candidacy, placement, and transition into ministry is an inherently spiritual affair.

You know this already; I don't need to be condescending about it, or act like I'm telling you something you don't already know.

And yet, in all of my research, in my interviews with others, and even (maybe especially!) in my own experience, I've come to recognize how easy it is to take this aspect for granted— or to neglect it altogether. When I first began my research into the topic of pastoral transition, I assumed the spiritual element; as I mentioned in the introduction, I conducted my survey with a default position that took for granted that those seeking to transition into ministry from seminary were prayerful about it, that they were regularly reading the Bible, that they engaged in worship often, and that they were sharing their souls with their family. I felt this was an area where I could safely make some presumption.

I have since learned that presumption in this area is anything but safe. Many of those I surveyed and interviewed reported how spiritually burned-out they were by the end of seminary. Often I learned that one or more fundamental areas of spiritual formation were simply neglected altogether. One interviewee said that he didn't read his Bible at all during his last year of seminary. Another, responding to a question on my survey that asked what they would do differently in their transition process, answered, "I would pray about my transition" (NOT, "I would pray *more*" but that they would pray at all!).

So I want to spend some time practically discussing how you might navigate the whole process of events in a spiritually-astute manner. I am going to assume that you know that you should be spiritually-engaged during this season of your life; but I'm not going to assume that you are actually doing it! Rather, I'll work from a pastoral perspective, trying to encourage you about each area, with some advice specifically on how you might spend your time in these basic parts of spiritual life.

Bible Study

First of all, you need to be reading your Bible.

This always strikes me as an almost-silly thing to say— yet, I find it easy to neglect my own Bible reading, and I know many other pastors who also struggle to read the Bible regularly. I knew a lot of classmates in seminary who were very disciplined about their devotional life, but I also knew plenty of others who, like me, have struggled with the spiritual disciplines.

If you are already disciplined about reading your Bible, I commend you, and congratulate you on a gift from God that not every Christian receives. You will still find some suggestions applicable to you in this section; toward the end, I'll offer some suggested readings related to the transition process.

On the other hand, if you struggle with Bible reading then I want to offer encouragement for you, as well.

Things to Remember about Christian Devotional Reading

Penance

We don't read our Bibles as a form of penance. Most protestants will zealously reject the Roman Catholic idea of penance in the form of atoning for sin by repetition of certain prayers a prescribed number of times, etc. However, many of us do the same thing in our own way: if we missed a devotional yesterday, we'll try to do penance by reading twice as much today. If we haven't read our Bibles for weeks, we'll demand of ourselves that we read for a half-hour every day without missing one.

We'll do this for other things, too: if we were mean to our wives, ignored someone's pain, or wasted time when we should have been working— and we feel convicted about those things— we might turn to Bible reading as a way to make up for them. Whatever our sin is, we frequently turn to self-flagellation of some sort to attempt to make atonement for it. Bible reading can be done as a form of such flagellation.

We don't need to atone for our sins, through Bible reading or anything else. Christ has already atoned for our sins! If you are in Christ, then you are free from the guilt of your sin, and free of any need for self-atonement. (Good thing, too, because self-atonement isn't possible anyway!) God doesn't love you any less because of your sin, and He doesn't love you any less because you missed a devotional, or a dozen devotionals in a row. God's love for you is constant because Christ has atoned for all of your failings.

Love-Earning

Likewise, we don't read our Bibles as a way to gain God's love. Too often we approach God as if His grace and love for us is one-dimensional: He is gracious and loving toward us in our sin, but in all other ways we have to gain His favor. This leads to a life spent in attempts to earn God's love and favor, to gain His blessing through meritorious acts.

This can be our motivation in our devotional time, also. We may think, "If I spend my time reading God's Word, He'll love me more! He'll give me more blessings! He'll be glad He bothered to save me!"

Just as God doesn't love you any less because of your sin, neither does He love you any more because of your obedience, your service to Him, or your piety. God already loves you as much as anyone can be loved— and He demonstrated that love 2,000 years before you were born, when He sacrificed His own Son to pay the ransom for your soul. God's love for you is never-ending, and it is already as great as it can possibly be. You do not need to earn God's love, even through your devotional life, for it is already yours.

Life Expressing

We read our Bibles because we will grow spiritually from reading the Bible. We read them because God communicates with us through His Word, reminding and teaching us of our need and His provision. We read them because we need the truths that the Bible contains. We read our Bibles because of our identity.

We have an identity through our faith in Christ: we, who were strangers and aliens in a foreign land with no home-country, who were orphans without a family or inheritance, who were enemies with the living God— WE are now the opposite of all of these. We are citizens of a holy nation, and part of the celestial city. We are no longer enemies with God, but are reconciled to Him, so much so that He has adopted us as His own and called us children of God! We have an identity, and it is in that identity that we do all that we do— including reading our Bibles.

We read our Bibles because, as children of the living God, we need to hear the words our Father would say to us. They are life-giving, strengthening, faith-building words, and they teach us of ourselves and our identity. They instruct us in what it means to be who we have become in Christ, and in how we might properly live according to the name we have been given.

Our Bibles are worth reading, not because doing so makes God overlook or forgive our sin, and not because reading them earns His pleasure; either of those perspectives subtracts from God's sovereignty and places the determination for our spiritual well-being on ourselves. Our Bibles are worth reading because the Word of God is good for our faith and for our spiritual health.

Strategies for Bible Reading
If you're stuck in a Bible-reading rut and need some un-sticking, here are some things to consider.

All Study Is Devotional
The odds are good that even in your last year of seminary, you have one or two exegetical and/or theology classes left. These may be the key to jumpstarting your devotional Bible reading.

"Wait," you say. "Those classes are part of the reason I feel so stuck!" It's understandable that, when studying the Bible for a class, your devotional approach to the Bible might seem to dry up. That can be true especially when you're asked to do things like making an analysis of the keywords in the original language or consider the text-critical differences of the early manuscripts. What do you do about the very technical and academic approach to the Bible that you are asked to regularly assume in seminary?

You must learn to embrace the spiritual value of those things, and you must learn that a division of the academic from the devotional— of the head from the heart, so to speak— is a false dichotomy. Everything that a seminary asks of you has devotional value, no matter how academic.[1] Remember, what you are doing in those classes is learning how to more closely and accurately determine the meaning and intention of

---

[1] I acknowledge that this is true more often in evangelical seminaries than in others; nevertheless, even in a theologically-liberal seminary where the authority and integrity of the Bible is highly challenged, there can be devotional aspects to the most critical exercises. Those men I know who came through a more liberal theological education with their faith intact did so because they saw every note of criticism and every challenge to biblical accuracy to be an opportunity for them to strengthen their own understanding and belief in Bible truths.

the text— which means that, through the most minute details, you will learn more of what the Bible says and how it says it.

Seminary is an opportunity to learn how to connect head and heart more fully in Bible study. Like so many aspects of seminary, this is vital preparation for real ministry. You will be faced with the same kind of work on a weekly basis, if not daily, and whatever difficulty you have with this now will carry over then; it won't get easier, it will get harder. What is more, if you cannot connect the study you are doing for sermon and lesson preparation with the devotional, heart and soul-oriented application, you will rob your congregation of the truths the Bible has for them.

Start learning how to approach your academic study devotionally. As you work through the assignments and exercises, ask yourself what application each assignment draws out for you. Consider how the information you gather through the exercise may aid in explaining the meaning of the text to others, and how it helps you understand the text on a personal level. Think about how this new knowledge might affect the way that you would preach or teach that passage. Determine whether the conclusions you draw lend clarity to the meaning, and decide if those conclusions are necessary and/or useful in a devotional sense.

Finding Time

Approaching your academic work with a devotional spirit is helpful, not only because it re-shapes the way you do your assignments, but also because it means that you've done some devotional reading already that day!

But you don't have those assignments every day, and there are times when you may have trouble finding time to do the devotional reading you want to do. It can be a lot easier to find time than you might think.

You probably own more than one copy of the Bible. Try keeping copies in different places all over your house. A Bible in the kitchen, another in the bathroom, one in the living room, and a copy by your bed— suddenly, anytime you have a few spare moments, you can grab a Bible and read it. Keep one in your car, too; how many times are you waiting in a drive-through line and could read a verse or two?

Remember that we must be careful not to be legalistic in how much time we must spend reading the Bible to consider it "devotional" reading. Is 15 minutes enough? How about five? How about just one minute, reading just one verse two or three times through? The length of time is not as important as how much God's Word is hidden in our hearts where we might meditate upon it. If you use a calendar to organize your day, look over it for occasions when you have small windows of time spent waiting. Maybe in the moments between when you get to class and when the lecture begins, the few minutes after you're ready but before your carpool picks you up, or the time in the grocery store line as you await checkout, you could grab some quick devotional reading.

Routines (Good & Bad)

Sometimes we can find help in routines for our devotionals. At other times, they can become a prison.

Perhaps, like me, you have struggled over the years with the warring desires of rising early for a lengthy and satisfying time spent reading God's Word, and the lure of a comfortable bed during the sleepy moments of waking. I have tried time and again to develop this discipline, to no avail.

I want to be careful not to fall into a mystical or legalistic concept of morning devotionals. I don't believe that rising early for devotional time is inherently any more special or powerful than Bible reading at other times during the day. But I love the thought of rising early and spending the waking moments in God's Word and in prayer.

Your routines, or desires for them, may be different. I had a friend in college who didn't feel like her devotionals were complete if she didn't have a cup of coffee with them, sitting in a certain place, and with absolute silence in her apartment. I knew someone else who felt like their time had been violated if they had an interruption— and he would bark at his wife or children if they spoke to them, "**I'm having my Quiet Time!**" How contrary!

Familiarity can be good, and the routines you establish for devotionals may be a great aid to you for their regularity. But they might also become enslaving, preventing you from any sense of having communed with God in His Word unless things were "just right." Or they could become mystical, where the very practice of certain activities (like nestling into a favorite chair with a cup of coffee at your side) take on voodoo-like ritual qualities. Use routines well; be careful that they don't begin to use you instead.

Re-Starting

If you have fallen out of the habit of reading the Bible, all you have to do is start again.

I once had a member in a congregation I served who came to talk to me about feeling distant from God. I asked her if she prayed regularly; she replied that she did, but that her prayers felt repetitive and dull. Then I asked her if she read her Bible. "Oh, yes," she said. "I try to read all the way through my Bible every year!"

"That's wonderful," I said. "How is your progress lately? How far have you gotten?"

She thought about it, and she couldn't remember. I asked her if she had read it that week, and she said no. I asked if she could remember the last time she read it, and she thought for a moment before replying that she couldn't. After a few more minutes of interrogation, it turned out that she had begun her reading plan in January, but had gotten bogged down in Leviticus sometime around early February and had stopped reading then. (It was June when we spoke.) After a few weeks of unfulfilled good intentions, she never started back up again, because she was so far behind she knew she would never finish her reading plan within the year. She figured she would just wait and start again next year.

I believe her problem is an all too common one: when we think about our aspirations for Bible reading, we often aim too high. We set a goal that we cannot reach, and therefore we are always discouraged. As I told my congregant, I think that reading through the whole Bible in year is a wonderful goal; but I also think that abandoning Bible reading altogether when it becomes clear that the goal won't be attained is a tragic consequence of too-lofty ambitions.

When you haven't read the Bible for a while, just pick it up and read. Open to a Psalm and read just one, or if you're ready for more then read two. Or go to one of the smaller epistles toward the back of the New Testament and have the satisfaction of reading all the way through a letter in one sitting! (Nevermind that it was only 15 verses.) Try the same with one of the Minor Prophets. Or just read the opening chapter of Genesis, John, or Acts.

In other words, ease back into Bible reading; don't approach it with a level of ambition you won't yet have the stamina to sustain. Work up to those larger goals.

Bible Reading Plans for Candidacy & Transition

Here are a few plans that may strengthen and encourage you during your season of transition.

- **Gospels.** Work through one or more of the gospels. Pay attention to (at least) two things: how our Lord accomplished the work of redemption for you, as well as for the rest of His sheep; and how He conducted His own public ministry. With regard to the latter, consider His boldness, His loving approach, His self-sacrifice, and his commitment to a singular message. Remembering that you are not Christ, nevertheless consider how Jesus' ministry style and practices might be put in place in your future ministry.
- **Pastoral Epistles.** Make a careful study of the pastoral epistles of Paul: I & II Timothy and Titus. Examine the advice that this apostle offered to these young pastors, and what priorities in ministry he urged them to embrace.
- **Paul's Epistles to the Churches.** Pick a letter written by Paul to one of the New Testament-era churches. Read through this letter, noting the sin and problems that Paul addressed. Notice also how Paul addresses them, and what answer he consistently gives to them.
- **Leadership.** Do a survey of those God names and calls to lead His people throughout Scripture. Consider each one's strengths and weaknesses, gifting, and the need he/she fulfilled in their leadership.
- **Spiritual Gifts.** Survey the New Testament teachings on spiritual gifts, and consider each gift separately. Focus especially on the spiritual gifts that are strongest in your life and ministry, and ponder how the Scriptures speak to the use and function of those gifts.
- **Psalms.** Read the Psalms, specifically with the worship of the local church in mind. Note how the Psalms might have served as the book of worship for the Old Testament people of God, and consider how the Psalter may also have use for worship in a church you might pastor.
- **Revelation.** Study John's Revelation, keeping (at least) two things in mind: 1) how did Christ speak to the churches that He addressed in the Revelation, and what did He address for each church? And, 2) what is the final fulfillment of all that Christ is accomplishing and has accomplished in His work of redemption? Through this study, consider how these two emphases are applicable to daily church ministry.

These are just ideas; all of Scripture is both useful and necessary for ministry, so whatever you choose to study will have application in that context. These ideas are not designed to be an exhaustive look at ministry in that way; rather, they are presented for the purposes of encouraging you as you prepare to enter into vocational ministry.

Prayer

Prayer, like devotional Bible reading, can often fall prey to neglect or disengaged routine. Without repeating much of what was covered in the previous section, there is still work to be done in urging and challenging you to give attention to this vital area of spiritual formation. I offer here encouragement to pray, and how you might pray.

Ways to Refresh Your Prayer Life
Pay less attention to length, eloquence, and orderliness. Remember that prayer mustn't be long to be effective. Sometimes a prayer may take the form of hours-long conversation with the Lord. At other times, an utterance as brief as, "oh, God!" may suffice. Likewise, how precise your language or articulation in prayer can become a distraction if you let it; remember how Paul encourages us that, when we lack words for precision, the Holy Spirit intervenes on our behalf.[2] Order in prayer— working through a particular list or making priorities— may also hinder you from praying freely.[3] In heart-felt and effective prayer, length, eloquence, and orderliness matter far less than honesty, fervency, and earnestness.

Soak yourself in the Psalms. It is easy to forget that God has provided us with a prayer book: the 150 prayers of the Psalms are themselves a rich resource for both learning to pray and for regaining a renewed vigor in prayer. Dietrich Bonhoeffer said, "The Psalter is the great school of prayer."[4] The Psalms contain every emotion that you will encounter, and they engage that emotion prayerfully in a manner that is biblically-consistent— after all, they are Scripture! Learn to pray the Psalms as a tool for prayer.[5]

Make use of good prayer resources. In addition to the Psalms, we have the blessing of generations of prayers offered before us— many of which have been recorded and offered as both models and aids for our own prayers. You may find collections like *The Valley of Vision* by Arthur Bennett to be a goldmine of worthy prayers. You might make use of a *Book of Common Prayer* or something like the Daily Hours. There are many of these available, and almost every tradition has one or more that are both consistent with the tradition's theology and helpful to work it out in prayer.

Get quiet. It is a challenge today to get away from noise and distraction. Most of us have constant access to music, the internet, and/or television. Few settings and contexts are free of other people to speak with or, at least, to watch. Our schedules are full, and our minds are engaged. You must therefore be deliberate to find times and ways to get quiet for prayer. This may mean setting aside time in your day for undistracted prayer, be it 10 minutes in the morning before you get dressed, some moments before you go to bed, or scheduled in the middle of your day. It might be as elaborate as some hours or a whole day when you will retreat to a quiet, private place

---

2   Romans 8:26-27.

3   Don't get me wrong here: often, making a list of needs for prayer, items of praise, and reasons for thanksgiving can facilitate focused prayer, and may allow you to pray more and longer than just praying off the top of your head. It may also protect you from meaningless repetition and babbling. But these tools, when held too highly, may also keep you from the intimate fellowship with God and means of grace that prayer is.

4   Dietrich Bonhoeffer, *Life Together* (New York: Harper & Row, 1954), 47.

5   Toward this end, I recommend Eugene Peterson's *Answering God: The Psalms as Tools for Prayer* and Stanley Jaki's *Praying the Psalms: A Commentary.*

for extended prayer. Or it may be one day a week when you commit to leaving your car radio off and spending all of your commuting time praying as you drive.

Meet with others. Committing yourself to an occasional or regular time to gather with one or several others for prayer can be both an intense opportunity for fellowship and excellent accountability to pray. There have been seasons in my life when such scheduled meetings were the only consistent time of prayer that I had. (There have also been times when I longed for the fellowship of prayer that these represented, and that was absent from my regular practice.) For two semesters of my time in seminary, I met every week with a classmate to pray for each other in our candidacy and placement; these semesters were, for me, a rich time of fellowship and a season of great spiritual growth in learning to pray for myself and for others.

Things to Pray for During Transition

Pray that God would lead you in your search. Pray for wisdom and discernment. Pray that He would grant you awareness of key factors for your decisions. Pray that your priorities would be rightly aligned with His for your particular calling. Pray for clarity, and that He would make straight your path to fulfilling your calling in service to His church and Kingdom.

Pray that God would lead the search teams you have contacted. Pray that they would be wholly submissive to His will and leading. Pray for their hearts to be made ready to follow the pastor He would call to them. Pray that He would give them wise and discerning insight into the candidates they are considering. Pray for the information that they need to make careful decisions to come to light quickly and clearly. Pray for their endurance through the search process. Pray that God would fill their pastoral needs in the timing of His will— and pray that His timing would be speedy!

Pray that God would protect your heart from discouragement and fatigue. Pray for Him to prepare you for the reality of rejection. Pray that you would be able to see His work of protection in those opportunities that tell you that you are not the right fit. Pray that God would protect your heart from bitterness and disappointment. Pray for God to raise up friends and supporters around you who will buoy your spirits and refresh your commitment to your calling. Pray that you would be able to press on when the search has become long and your endurance is tested.

Pray that God would protect your heart from a competitive spirit. Pray for earnest hope and expectation for yourself and for your friends who are also seeking placement. Pray that you would know how to love and support one another through the season of candidacy that you will all face together. Pray that you would be able to rejoice with those who find placement before you do, and that others would rejoice in your placement in spite of their own lack of it. Pray for God to overcome on your behalf those temptations to envy, jealousy, and slandering of others in your heart and mind.

Pray for God's sustenance of congregations during the difficult seasons of transition they are encountering. Pray that the churches that you have encountered who are seeking a pastor would be sustained by God's grace, and would weather the season of transition in a healthy manner. Pray for the members of the congregations to be made ready for their new pastor. Pray that God would tend and care for them through the leaders that are present, as well as through sister congregations and others who may come alongside them during this season. Pray for their patience and perseverance through a time of unknown and uncertain future.

Pray that God would make you ready for transition into ministry. Pray that the remaining weeks/months/semesters that you have in seminary would be useful for your pastoral preparation. Pray for your spiritual health and maturity to be well-founded and grounded in His grace, mercy, and love. Pray that you would gain the knowledge you need, as well as the experience, wisdom, and love to lead a congregation or ministry well in the capacity to which you will be called. Pray that He would prepare you (and your family) for the joys, difficulties, successes, and trials that lay before you in your calling to ministry.

Like the suggested Bible studies, these are just starting points. You might add more than double to this list, or it may be sufficient for sustaining your prayer life with regard to transition. And there are many other needs in your life to pray for— many of which, you alone will know. Nevertheless, it is my prayer that these suggestions will be nourishment to your soul through transition.

Corporate Worship

Are you worshiping well?

Worshiping while in seminary can present one of the greatest challenges of that season of life. In fact, I knew a handful of classmates who confessed that they felt they had lost the capacity to worship, because (among other things) their seminary education had presented too many stumbling-blocks.

What were/are some of their struggles?

- **Temptation to critique.** Often, our own study of things like homiletics and worship leadership will create a default-mode of critical examination for sermons, music selections, prayers, and other parts of the public liturgy. It is easy to think, "I would have preached that sermon differently" when you are not the one preaching it.
- **Racing minds.** Anyone who has been in seminary for a while has a mind that is in a near-constant state of high-gear. It is tempting to think about everything but the worship of God.
- **Burdensome work-loads.** The seemingly never-ending state of unfinished assignments presents an ongoing burden of interruption to the worshiper. This is true for everyone, and no less so the seminarian.
- **Knowledge distractions.** Something said (or unsaid) during worship will spark an idea that a knowledgeable mind wants to engage. We have learned so many wonderful and fascinating things! We want to allow those thoughts to mature right away— even at the cost of our worship.

I'm not listing these to suggest new ways to worsen your worship! Rather, my goal is to point out some of the things that might be preventing you from worshiping well.

What can you do about the struggles of worship?

You can start by *seeking to be well-prepared for worship*. This subject is worthy of a book in itself, but a few ways to better prepare for worship include approaching corporate worship prayerfully; reading the sermon text ahead of time, if possible; learning to anticipate corporate worship with eager expectation; seek forgiveness from those you have sinned against, and extend forgiveness to others; disciplining your heart and mind for focused, concentrated worship; and getting a good night's rest. Strive for learning how to worship well as a member of a congregation, even in the face of the knowledge and experience you are gaining.

You should also *spend concerted effort on seeking humility*. Many of the struggles that I and others faced in seminary(that perhaps you are facing, as well) stemmed from a prideful approach to worship and the pastors/leaders who served us. Remember that they, too, struggled through the studies that you have taken up— and unlike you, they finished those studies! Your pastor(s) have experience, wisdom, and training that you do not yet have; it is nothing short of arrogance that a seminary student might criticize the leadership and/or preaching of his pastor the way that some do.

Remind yourself of the magnitude of the Gospel. We worship God because we are aware of how worthy of our praise He is; how much He has accomplished on our behalf; how dependent upon Him we are, daily; how much He loves us. If you're struggling with worship, ask yourself how much you are remembering the Gospel during it. Have you forgotten His grace? Have you taken for granted His mercies, new every morning? Have you made little of your sin? Reclaim the place at His feet that He has secured for you.

Ask your professors how they have learned to worship well. One of the greatest indirect ministries that I received from my seminary professors was watching them worship with their families in our congregation. And one of the most interesting conversations I had with a professor was talking about how he worships with his family: they had arranged to have the hymns for the coming Sunday e-mailed to their house, and they practiced them with their children. They held hands during the congregational prayers, and sang harmonies together. They encouraged one another with what they had heard and learned during the sermons. Most of all, though, my professors (all of whom had been pastors themselves, at one point) came humbly and readily to sit under the leadership and teaching of a man they had helped to train for ministry, and they willingly submitted to their congregation in worship. Your professors may be the best models for you in worship.

Your private and family devotional life will also shape how you worship. If you are neglecting your personal Bible study and prayer during the week, of course you will struggle to worship on Sundays. If you and your wife have unforgiven sin between you, naturally you will not be ready of heart and mind for worshiping God. Attend to your private worship, be diligent in your family devotions, and corporate worship will come more naturally to you.

Commit yourself to set aside the time for worship. Worship and rest are inextricably connected in Scripture, and for good reasons— one of which is that you cannot ably worship with a mind that is not at rest. You must learn the discipline of putting aside the unfinished work that is before you: regardless of how many pages you have left to write, how much reading is still incomplete, or how big the pile of dishes you haven't yet washed, you will never worship fully and devotedly without learning to turn away from the work and turn to the Lord.

Don't neglect to pray that you would become a better worshiper! This is a prayer item that you will never exhaust. Pray that the Lord would teach you to worship in spite of yourself. Pray for the humility that you need, and the awe and wonder at Christ's grace that would move you to worship Him fervently. Ask God to draw you to Himself and bind you to others in your congregation as you worship together.

Why is it so vital that you worship well? First, because you were created to worship God, and to bring Him glory. You will never enjoy Him more fully than in corporate worship. Second, because our worship is a reflection of what we love— and if we struggle in worship, it means that we have either begun to idolize something else or our love for God has dulled. Third, because it will give you the nourishment and sustenance that you need to persevere through your work as a student (and other work).

And finally, because you may never again be free to worship God in the way that you are now free to do so. Most pastors have some level of responsibility during (or surrounding) the corporate worship that they engage in through their ministries. Many (like myself) serve in a setting wherein we are leading a central part of worship almost every week. This may be your last season of worship that is unfettered by the responsibilities of ministry.[6]

Learn to worship well, and delight in the worship that you get to participate in during seminary.

Family Life

You may not immediately think of family as a context for spiritual engagement, at least in the same way that Bible study, prayer, and worship are. *But it is such a context.*

Every seminary family is different: some spouses are much more active on-campus, attending or taking classes and perhaps even earning degrees themselves, while others (by choice or necessity) have not been as present. Some relationships were forged in the seminary context, while others were longstanding before seminary was a nascent thought. Some are eager and supportive of their spouse as soon-to-be pastor, while others are much more reluctant and even apprehensive about that prospect.

Regardless, if you are married then neither your marriage nor your ministry will survive for very long without the unequivocal support, cooperation, and participation of your spouse. Therefore, your family life (to whatever degree you have a family) must be a part of the process of both the preparation for ministry and the transition into it.

This must begin at the spiritual level. You cannot neglect the engagement of your spouse in the spiritual relationship as you prepare to move into pastoral ministry.

What are some ways that you may do this? How do you enter the season of transition, spiritually, with your mate?

Read the Bible together. You need to spend time as a couple[7] in Scripture together, seeking wisdom and growth from the Lord. Share with them what you have been reading lately, and talk about it with each other. What has she been reading for her devotionals? Where has he felt like God has been ministering to him from the Word? Open your Bibles and build one another up with the Word of God.

Talk openly and frequently about transition. Work hard to get on the same page about where you both are in the transition process, and where you need to be. How do you

---

6 Which is not to say that you won't be engaged with the worship of God in your ministry! On the contrary, it is a privilege to worship God in the way that pastors get to worship weekly. But it won't be the same— and those differences are significant.

7 And as a family, as appropriate.

feel about transition right now? Excited? Scared? Nervous? Frustrated? Motivated? What is on their mind about it? Are there any opportunities that stand out to them? What priorities do they believe are important? How ready do you both feel for the candidacy process? How about for the transition? Dig in and shoot straight with each other about what's on your heart and mind regarding your transition into ministry.

Be encouragers. This is a difficult season to go through— even if you're not going through it alone. You both need the vitalizing support of the other. Where do they feel ready and prepared for ministry? In what ways do they need to be built up? How about you? Learn ways that you need encouragement from each other, and then provide that encouragement.

Pray for one another. You will face the transition differently, and you will have different needs. Be faithful to lift up the other's needs before the Lord in prayer. Does your spouse feel differently than you do about where you are in the process? Are they trusting in God's leading as they should? Do they struggle with discerning what is best? Do they know how they can be praying for you, as well? Support one another by praying for each other.

Pray with each other. Don't just pray **for** your spouse— also pray **with** them! Share with them in the fellowship of giving praise to God, offering thanksgiving for the call into ministry, and asking your heavenly Father for His hand to be upon your candidacy and transition.

Take advantage of this window of time, with its focus on your future ministry together, to continue, renew, or establish patterns and habits for spiritual engagement with your family. You'll grow from it during your transition, and you'll have a strong precedent to begin a new ministry together.

Other Spiritual Development

Two other areas that might deserve some focus for spiritual formation are reading and discipline.

In the midst of finishing seminary, you may not think more reading is what you need! But it may actually be exactly what you need: reading that is devotional, that encourages your soul toward readiness for ministry, or that gives you a healthy break from your study can be restorative to your soul. Pick up a book by Henri Nouwen, Brennan Manning, Walt Wangerin, or Jerry Bridges to encourage your weary spirit. Take up and read Richard Baxter's *The Reformed Pastor*, Martyn Lloyd-Jones's *On Preaching & Preachers*, or one of Eugene Peterson's books on pastoral ministry to encourage you in preparation for your soon-coming transition into service.

Likewise, do not neglect the other aspects of spiritual discipline as further focus on your spiritual formation. One approach to these might be to consider the fruit of the Spirit from Galatians 5:22-23. How are these aspects of the fruit of the Spirit made manifest in your life? What areas of spiritual discipline need greater attention in order to better see these borne more fully in your life? (You also might re-evaluate the other areas of Bible study, prayer, corporate worship, and family life in light of the fruit of the Spirit.) Other disciplines also come to mind, as well: for example, whether or not fasting has been a part of your spiritual practices, it may be worthwhile to begin occasional or regular times of fasting as support to your prayer and worship. Jesus expected his disciples to be people who fasted,[8] and pastors (as well as those preparing for pastoral ministry) should take up the practices that Jesus expected of his disciples. Likewise, therefore, ministry of caring for the poor (almsgiving) may be another spiritual discipline that you consider redoubling your attention toward during your time in seminary.

Pastoral ministry is a spiritual work, but your personal spiritual practices won't change substantially from seminary into ministry. The practices and disciplines you establish now, and that you have been establishing up to now, will be what you can expect your ministry to enjoy down the line. Re-commit yourself to a devotional life!

---

8 "And *when* you fast, do not look gloomy like the hypocrites, for they disfigure their faces that their fasting may be seen by others. Truly, I say to you, they have received their reward. But *when* you fast, anoint your head and wash your face, that your fasting may not be seen by others but by your Father who is in secret. And your Father who sees in secret will reward you" (Matthew 6:16-18, emphasis added.)

Attitude Adjustments

In the second chapter we talked about what needed to be done before finishing seminary— and a lot of that was simply working on our mindset and attitude about seminary and ministry. The third chapter offered some guidance about the spiritual aspects of the candidacy process. Now it's time to work on our mindset and attitude about candidacy and placement.

I know a man who finished seminary more than 10 years ago; at the time, he was working for a church in youth ministry, and was ordained while he was in that position. He left it not long after, however, and though he has persistently searched for another placement since then, he has never found one.[1]

I'm certain that there are a number of reasons why my acquaintance has had difficulty. For example, he has a couple of theological views that narrow his field of options. But I'm convinced that one of the main reasons he hasn't been placed (and possibly *the main reason*) is because of his attitude.

Good search teams use the search process to gain an estimation of how a man will function as a pastor. That is, they correctly assume that the attitude that is displayed by candidates during the search will also be the attitude with which he approaches pastoral ministry. While there are some limits to how rightly they can estimate this— not least because the context is very different in a search/interview scenario, and because they can get to know him only so much during it— this is largely accurate.

The man I spoke of above has the wrong attitude. He often comes across as if he has a chip on his shoulder: he is defensive about his theological views, his spiritual maturity, and his training and fitness for ministry. There is little humility in the way he is perceived. I am sure these things come across in his candidacy, and I am equally sure that they would be characteristic of his pastoral ministry as well.

How can men find effective placement for gospel ministry? By changing their attitudes. What should a candidate's attitude be? There are several things that a candidate should keep in mind throughout the candidacy process:

- He needs to take himself seriously, but not too seriously
- He should be cautious about candidacy and his sense of "competition"
- He should approach churches in a similar way that they approach him: as candidate-churches
- He ought to be willing to be totally vulnerable in the candidacy process
- He must see that his next ministry begins with the first point of contact in candidacy
- He must understand the different stages of candidacy and where he fits in them

---

1 At the time of this writing, at least.

Understanding these will amount to the attitude adjustments that are necessary for effective placement.

Don't Take Yourself Too Seriously

One of the most difficult lessons I had to learn in candidacy (and in ministry) is not to take myself too seriously. I don't like to be teased, and when I mess up I would prefer for others not to notice— let alone point it out and have a laugh.

But I've learned that I need to laugh at myself more frequently. As I have realized my own brokenness more thoroughly, I've learned that must I admit that I am both unworthy and unable to accomplish the things I set out to do, without the work and strength of my Savior. Rather than hiding my failures, by acknowledging them I can give glory to God that He is able when I am not.

When it comes to ministry, this is essential. Pastors and ministry leaders are already set apart and viewed differently from their constituents. It is easy for someone like me to play into this, allowing others to believe that I am able to do so much, when honesty would reveal that I am afraid of failure and of being found out as a failure.

A conversation with a search committee member brought up the possibility of someone being "over-qualified" for a particular position. I don't think it is possible for anyone to be over-qualified for pastoral ministry. There is a big difference between being trained and experienced and "qualified" in the common sense of that term, and anyone who thinks they are over-qualified is probably someone to be wary of.

(Of course, the real qualifications for ministry are weakness, humility, and vulnerability. Unfortunately, I'm too prideful to even have those down— and so are most pastors and pastoral candidates! But I hope most of us are much closer to that than to the other extreme.)

Another lesson for ministry was learned from a hero of mine, Joe Novenson— who I am proud to also call a friend— is that being broken, weak, and unfit is not an obstacle for God to use us for great things in ministry. Instead, it is something that, when owned and faced, can allow God to bring glory to Himself all the more.

Joe frequently tells of a point when he felt low in ministry, and all of the confidence that had carried him so far had left him. He went to his elders sheepishly, certain that they would ask for his resignation when he confessed this to them. "Brothers," he said, "I'm terrified that I just don't have the strength or ability to do what I need to do." Their response surprised him (and ought to encourage anyone who aspires to work in a church context): "You mean you have been trying to do this in your OWN strength? Let us pray for you that you will find His strength in your weakness."

Joe has ministered out of his weakness from that day, and I can tell you firsthand, alongside the testimony of dozens if not hundreds of people I have met, that Joe's ministry has been a glory to God and a power in the lives of those that Joe serves. In my own ministry, I must remember Paul's words regarding how the Lord's work doesn't depend on me:

> "What then is Apollos? What is Paul? Servants through whom you believed, as the Lord assigned to each. I planted, Apollos watered, but God gave the growth. So neither he who plants nor he who waters is anything, but only God who gives the growth. He who plants and he who waters

are one, and each will receive his wages according to his labor. For we are God's fellow workers."[2]

Competition And Candidacy: Watch Yourself

Is there competition in candidacy?

A friend and I once talked about how you should handle situations where you and friend are both candidates for the same position. As American men, perhaps our sense of competition rises to the surface too often, which is poignantly revealed in the tendency toward gambling. (I'm reminded of two anecdotes: first the Seinfeld episode where Kramer fell off the gambling wagon by betting on, of all things, which flights would arrive next at the airport;[3] second, an account on the radio program *This American Life* where an interviewee tells host Ira Glass that he lost $5,000 in a round of "Rock, Paper, Scissors."[4])

But in ministry there shouldn't be a very strong sense of competition with regard to candidacy. When you are one of several (or more) candidates for a single position, you are— at most— competing for the time and attention of the search committee.

Beyond that, I think you must view candidacy from a perspective larger than yourself. This process is not all about you. Though you need to make wise decisions (and you need to ask the questions and get the information needed to be discerning), in the end you must put the needs of the congregation above yours. It is God's church, and He has chosen precisely the man for the position you are being considered for. And that might not be you. As one of my friends once said, "God still has plans for you, even if you aren't the one for that particular position."

Whether the "competition" is a close friend from seminary or nobody you know, don't be overly disappointed when someone else gets the call. You need to be emotionally invested in the process, but guard against taking it "personally" when you aren't chosen. It isn't rejection— it is a victory for that congregation to have the man God has called. And if that man isn't you, you don't want to be there, anyway.

I grew up a fan of the South Carolina Gamecocks— I lived in the city of Columbia, SC (where the University of South Carolina is) until I was in my mid-20s, and I attended that school for undergraduate study. If you know anything about Gamecock athletics, you know that— apart from some success in basketball in the late 1960s and early '70s, more recent accomplishments in baseball, and occasional victories in more minor sports— we've always faced a certain level of regular defeat. I often joke that, if you are a Gamecock, you either have your sense of competition severely tempered or you lead a life of despair.

Yet, in spite of my ambivalent history in athletic competition, I too have struggled with a competitive spirit when it comes to ministry placement. My attitude on this has been helped by the wisdom of a 15 year-old. She was on the search committee that brought me to one of the youth ministry jobs I held. Her words stand out to me, not so much as an affirmation of me, but as a testimony of her faith. After I had

---

2   1 Corinthians 3:5-9.

3   *Seinfeld*, episode #108, "The Diplomat's Club," by Tom Gammill and Max Pross, directed by Andy Ackerman. NBC, May 4, 1995.

4   "Meet The Pros," episode #192, *This American Life* by Ira Glass. American Public Media, August 31, 2001. http://www.thisamericanlife.org/radio-archives/episode/192/meet-the-pros.

begun serving in that position, her father told me about what she said. It seems that she came home from the interview and told him, "If this isn't the guy that God is bringing here, I'm really excited about who it must be!"

I translated this into candidacy when I faced the struggles of feeling rejected: no matter how great a particular opportunity seemed, if that wasn't the church God had for me, I should be very excited about the one He does have. And I should give glory to God that He sees fit to place another (better) candidate in the position that I was rejected for, and not consider myself better than others (Philippians 2:3).

You will do well to adopt a similar attitude. Pray that God would temper your spirit of competition.

The Candidacy Of Churches: A New Approach

When it comes to how we approach candidacy, we must recognize that there are candidate-pastors and candidate-churches, not simply churches and candidates. To me, it is a no-brainer; the pastor is certainly candidating for a position, but the church is also candidating: for a pastor, called by God to care for and shepherd the people in their faith.

Let me clarify: pastors and graduating seminary students, seeking a new position in ministry, understand what it means to be a candidate (and if you don't, you soon will!). It means that you must show yourself to be right for the position— demonstrating that God has equipped you with the gifts, abilities, and vision that are best for the ministry that you will lead and serve— and then you must seek God's confirmation that you are the one for the position in question.

What would it look like for a congregation to view itself in a similar way— as a candidate for any particular pastor? The outcome would also be similar: the congregation would need to show that it is the best fit for that pastor, because the make-up of the church in its ministry emphases and direction mesh well with his giftedness and vision. And it would see that the decision is not merely theirs; rather, it is a decision between the congregation (as candidate-church), the candidate-pastor, and God.

If a candidate-pastor does not approach the process from this perspective, he undermines the significance of the calling given to him by God, and he will fail to examine the candidate-church carefully because he will not see the need for it. God, and God alone, calls a pastor to the ministry; he receives a specific call from a local congregation, it's true, but his calling should be certain and confirmed by others (hopefully by entire institutions— his home church, a presbytery or synod, a seminary and its faculty, etc.) long before candidacy actually begins, so that he is not tentatively, cautiously hoping that someone— anyone— will finally affirm this calling by giving him a job. God's calling on a man is significant; anything short of viewing a potential church as a candidate-church will shortchange that calling. This will lead to an inevitable failure to consider the many complexities of the church he is pursuing (or at least a failure to consider all of them fully), because he will begin to think that it will not matter anyway.

If a candidate-church does not approach the process in this way, this too will strip the candidate-pastor's calling of significance, and it will also threaten the actual effectiveness of the candidacy process. The latter fact is the great irony in the problem. Not only do churches who view the search process as little more than working over resumes and interviewing possible hires for a job either overlook and/or subvert the dignity of the calling of those they interview ; what is more, they set themselves up for potentially-colossal failure, as they are ignoring the pre-eminent importance of God's calling in the process. If God is at work in the matching of a pastor with a church, then churches seeking a pastor must submit themselves to the candidacy process just as much as the pastor seeking a church. If they do not, then the process is an idol; the candidate-church has established some system or measure for determining who is the best pastor for them other than seeking the will of God through submission to Him.

On the other hand, what would happen if they viewed themselves as true candidate-churches? They would treat the candidate-pastor that they interview with dignity and respect, wanting to know his needs and desires, his vision and goals, and they would want him to find the place most well-suited for his calling. They would seek after their own desires also, but these would be secondary to their true needs. And, most of all, they would recognize the place of God's will in the process, shunning the idolatry of a more utilitarian, pragmatic system.

It seems like churches often miss this. In my experience, this seems to be a greater problem with the "secondary" ministerial roles: youth pastor, music minister, director of Christian education, etc. When it comes to the search for a senior pastor, a church (or its search committee) will take the "church-as-candidate" approach more readily, but with other positions it will deem the search process as more efficient if they simply treat it as more of a Human Resources function: sort through the resumes and find a qualified hire, expecting him/her to concede any expectation of equal sharing of information and expectations. They don't act as if they must meet anyone's "fit" because they have a veritable hoard of pastors to choose from. They don't seem to realize that either God is in the process or He isn't. They act as if they believe that God is concerned only for what they want in a pastor, not what they need. Nor is He concerned for the needs and desires of the man He has called to be a pastor. And the great shame is that, in missing it, they only hurt themselves in the long run.

But a candidate-pastor must not miss it. As you begin to explore the candidacy process, you must take care to protect your sense of calling and the dignity that it demands. You must expect that churches are as sensitive to what the Lord is leading them to do as what the Lord is leading you to do, and expect them to value your gifts and needs as important factors in the decision. If they do not— if they fail to see themselves as a candidate-church, and therefore treat you as if you are at the whim of their decision— then that is a sound indicator of how thy will also treat you as their pastor.

The third attitude adjustment then is to begin to think of the candidacy process as a two-way endeavor.

Bow Ties & Boxer Shorts: Vulnerability In Candidacy

There are definitely times when the candidacy process seems like a beauty pageant— the candidate-pastor is carefully rehearsed, dressed in their best, and trying to win the contest of placement. This is definitely the case when a church does not see itself as a candidate-church. As a metaphor, the beauty pageant idea is fitting, and as a practice it is too common.

One church I candidated with for a position as associate pastor did this, to an extent: they went from a "final four" to an elimination of two, and they brought both in for a beauty pageant. In other words, show the senior pastor two candidates and ask him to pick between them. At one point in my process with them, I was talking to an acquaintance about it. When I told him they had recently included me as they narrowed their search to four candidates, he said, "Final four! Are you gonna get bracket t-shirts made?"

He was kidding, of course, but the mental image of a "final four" bracket with mine and three other candidates' faces representing each semi-final branch was both humorous and scary. It seems to me that the metaphor of creating a "final four" bracket is far too accurate— that the search process appears to mirror such an elimination process a bit too much. And, when churches choose to continue to "comparison shop" for their candidates— i.e., when they work too hard to figure out which one is "better"— they are only hurting the process of finding the best candidate.

This is problematic across the board: in my case, the search team was asked to find the best candidate, and they left the job half-finished and returned a comparison study instead; the senior pastor (who had intentionally distanced himself from the process up until the last stage) is forced to pick by comparison instead of evaluating what others believe to be the best man for the job. Nobody wins.

The lack of consideration of anything but what is immediately in front of you may sound very appealing to those who have little experience (or bad experiences), but it isn't honest or authentic. In grammar terms, this is choosing the comparative over the superlative. But in the words of Steven Curtis Chapman, "God wants our best and not our 'better-than.'"[5]

Back to the candidacy metaphors: one friend said that his view of candidacy has always been stripping down to his boxer shorts and showing everything he has— warts and all— but the problem is, he said, that most churches would rather see you in black tie and tails.

I prefer the boxer shorts metaphor, myself— it speaks to the sort of vulnerability that is needed to find truly effective placement. Don't allow yourself to be forced into the "beauty pageant" mold; instead, persevere with the vulnerability.

Ministering Through The Process: When Ministry Begins

In the midst of all the stress and effort of pastoral candidacy, it is helpful to remember frequently that the pastoral transition process is very difficult for a church.

Oddly enough, I have never been a part of a church that was completely without a pastor. I have been in churches during the transition of an associate pastor, youth minister, or the like, but even then the process has turned around quickly enough that a replacement was found before there was a vacancy. Because of this, I have never personally known what it would be like to have a hole in the ministerial staff of a church— or the total absence of a ministerial staff, as is the case in many of the churches looking for pastors.

---

5 Steven Curtis Chapman. "You Know Better," *More To This Life*. Sparrow, October 5, 1989, compact disc.

Attitude Adjustments

But I can imagine what it must be like. I suppose it would be quite difficult indeed. A small church without a pastor could suffer tremendously, and even a larger church that goes without a key pastoral staff member— like a youth pastor, for example— would feel the crunch of their absence.

In light of this, I set out to minister to the churches that I candidated with in every way possible. I asked myself: how could I serve them? How could I pray for them as a congregation? How could I be praying for their search? How could I encourage them in it— even as they decided that I was not the one for them, and face the certain discouragement of yet another candidate-pastor who will not be ministering to them permanently?

I am called to be a shepherd to the Church— not just to a particular, local church, but everyone in the Kingdom as it is appropriate. Therefore, I viewed my role as a shepherd as being applicable in the placement process. Perhaps never more so.

I interviewed a member of a search committee who spoke of this as a key factor in thier decision (although they didn't anticipate that it would be). She said that they had one candidate that they considered strongly, even inviting him to visit and interview in person. When he arrived, however, it was clear that he was weary from his own search and the conditions of his present ministry; he needed to be *ministered to*, rather than to be in ministry to others. On the other hand, the next candidate they considered (who they eventually called) brought an attitude of readiness to minister to the entire visit, despite also having wearying circumstances; in every conversation, he earnestly sought a way to ministry Gospel grace to the people he spoke with. The search committee was unanimously agreed: this man was ready and equipped to minister to their congregation.

One of the things that Mark Dalbey said in his Candidating and Transition into Ministry class was very well-stated:

> *"You need to remember that, on the interview weekend you are beginning your ministry to that church, if you end up going to that church. If you don't, then you have a weekend of ministry at that church."*

I think this is so important to remember, and far too easy to forget. This is a key part of viewing the process itself as a ministry, and if more candidates approached it this way they would fair far better.

The leader of another search team I spoke with also commented on the way that candidates approached and communicated with his team. He said that many candidates had an almost aggressive attitude, demanding that he respond on their timetable and acting with suspicion at every question.

Why would candidates do this? It may be that they have baggage that they aren't aware of: they've been burned by a trick question in the past, or they have had a church fail to respond to them in a timely manner (or at all). Or it may be that they are forgetting the very impetus for their contact with that search team: they are hoping to be considered for a pastoral role.

Dalbey's words are a good reminder: you won't suddenly change once you have a pastoral call, get ordained, or are granted title of "pastor." You'll still be the same broken, weak person you are today— utterly useable by Christ for His glory, and strong in His strength through your weakness. How you treat a search team today is how you will treat your congregation of tomorrow— after all, that search team could be your congregation of tomorrow.

Candidacy As "Dating": Stages In The Process

At one point my friend Craig asked me about my progress in candidacy, and he particularly inquired about whether I would slow or stop my pursuit of other opportunities just because I had gained some ground on a few.

In short, my answer was, "no."

Some folks have used a dating analogy to describe the candidacy process. There are two problems with this: first, as Mark Twain said, "every analogy has a limp." They always break down at some point, as Craig reminded me. But they have a useful function until then.

The second problem is that most mis-apply the analogy in the case of candidacy as dating. Here is how many see it:
- Finding a likely fit = falling in "like" (i.e., beginning to date with serious intent)
- Getting a phone interview = entering into serious courtship
- Being invited for an interview weekend = engagement
- Being offered a call = marriage

When you view it this way, however, your progress is slowed with any other opportunity, and you have misinterpreted the communication from the present opportunity.

I account this improper application of the analogy to the fact that most Christians today do not understand or practice the kind of "casual dating" that our parents did. When viewed from that perspective (the one with an understanding of casual dating), the analogy actually works:
- Finding a likely fit / making initial contact = meeting others in a social context (Craig called it "hitting the singles bars;" you could also just think of it as being ready to date)
- Getting a phone interview = being asked out on a date
- Being invited for an interview weekend = beginning a more serious dating relationship / courtship
- Being offered a call = a proposal for engagement
- Accepting the call = accepting the proposal
- Beginning to serve in that call = marriage

After this, the analogy breaks down, because serving the full-term of one's ministry does not necessarily equate with "'til death do us part." But in understanding the stages of candidacy, the analogy is helpful—IF it is applied properly. Be careful, though, to understand where you are in the actual stages of the "dating" relationship; just as in real dating, it is too easy to think that the relationship is further along than it is, which inevitably leads to someone getting hurt.

Real Attitude Change

All of these are important shifts in attitude. But be warned: it is possible for someone to "fake it" when it comes to attitude. Don't do that!

You need to be true to yourself. If the attitude adjustments suggested above aren't accurate descriptions of who you are, you shouldn't be deceptive in your self-portrayal.

At the same time, men who aspire to pastoral ministry should embody the attitudes described here, as Scripture itself confirms. Therefore, if you find that the attitudes above are inaccurate when it comes to your own, you must pray that the Lord will change your attitude!

I'm advocating **real** and genuine change where change is needed— not simply the assumption of a façade that, in time, a congregation will see through. Such would be a significant departure from the third aspect of effective placement (which will be detailed in the next chapter): a context for full-term ministry.

Factors for Effective Placement

What is effective placement?

I have been asking this question for years now. This question has led me to conduct a survey, administer interviews, and read books. It has called me to be introspective about my own experiences, and to investigate corroborative aspects of others' experiences. It has motivated me to brainstorm, to write, and to give lectures and seminars. The question of effective placement is one of the main reasons for this book.

I have generally concluded that there are three defining elements of effective placement— three benchmarks which, if met, indicate that a placement into ministry was everything that it could be. They are:
- Fulfillment of one's calling
- A fruit-bearing ministry
- "Full-term" service

To begin with, gospel-centered ministry is predicated on the calling by Jesus Christ of individuals to service in His Church and Kingdom. Just as Jesus' life and ministry was focused on God's Kingdom (Matthew 3:2-3, 11), so too the Redeemed, called by God, are focused on ministry within the Kingdom in accordance with their calling. All believers called by God to faith are also called to service in His Kingdom, and are uniquely gifted for that purpose (Romans 12:1-8). Every Christian has the privilege and responsibility to discern God's particular calling for him, and to act upon that calling, ministering to others, and being ministered to by others, for his lifetime.

This is no less true for the pastor called into vocational ministry. Effective placement into a vocational ministry position, then, inevitably includes the utilization of a pastor's giftedness. A pastoral call must be a good fit for both pastor and congregation. However God has gifted and prepared a man for ministry, that is how he should serve God in ministry (Romans 12:6-8).

If a pastor is to serve out the calling God has given him, he must either fulfill this in the unique way that he is crafted or face eventual failure. Some men are capable enough that they might work outside of their giftedness for a season; a very few are remarkable enough to do this for an extended time. No one, however, can sustain work in ministry (or in any other vocation) indefinitely. All eventually burn out.

On the other hand, if a pastor is allowed to focus on the areas where he is gifted, his work will delight him rather than leaving him spent. This implies two things: first, a pastor (or pastor-to-be) must have a clear sense of how God has gifted and shaped him for the work of ministry, as well as a clue about where he is too weak to spend much time or effort. All of us have our weaknesses, and if we aren't aware of them then we cannot find appropriate complements for them. Pastor, know thyself.[1]

---

[1] Dr. Philip Douglass at Covenant Theological Seminary wisely applies something very like the Pareto Principle to this idea: the Pareto Principle is the well-known "80/20" rule. Often, for example, a room

The other implication is that both pastor and church must recognize when a pastor, uniquely suited for a certain kind of ministry, is a good fit for the position they are filling— and when he is not. Neither pastor nor congregation should be afraid to simply say, "it's just not the right fit." Obviously this must be done tactfully and graciously, but it must be done. Then, if feelings are hurt or egos bruised, that suggests that the wrong approach or attitude was taken in the search process.

A good fit or not? When the candidate-pastor and the candidate-church both know what would be a good fit for them, the question should be fairly straightforward. Anything else denies the possibility of genuine fulfillment of calling.

Also, an effectively-placed pastor should see the fruit of his labors. This fruit will primarily manifest itself in the replication of the pastor's ministry into the lives and ministries of others (2 Timothy 2:2). Some pastors are natural equippers, and therefore will demonstrate this criterion more fully than others.

However, even the pastor least inclined to serve as an "equipper," if he has been well-placed, will be a benefit to some in this way. Perhaps it will merely be his example to his elders or deacons, or perhaps he will lead a revival in the emergence of lay-leadership in his congregation. The ministry of a man who is well-placed as a pastor will continue to impact that church for years—even generations—after he has left the church. Such a ministry will be a legacy of blessing to pastors who follow.

The result of effective placement, then, is completion of a full-term ministry. This may mean lifelong service to the same congregation[2] or a considerably shorter charge; length of time is not as significant in our day as the opportunity to complete the task before them. A church planter may find that the full term of his ministry is a three or four year span, during which he shepherds a core group or leadership team through growth and progress to become a self-sustaining, particular church— then passes on that congregation to another pastor while he goes on to plant another church. The full term of a pastor gifted at taking a ministry or congregation to the "next level" may be six or seven years, leading that congregation through that transition and positioning them for healthy continuation after he leaves. A revitalization pastor may labor for a decade or more in his full term of service, while the "lifer" may serve the same congregation for twenty or more years as he strives to "finish the race" (2 Tim. 4:7).

When a pastor can serve his flock to the fullest of his abilities, without threat of burnout and with a productive and fruitful ministry, he is able to remain in his ministry until the Lord truly calls him elsewhere— whether elsewhere is another ministry, retirement, or a call into glory. While this criterion is difficult to quantify,

---

that is 80% full will feel as if it is at capacity, while a room that is less than 20% full will feel "empty." (An important idea to remember in thinking about worship space, incidentally.) Dr. Douglass's variation, applied to fulfillment in ministry, is a 60/40 principle: if you are spending consistently less than 40% of your time in your areas of giftedness, you will eventually burn out. Meanwhile, if you spend 60% or more of your time serving in your areas of giftedness, you will normally always have a sense of fulfillment in ministry. Therefore, you might evaluate potential ministry opportunities based on how likely you are to hit somewhere at least between that 40% and 60% range, and ideally even more, in your areas of giftedness and ability.

2 This is clearly what a good fit meant to previous generations. Studies of early North American churches and pastorates, for example, suggest that the typical pastor served three or fewer congregations during his lifetime — yet most of these pastors remained in pastoral ministry for the whole of their adult lives.

Factors For Effective Placement

it is nevertheless a helpful guiding principle that is significant in the definition of effective placement.

On "Full-Term" Ministry

The last mark of effective placement is also the most difficult to measure, as it typically can only be determined well into a particular pastoral call, or perhaps not until after it has been completed. It may be helpful, therefore, to think about two aspects that can give better definition to the idea of a full-term ministry.

Obstacles to Full-Term Ministry

There are a number of things that may stand in the way of a full-term ministry. What follows below is not an exhaustive list; still, these ideas will certainly give a good starting-point to thinking about what may prevent you from full-term ministry, and therefore from effective placement.

Geographical Obstacles: pastors (and their families) who are geographically far from family members with whom they are close will certainly face difficulty in their willingness to serve out a full-term of ministry, particularly in a ministry where a longer timeframe is called for. While there are many in ministry who move far away— even to the "other side of the world"— from their families and find complete fulfillment in doing so, such a decision is not an easy one for any but the most disconnected. Everyone who is called to gospel ministry should be willing and ready to forsake their families for the sake of the Gospel, and yet there are good reasons why others will find family a legitimate and godly rationale for staying closer. Be careful of geographical obstacles.

Cultural Obstacles: much like with geographical obstacles, those called to service in gospel ministry must be willing to love and embrace other cultures if the Lord so calls them. At the same time, be aware that cultural differences— even slight ones— can present a substantial obstacle to effective and lasting ministry. Remember, too, that crossing cultures isn't simply a phenomenon that occurs when moving to another country, or even to the other side of a country. The differences between the American mid-west and mid-south, though separable only by a few hundred miles, can be striking; likewise, one part of the "deep south" may be a very different culture from another part, and the region known as the Mississippi Delta, though only a few miles from other communities of that area, is utterly different culturally. Even the differences of moving from a bedroom community into true suburbs, or from one urban part of a large city to another borough, can be significant. Do not underestimate the substance of cultural obstacles to full-term ministry.

Relational Obstacles: you may find an opportunity that is a great fit culturally and geographically, and that has everything that suits the needs of your family, and yet you might find yourself isolated and alone as the only pastor (or the only similarly-minded pastor) within a hundred miles. Or you might find that everything fits you perfectly, but your spouse has no peers to befriend, or your children are friendless. Such relational obstacles are not to be taken lightly: your long-term spiritual health, and that of your family, may be in jeopardy in the face of them.

Generational Obstacles: it is certainly not the case that one generation cannot effectively minister to another generation; indeed, the Scriptures make it clear that multi-generational ministry is vital to a healthy congregation. You shouldn't shy away from an opportunity only because there are generational differences between you and them. At the same time, there will be difficulties in cross-generational ministry, and sometimes these are more substantial than at other times. It may be difficult to assess during the candidacy process, but identifying whether true generational obstacles are present may be the key to a truly effective placement.

Personality Obstacles: it's true that opposites attract, and that is often the case for pastors and congregations as much as it is for one-on-one relationships. But more often than not, such opposites in pastoral ministry will not make for a long-term (or even a shorter full-term) ministry. Part of knowing yourself is to know your personality, and how that personality affects your ministry. If you encounter an opportunity that is clearly a fairly different personality, there may be reason to believe that it will work out nevertheless; at the same time, without a clear reason for why you believe it will work, be very cautious of personality obstacles.[3]

Ministry Obstacles: what does effective ministry look like for you? What results does it produce? You should have a clear picture of this by the time you begin candidacy— and you should also begin to learn how to recognize when those approaches, priorities, and goals are not shared by a potential congregation or ministry. They may have a similar, but not identical, set of core values, in which case the fit may still be a very good one. They may also have a very different set of priorities that are just as legitimate as yours, but which may indicate an obstacle to full-term ministry. Or they may have a few measures for "good ministry" that aren't biblically-based or even biblically-sanctioned, but are at the core of their identity nonetheless. Watch out for divergent ministry values.

Seasons of Ministry

Another thing to think about are the seasons of ministry that you will inevitably face. It may be the case, for example, that you serve out the full term of several seasons of ministry in a single congregation, making for a long-term tenure that consisted of several ministry terms.

When I was in college, I attended a church that was over 20 years old. The senior pastor then had planted that congregation more than two decades before then (his first season of ministry), had shepherded the church through early "establishment" years (his second season), and was well into a longer term of solid, established ministry (his third season). During that time, they had changed locations three times, gone through three building projects, and had sent out two daughter congregations (with a third in preparation). They had expanded their staff to include three other pastoral staff members and multiple members of an administrative staff. They had begun a school, and were instrumental as a congregation is seeing a number of service organizations begun in the area— all under the leadership of a single (very capable) senior pastor. But while he had served that congregation for a long tenure, his ministry had actually spanned several "seasons" of the congregation's life.

---

3 To better understand the implications of personality and temperament on ministry, I recommend my friend and former-professor Philip Douglass's book, *What Is Your Church's Personality?* Learn more about this book in the appendix of recommended reading.

Be aware that the close of those seasons may also signal a time to move on. I've known several pastors who perhaps should have left their current congregations years before, both for their own fulfillment of ministry and for the health of the congregation— yet they stayed, to the detriment of both. When the Lord brings a season of ministry to the completion of its full term, it may be time to go, regardless of how long a pastor intends to stay.

In my own experience, there have been times when I have clung to the idea of a "long-tenured" ministry as an ideal that I felt determined the inherent value of my ministry. I confess that such an approach, having no regard for whether the Lord would have me stay for a longer term, is more idolatry than it is faithfulness in ministry.

Introducing The Factors

So how do we get there? What are the steps to attaining effective placement?

In some ways, that is what this whole book is about. I want to see as many effective placements as possible, and every step I outline in this book— for the time before candidacy, the search process, and the transition— is intended to help you find effective placement as you finish seminary and move into ministry.

That said, there are five factors that my research reveals— and my experience, and that of others, testifies— are keys to getting started in the right direction. They are the main points of a "philosophy of placement" and the essence of your advance preparation for candidacy and placement. The rest of this chapter will cover the details of each of these factors in abstract form. In later chapters, I'll work through how each factor is applied to the process.

The five factors are:
1. A healthy candidacy and placement "work-ethic"
2. Connecting with God's Church
3. A strong awareness of calling
4. Remaining flexible about fulfillment
5. Humility and submission in the end goal

The first two factors are the primary factors, while the remaining three are secondary. Or, thought of another way, the last three are the foundational elements that give shape to the first two, while the first two are the "fleshing out" of the last three.

Factor #1: A Candidacy Work-Ethic

A big piece of the puzzle is what I call the "placement work ethic." In a way, what I've found about this is surprising: many seminarians (and many pastors) are shockingly lazy when it comes to their ministry placement. Most seminary students that I know are hard-working guys, so I am sometimes stumped when I find that they are taking their placement very lightly.

During seminary, I inevitably encountered this in an informal way: a friend, graduating in the coming months, and I would be talking and I would ask, "how is your search going?" "Okay, but I don't have a lot of things in the works," their response might go. "Tell me," I would prod, "What has your search process been like? How have you been pursuing opportunities?" "Oh! Well, I've been checking the Hot List!"[4] Then comes an awkward pause while I try to find a tactful and loving way to say, "That's it? **That's ALL**?!?"

I didn't think these guys were being intentionally lazy or neglectful of their placement process, but I do think they were approaching placement with a poor work-ethic. Perhaps they believed that if they could simply get the divinity degree, things would just fall into place for them. Some of them over-spiritualized the process, wrongly applying Jesus' admonition not to "worry about tomorrow" to their placement. Some were simply working off of assumptions that it really isn't that difficult to find a pastoral call.

My own experience told me already that none of these assumptions were right— and my experiences since then have only confirmed that. It is hard work to find a pastoral call— in fact, it should be considered another part of the difficult labor of seminary, just as ordination should be: you haven't finished the work just because you have graduated, but still have the steps of placement, transition, and ordination to complete. God is indeed sovereign over the process, but that doesn't remove our responsibility to be faithful, diligent, and obedient in our participation and work toward finding placement.

My research confirms my own experiences. Many of the respondents who were placed quickly listed a wide variety of ways they had been working at finding placement. Those who fit the description of "effective" placements always demonstrated a strong work-ethic. These graduates indicated that they began their search very early— often as much as a year in advance— and diligently followed up on new leads and established contacts. They utilized as many points of contact as they could find and had an easier time finding the right fit. And a major theme that arose in response to the question, "what would you do differently?" was the theme of working harder— starting earlier, making more efforts, contacting more people, exploring more directions.

Sometimes in my conversations with fellow students, I would say to them, "It would be great if God suddenly put you in contact with just the right congregation, out of the blue. In fact, it would be almost miraculous, wouldn't it?" And then we would discuss a theology of miracles. If they were sick and in need of healing, they would pray that God would miraculously heal them— but, knowing that by definition a "miracle" is something that is not ordinary but extraordinary, they would also proactively pursue medical care for healing, trusting that God may also use common and ordinary means to bring about His will. Why would they believe that it should be any different in their placement?[5]

Clearly, the work-ethic is a big factor in successful placement. I like to think of the adaptation of an old mantra: Al Capone urged Chicago citizens to "Vote early and vote often." My motto is: Candidate early, candidate often. Words to live by.

---

4 The "Hot List" is a list of opportunities that my seminary published in-house for its students and graduates.

5 A friend told me of how one of his seminary professors addressed this before their class: he compared it to the girls he had known in his campus ministry days who were simply waiting for a godly, mature Christian man to suddenly ask them to marry. His words to these well-meaning ladies were the same to the seminary students: if you need a taxi, you have to hail for one!

Factor #2: Networking— Who Do You Love?

Apart from the timing in candidacy, the biggest issue facing a candidate is networking— that is, making essential connections within the larger Church.

Networking sometimes is on the receiving end of fairly harsh criticism in the Church. Okay, some business executives take it too far, and they only network for personal gain. Yes, some people are manipulative with their relationships. No, we can't expect relationships to avoid the fallenness that affects all of us. And I'll grant that networking can sometimes dwindle down to little more than selfish abuse of the existing relationships of the Church for "my purposes" only. But those who are unwilling— or even reluctant— to recognize the connected nature of the Church, particularly with regard to pastoral placement, are missing a key biblical element to the way that the church works.

In my research, I found that a lot fewer people have a negative view of networking than I would have guessed. Less than 2% of respondents to my survey said outright that networking is "an unhealthy idea." Another 13% called networking "a somewhat professional approach" to placement (seeing "professional" to be a bad thing in this case). On the other hand, almost 80% indicated a favorable view of networking, acknowledging its value in the placement process.

And as I read through the qualitative portions of my survey, networking improves its standing even more: even those who downplayed the importance of networking quantitatively (e.g. they indicated that they did not utilize a network to a very great extent in their candidacy process) suggested or stated outright that the relationships they had (read: "network") were significant in their candidacy with the particular church or ministry where they accepted a call. In other words, they may not have networked at all for 95% of the churches they candidated with, but the relationships of their network played an important role for the church that mattered— the one where they ended up.

Networking at Work

"It's like 'old home week' for you," my friend Craig commented to me. We had only been at the Presbyterian Church in America (PCA) General Assembly for a few minutes, but I had already greeted a dozen people. What gives?

What gives was the very reason I went to General Assembly: what happens in the Church is all about relationships, and Craig saw this starkly in only a few moments. If anything, my hypotheses about networking and the placement process were confirmed and strengthened by my brief time at G.A.

Since I've been in the denomination for a while, had a mentor early on who took the time to help me build relationships with PCA folk, and attended the PCA seminary for over four years, I was already fairly well-connected in the denomination. What Craig saw was the fruit of that. In spite of this, however, I would be presumptuous if I had assumed that my relationship-building work was done.

Based on what I knew about my own sense of calling, I set up meetings at General Assembly with key people from PCA presbyteries where we would like to move. For example, I met with the chairman of the Mission to North America Committee from one presbytery in my wife's home state. We had a great conversation about my passions, burdens, and sense of calling for revitalization, and he indicated that he was encouraged that I would be interested in coming to his presbytery to minister in that capacity. He was not in a position to recommend a particular opportunity to me at that time, but simply having met him and gotten to know him— even briefly— seemed like it would make a difference in the placement process.

More than ever, I was convinced that networking and relationships are the key to placement.

Answering Concerns
After our trip to General Assembly, Craig challenged me about my views on networking, "Can you pursue placement through networking, as you suggest, with true integrity?" Good question— and it brings up a significant issue that a candidate-pastor must address: does a placement effort done with pure motives mean that networking is not an option?

As I've already mentioned, business-world networking is often motivated out of a self-serving, "close the deal" attitude: business professionals network because, frankly, their work requires them to do so. Contracts, sales, mergers, promotions, and new jobs depend on who you know— so smart professionals make it their business to add as many people as possible to their network. This view of networking, regardless of effectiveness, pushes against the edge of ethical and social propriety, and sometimes crosses it boldly. Not all business professionals do this, but there certainly are some who do.

So the critique stands as this: can we, in good conscience, engage in a practice known for being a vehicle to use others for personal gain, simply because it is an effective means of finding placement? Or is the demand on Christians to do what is right— not simply what works— sufficient grounds to abandon the practice of networking as a instrument for placement?

One of my professors wisely and regularly reminded us of a key idea to understanding this paradox: "The abuse of something does not negate its proper use."[6] Just because people abuse the Internet (for pornography, online affairs, soliciting inappropriate or illegal activity, etc.) does not mean that the Internet is all bad. Someone could use a baseball bat to hurt another person, but baseball bats would still have a valuable function in the game of baseball. Anyone who has understood the argument that, "Guns don't kill people; people kill people" can grasp this.

If there is indeed a proper use for something (and there are things that, I believe, have no proper use), that usefulness should not be overlooked because of other uses. Networking, then, should not be discarded inherently because it has become a tool for some business professionals to manipulate or politick their way to greater success.

On the contrary, I would argue that networking is biblical, and that a networking model for placement is how God intends for pastors to find a call. One of the main themes of Scripture is the idea that God's people are a community. The New Testament uses several metaphors to describe the Church: the family of God, the Body of Christ, the Bride of Christ. Jesus used other metaphors: the Vine and the branches, the Shepherd and His sheep. What is common to all of these metaphors?

---

6   This principle, which is actually a loose translation of an old latin phrase, *abusus non tollet usum*, is actually an old and well-established philosophical idea.

A connected, relational nature, not just between the members and Christ but one to another, as well.

We exist in a community for a purpose, which is to collectively seek God's glory. How does this happen? Unless your view of your faith is very narrow— so that worship, a life of faith, and bringing glory to God are reserved for the particular geographic, temporal, actual context of Sunday worship— then a collective effort means that what you do day-to-day is not only your concern, but the concern of everyone else in the Church as well. This is why accountability is so crucial.

This is also why networking is so essential to pastoral placement. No one in the church is isolated from the rest of the Body (not even pastors). We must rely on one another, and we must bear one another's burdens, for the support our ministries need. And never was this more important than in the placement process.

At its best, then, networking is a contemporary term for an ancient idea: that we need each other for our own effectiveness and success. If I am to find the call God has for me, I am dependent on His Church to lead me to it. When I do so, I'm not using the Church for my own benefit— God is using the Church for her own benefit.

Factor #3: A Candidate's Sense Of Calling

The next factor for effective placement that emerged from my research is having a strong sense of calling as a candidate. My own struggles with this question— specifically, understanding (and misunderstanding) what it means to have a "calling"— have helped me understand why this is such an important factor. It also seemed to be something that many of my classmates struggled with, as well.

When we first began seminary, I had left youth ministry and was looking in many different directions. I thought about college ministry, teaching (and possibly Ph.D. work), church planting... I was generally open to just about anything. What I knew was that I didn't think I would do youth ministry anymore. Add to that equation the fact that we left a difficult situation, and you can bet that I was practically schizophrenic about our calling.

Graciously, the Lord whittled away some options and focused me on others. This meant that, going into candidacy, I had something of a grid to sift through the many opportunities. In fact, this was one of the reasons that the survey respondents gave for the importance of knowing your calling: it helped them to know whether a position or listing was "good" (as it related to them) or "bad" so that, from the outset, they could eliminate some otherwise-viable opportunities. And during the candidacy process itself, it also gave them a measure for discernment.

As a case study, consider "Jeff" (not his real name). Jeff knew he was called into youth ministry; that, in itself, eliminated dozens of prospects from the job listings. But more than that, he knew that he wanted to stay in a particular geographic region (due to a sense of calling to family obligations) and in a certain denomination (as a result of his calling for theological convictions). That limited him to less than 20 churches— there just weren't that many that fit all of those criteria and were also large enough to hire an ordained or ordainable Youth Minister.

As Jeff went through a few interviews, he eliminated even more of them, because Jeff was committed to a certain philosophy of youth ministry, and it was simply incongruent with what some of these churches wanted in a Youth Minister. Jeff was left with only 5 or 6 churches that could even be on the short list, and none of them were hiring. But Jeff was doggedly committed to what God had called him to do, so he waited until an opportunity arose, and when it did, he was perfect. Jeff is a prime example of an effectively-placed graduate, and he has remained in that position for close to 10 years already as of this writing. I anticipate that he'll remain in his current calling for a long time yet.

Waiting, as Jeff did, is not easy— particularly when your classmates are getting placed— and can even feel threatening, causing you to question your decisions and your calling itself. But here again, having a strong sense of calling helps immensely: it provides a sense of confidence and direction when doubt arises. After all, God is calling you to a particular ministry in a particular place and time. Thus it is not simply our own discernment, our own preferences, or our own determination that will get us placed, but God's work through us, our circumstances, and the Church at large.

How can you develop a stronger sense of calling? I see two ways, both through the responses of my survey's respondents and through what the Scriptures themselves teach. First, know and understand yourself, then have others know and understand you.

"Know thyself" said the Philosopher, and he was right. The Scriptures repeatedly discuss our giftedness, our functioning as a part of a larger whole, and as the new creation we (the Church) are in Christ. At the root, these passages are identity passages, and understanding our identity in Christ means, in part, understanding who and what we are called to be and do. The better we understand our identity in this way, the better we will place into ministry. Survey respondents agreed: they directly affirmed the importance of knowing what you are called to do, as precisely as possible.

One of the best books I've encountered on this subject is *Maximizing Your Effectiveness* by Aubrey Malphurs. As I mentioned in a previous chapter, we were fortunate to have a professor at my seminary who required all ordination-track students to work through a process very similar to the one outlined in this book; on top of that, he is one of the most intuitive, discerning, and encouraging men you will ever meet, and he counsels each student personally about their calling. Not every seminary has someone like that; if you are struggling in this way, you might find help through a professor or pastor.[7]

The other way that we can strengthen our sense of calling is to test it— that is, to show others ourselves, and allow them to understand us in ways similar to how we understand ourselves. When in seminary, this means internships, field education, and general service in the local church. But beyond seminary, it means simply being involved in the church of which you are a member. If you are involved (as a layman, an intern, a volunteer) then those in the church will know you. Be assured, they will let you know how you are doing in one way or another. This is the testing grounds: this is where you will learn if you know yourself well. This is where you will discover exactly how you are gifted, where your strengths are, and (most importantly) where your weaknesses are. As James says, consider it a joy when you face these trials, as they lead to steadfastness and completeness.

---

7   I've included a list of several other books like Malphurs's in the appendix of recommended books.

Factors For Effective Placement

Testing will lead to confidence in some areas and uncertainty in others. But this is good, because it means that you understand yourself that much more. Knowing your calling is not simply an ability to list off what you are good at; it is also knowing how you communicate, what you're passionate about, where you need help and complementary staffing, and what you should stay away from altogether.

Get to know who you are and what you are called to, and you will be miles closer to an effective placement.

Factor #4: Remaining Flexible

The next factor could be summarized as, "keep your eyes open."

At one point in my candidacy I was approached about considering a position that I would not have thought twice about had I seen an advertisement for it. It was a position as the Head of School at a private Christian elementary school. Even though I was focused on a pastoral ministry position, I was a little surprised at how my interest was piqued by this opportunity.

There were essentially four reasons why I was open to considering it:

1. First, my disposition toward candidacy included the idea that, in the event that I was approached with an unsolicited request to consider a position, I would consider it. This was because I wanted to be sensitive to the facts that a) the Holy Spirit works through a variety of means, and b) I am not wise enough nor prescient enough to be certain that I know the trajectory of my future. (Incidentally, this same disposition later led me to consider a church simply because four different people, at separate times, suggested that I might be interested in it.)
2. Also, my experiences in Christian Education, gained almost completely at the school where I taught while in seminary, had been so delightful that I was all but required by them to keep an open mind about a future in Christian schools. I enjoyed every aspect of teaching at the school where I taught, and felt quite fulfilled in that position.
3. The school that approached me was, for lack of a better label, a "revitalization school." That is, it lacked vitality and direction, and needed a Head of School who would refine their focus, cast a vision for their future, and lead them in accomplishing their goals. Since I was fairly certain that God has prepared me for a ministry of revitalization, it may have been that I simply needed to broaden my understanding of what revitalization ministry includes.
4. Finally, in the survey that I conducted, when asked "what one thing would you do differently?" many of the respondents answered that they would, "keep an open mind to a wider variety of possibilities." Naturally, I thought that wouldn't apply to me, because I believed I had a clear mandate from God for what I would do. I had to question whether my "mandate" was really so clear when faced with this opportunity; maybe the survey had wisdom for me here.

Re-Thinking the Idea of "Calling"

Until my last year of seminary, I would have defined a calling as a specific end-result— usually, a particular job or position. Thus, my calling, as I understood it, was to be a pastor, probably a solo or senior pastor, and probably in a particular kind of church. In my mind, as God made my calling clearer, the scope of possible positions narrowed in a direct correlation: the more precise my sense of calling, the fewer the positions that fit the bill.

There was a good reason why I defined calling in this way: a position as pastor, assistant pastor, etc. is colloquially referred to as "a call." When I later received an offer of a position as pastor, I had a "pastoral call." Not surprisingly, in my mind I drew an equation between the idea of my "calling" and what would eventually be my "call." While this is not illegitimate, there is also not a direct equation. In other words, it is not the case that "calling = call."

A helpful analogy came to me from Greek syntax, of all places. Perhaps you will remember this distinction from your early seminary studies: when working to translate from one language into another, you are concerned with semantics— that is, word choice. There are two categories that must be considered: the semantic "range" and the semantic "field."

The semantic range of a word is simply the different meanings or definitions that the word might have. Thus, the semantic range of the word "class" includes two different ideas: the academic one, where "class" means a group of students that meet together to learn; and the socio-economic one, where "class" denotes a particular level of status. (There are more ideas, but these two are good examples.)

The semantic field of a word is, in a sense, the converse: it is the different words that fit into a given definition. The semantic field, then, of the word "food" includes green beans, steak, bread, and birthday cake.

Depending on the level of precision in a given word, there may be a semantic range that is very narrow indeed. That precise word, however, might fall into a semantic field that is still quite broad. For example, a semantic field of "food" may include the fairly broad "bread" and the quite narrow "Hudson's famous Hush Puppies," yet both are a part of the same semantic field. But to translate properly (which assumes a clear understanding of the word being translated), both the semantic range and the semantic field must be considered. That is the beauty of language— it affords us many ways to say what we mean, thereby allowing exacting precision in our statements, questions, and opinions.

Here's the analogy: I had been thinking about "calling" with regard to, if you will, the "range of calling" but ignoring the "field of calling." That is, I focused on the precision of my calling— narrowing the definition of what I'm gifted for, passionate about, experienced with, and burdened for. Yet, I ignored the field of what that precision could lie within; I assumed that the field was as precise and narrow as the range. This was my critical mistake.

To flesh that out a bit: my "range of calling" is fairly narrow. I know that I am equipped for teaching/preaching, leadership development, discipleship, administration, and vision-casting and implementation. I am passionate about my love for the Church and my care for her leaders. I have experience in a wide range of ministry, but primarily in preaching, teaching, discipleship, and leadership development. And I am burdened for the long-term health and advancement of the Church.

For a long time, I assumed that my "field of calling" was also narrow: small church ministry (probably in a revitalization context) as the solo or head pastor for a long-term service of ministry.

But I began to wonder if that was a fair assumption. I had to ask myself: are there other positions ("calls" if you will) that would scratch those itches and fulfill my calling just as well? Might a different position (other than as solo/head pastor) in a local church fulfill my calling? Could I serve a school, a presbytery, or even a denomination, and accomplish the same or similar results?

Keeping an Open Mind

Obviously, the answer to these questions is "yes"— which means that my notion of "calling" needed amendment. Many of my survey respondents discovered this, as well, as they went through candidacy.

"Steve" is a great example of this. Steve's sense of calling was clear: he had strong gifts for preaching and teaching, and also for working one-on-one with young, maturing believers. Steve, who was from the Carolinas, was convinced that these gifts meant a call to be a solo pastor at a small church in the south, and initially began exploring that direction; in fact, there were several opportunities that he interviewed for, and he was even offered a call with one of the churches. But Steve was not convinced that God was calling him there, and he turned it down.

Meanwhile, the youth pastor at the church Steve attended during seminary left, and on the same day he turned down the other opportunity, the leadership at Steve's church invited Steve to explore the youth pastor position. Although Steve had not previously considered youth ministry as a direction his gifts and calling would take him— and certainly not in the midwestern city where he went to seminary— he decided to consider it anyway.

To his delight, Steve found that his seminary church was looking for someone who would offer these students strong biblical teaching and give them individual attention for accountability, mentoring, and guidance as they developed their young worldviews. They also wanted someone who would serve as the second-in-line to fill the pulpit behind the senior pastor. In other words, everything Steve was looking for— everything he believed God was calling him to do in ministry— was found in this youth ministry opportunity.

Steve's advice to others is helpful. "Reflect on the gifts & tasks of the job rather than demographics, etc.," Steve says. "Be honest about who you are & what you want to do."

Factor #5: Remembering What Is What

"Pray expectantly that God will lead you— even if it means that you will take 'the lower seat' in terms of your own ego and agenda…"

I consider this advice from one survey respondent as one of the biggest take-aways that my research has produced. Humility is a requirement for the honor of what a pastor is called to be and to do. And finding the balance between proceeding with confidence in your calling and staying flexible in following God's lead to a specific call demands prayerful submission to His will.

Pastoral ministry is simultaneously humbling and self-aggrandizing. Pastors are role-models, mentors, confidantes, and counselors. They become one of the most important people in a lot of lives— it is hard to imagine the prominence not becoming a struggle at some point. At the same time, any pastor who takes seriously the substance of his job is humbled by the gravity of it.

The same is true in the candidacy process. A pastoral candidate is often flown in for an interview weekend and treated like a celebrity for several days. When more than one church is interested, candidacy can begin to feel like a bidding war with the candidate as the prize. Naturally, these circumstances can lead to an inflated ego, and can leave a candidate feeling as if he is in control.

But he isn't. In truth, God is Lord of the pastoral search, even when we fail to acknowledge it. Further, when our agenda becomes too important we can lose sight of God's hand of providence, hindering our discernment. A persistent humility is required for effective placement in candidacy. Without submission to God's leading, we will inevitably make mistakes in our decision-making.

There is a difference between pastoral candidacy and any other job search. While the work of every Christian is inherently valuable to God as vocational service to Him, most Christians readily agree that there is still something different about pastoral ministry. One survey respondent commented, "Too often, perhaps, we see the candidating/transitioning process as simply a 'job hunt.' but in the same way that there is a distinction between 'calling' and 'career,' there is a significant, glorious difference between 'candidating' and 'job hunting.'"

Candidacy for pastoral ministry is not career advancement, but Kingdom advancement. And the Kingdom is not all about you; remaining humble and submissive to God in the candidacy process is one of the most substantial things you can do in your candidacy.

If You Build It, They Will Come

When it comes to candidacy, the best things you have going for you are the relationships you have with others. The church is inherently relational— after all, it really isn't good for man to be alone— and those relationships form the framework for how God brings many things to pass: friendships for accountability, introductions of future spouses, and career connections.

Never is this more present— or important— than in the placement of pastors in ministry. Chances are, you met your best friend, a key discipleship leader in your life, and your spouse (if you're married) through the relationships you have with others in the church. Why wouldn't you expect to meet your future congregation or ministry in the same way? God uses His body, through the relational connections within it, to bring pastors into contact with churches. Including my most recent placement, all five of the ministry positions I have occupied have been the product of direct, relational connections between me and others. Fellowship is clearly portrayed in Scripture as a participation in one another's lives to such a degree as to serve and help others. The same sense extends to vocational concerns as well.

As someone on a trajectory for future ministry, you would do well to attend to the nurture of your "network" toward this end. It is important to realize that you need to do more than simply to call up or e-mail contacts in your address book, many of which are vestiges of long-defunct friendships, and asking if they will offer you some help or support in your pastoral search. You need to be in contact now, and already, with the people you intend to call on for recommendations.

In this chapter, we'll try to get our heads around how networking works in the church— and how we can build, grow, and maintain our networks of relationships. I'll also show you some examples of how it works in the candidacy process, to prime the pump for the rest of the book.

How & Why Networks Work

For starters, let's go back and refresh what a "network" is (according to my survey, and as far as this book is concerned). A network is not:[1]

- An unhealthy idea, common in the business world, in which every relationship is viewed from the perspective of personal gain.

---

[1] I alluded to this part of my survey earlier. These were the multiple choice responses to the survey question, "What is your view of 'networking?'" Of my respondents, only 2% believed that it was a completely unhealthy idea, while another 13% considered it a "somewhat professional approach." Meanwhile, 60% saw it as a natural process of relationships, while 26% said it was a benefit of community. Interestingly (as I mentioned before), 72% of those who those that networking was either "unhealthy" or "professional" STILL found the call they eventually accepted through networking— including 100% of those who labeled networking as "unhealthy!"

- A somewhat "professional" approach to relationships, in which some relationships are seen as beneficial beyond the normal extent of friendship and acquaintance.

In contrast, a network **is**:
- At least— a natural process of relating to others, sometimes benefiting from them and sometimes being of benefit to them.
- Optimally— a sense of community in which everyone serves one another toward the common benefit of all.

So, at least we're looking at relationships where we hope we might benefit and be a benefit. And here's the plain truth about networks: as Jesus said in Luke 6:38, the measure you give is the measure you get.[2] In other words, if you want to enjoy the benefit of a healthy network, first you must have a healthy network— and to get one, you must have been of benefit to others.

To do that, you can't simply call up strangers— or practical strangers, like the folks who have been in your address book since your freshman year of college but who you haven't talked to since sophomore year— and expect them to help out. Instead, the benefit you are able to ask of your network is directly proportional to the amount of relational energy you have spent in building it.

Think of it like an endowment. When a school or other organization has an endowment, there is a substantial stash of capital put away in an investment, and the interest from that investment pays for whatever is endowed. A network is like this, too: you need to have enough relational capital with the folks in your network that you can "live off the interest," so to speak. (Pastoral ministry is like that too— so you can consider this further training for ministry.)

Thus, the first lesson about building and maintaining a healthy network is this: how much have you invested in building the relationships you will tap during the placement process?

If you're following me, you may have realized that you should have started a while ago; years, even. That's true, and if you're just about to launch into your candidacy process there is probably very little you can do about it. It isn't hopeless, though— as we see when we look at the question, "Who's in your network?"

Who Is In Your Network?

The first part of understanding ministry networking, and of seeing your network become the catalyst for your future placement, is recognizing who is in this web of relational connections. These are the people in your world, in your pool of relationships, who do and will see themselves as "stakeholders" in your life and/or ministry: they have a personal stake in whether you succeed or fail, burn out or thrive. So, who is in your network?

When you're thinking about building the network you'll need[3] for candidacy and placement, it is helpful (and encouraging) to consider who is already in your network.

---

2 Okay, that text doesn't mean exactly the same thing that I mean here, but the principle is still found within that sermon.

3 I say "need" because I'm firmly convinced that you will most likely find effective placement through your network. As the results of my survey showed— which you will see shortly— by far most of the graduates surveyed found their placement through their network; more than that, the effective

If you're late to the game, this is all the more important. When I've taught on this subject, and when I've counseled with those going through the candidacy process, I often work through this with them to demonstrate how their networks are already far more robust than they know.

This question was asked directly of me by a student who had taken the class at Covenant Seminary in which I lectured. He stated that, for reasons I won't go into (but they made sense), he had not connected with a church in our denomination for the six years prior to coming to seminary— thus, he feared his network would be severely lacking as he began his candidacy. "Who," he asked, "is in my network?"

In considering the question, I'd like to point out that he had a reasonable concern: a substantial contribution to your network is made from your previous church(es), in the form of pastors you knew there, well-connected elders and deacons, and simply having lay-people who knew you and can speak to whether you will be effective in ministry. The first question I usually encourage others to ask, then, is: "Who knew you in your last church that you have maintained some sort of relationship with?"

Since in this case that question did not apply, I encouraged him to dig deeper: how about other churches he had been affiliated with? Maybe he was involved in a campus ministry in college; is there anyone he still keeps in touch with from there?

Having examined your personal history, now turn to the more recent past and present. After all, you've been in seminary for several years; surely you have met new friends and acquaintances who are now in ministry. You know many professors, and some better than others. And, of course, you have been attending a local church while in seminary (and hopefully you've been active in ministry there, as well). All of these represent parts of your network.

And don't forget— or underestimate— your family. These will be the biggest stakeholders of all, in some ways. Depending on your background, you may not feel that these relationships are directly helpful for ministry candidacy— but you would be wrong. You should never assume that any relationship will not be potentially the very contact you need to be in touch with the church God is calling you into.

Furthermore, realize that the members of your network don't include merely the relationships that you have and maintain, but all of their relationships as well. This is how your network will work with you to help you find placement.

So, who is in your network? Here's a list of starting points:
- Family members
- Seminary classmates
- Seminary professors
- College friends
- Other friends
- People from your home church(es)
- Former campus pastor(s) or ministry worker(s)
- People from presbytery, synod, or regional association

---

placements among them were almost all through a network. In my own experience, as I've already mentioned, every ministry position I have ever had— including my ministry opportunities in seminary— came through my network.

- Visiting pastors and/or speakers whom you have gotten to know while in seminary
- Present and former co-workers

As you can see, this list alone could generate dozens of names— depending on your life circumstances, perhaps even hundreds. And that is just a beginning; your circumstances will dictate how many more people you can add to the list.

So to get started "building" your network, make a list of everyone who fits into as many of these as you can. Do you have addresses, phone numbers, e-mail addresses for them? If not, who would you call to get them? Collect all of these together— in your computer address book, in a notebook or planner, or however will be the most effective way to collect your names and contact information.

Don't look now, but you have a network!

Building Your Network

Now that you know that you have a foundational network in place, how do you add to it? How do you grow it into a larger network? Do you even need to grow it bigger? To answer the last question first: you may not need to build it bigger. The Lord knows exactly how many of His people you need to know in order to be led to the place He has for you!

But you also need to be a good steward of the opportunities for new relationships God puts before you. After all, when we're talking about "building your network" then what we really mean is adding new relationships to your life. And these relationships will either be as brothers and sisters in Christ, or people who do not believe but who nevertheless may enrich your life (and who certainly need the Gospel!). One way or another, can anyone say they have "too many friends" or that they know too many people?

So really, building your network is about taking advantage of the social opportunities that are naturally a part of your life, and seizing those that are offered to you. What might this look like? Here are a few examples:

- **New classmates.** It is unlikely that you will know every classmate in your classes at seminary. If you make it a point to sit beside someone new in one class every semester and befriend them (or even just get acquainted with them), you'll gain 6-10 new friends every semester.
- **Leaders at your "seminary" church.** As you live an active life as a member of the church, and get involved in leadership and service there, you will inevitably get to know a few of the leaders in your congregation.
- **Members of your "home" church.** If you go to seminary in a city different from your hometown, your home church (in your hometown) will be interested in your progress at seminary. They may even ask you to give a report on what you have been doing and learning when you return home. Take note of the people in your home congregation that take especial interest in your seminary training— these will be the ones who see themselves as stakeholders in your current and future ministry. And here is a great opportunity to build some new friendships with people who care about you.
- **Co-laborers in ministry.** If you're involved in ministry during seminary (and if you're not— or haven't been— then I question whether you are

truly being well-trained for ministry), then your co-laborers in that ministry are a part of your network: they have seen your gifts and abilities for ministry at work, and can testify to your fitness for ministry. They'll understand as well as anyone what sorts of ministry opportunities you are best suited for.

Again, this list isn't exhaustive— there will be other opportunities for you to build your network. The point of this list isn't to name all options, but to point out how your relationships with others in the Body of Christ serve to advance your network.

Maintaining & Growing Your Network

Now that you've begun to build your network of relationships, how do you maintain them? How do you grow them?

There are two angles, or approaches, I want to cover about that: I'll call them the organic and the technological approaches. First, the "organic" approach.

There are entire books written about how to build friendships, how to develop relationships, how to grow your "network" in an organic way. Frankly, some of them are awful: they are part of the reason why some in the church have the negative opinion of "networking" that they do. But many of them are incredibly useful, and it would be a mistake to try to re-create here the great work of others. (I've made some recommendations in the appendix.)

That said, I'll list a few principles that are crucial in relationship development.

Be genuine. You're setting out to build real relationships with real people; by definition, a relationship is a commitment. If you're not truly interested in building the relationships you are pursuing, stop now. (For that matter, you might seriously reconsider your calling to the ministry.)

Be available. When opportunities present themselves for connecting with friends— new and old— then you need to be flexible enough to accept them, at least with regular frequency. You don't have to forsake your family life or passing your classes to do it, but you ought to be willing to turn aside from writing the perfect paper or polishing your sermon to acknowledge and relate to a friend or family member.

Be a listener. Sure, you want them to get to know you— how else will they really be a friend to you, or have any sense of stake in your life and ministry? But to build a real relationship you must listen. This doesn't mean solving their problems, offering great advice, or giving an ideal book recommendation. (Well, sometimes it might mean one of those.) It means knowing who they are, the details of their lives, and what their struggles and delights are.

Be pro-active. Sometimes you need to seek them out and be their friend. Whether its a phone call, a note or card in the mail, an e-mail, or lunch or a cup of coffee together, some of the relationship needs to come from you. Don't be one of those friends who never initiates.

Be attentive. Remember their birthdays. Include them on your Christmas card list. Be aware enough of major life changes to note them. And if you know about something significant— like that their dog died, their mother is sick, they are looking for a new job, or there is a problem in their church community— then check in with them about it occasionally.

All of this is exactly what you'll be doing with the people you'll minister to in your pastoral ministry. This is the life you will live as a pastor. If you learn the skill of relationships that these principles speak to, you will be far better prepared for ministry.

And really: isn't this simply "making friends 101"? You've done this before! Don't treat it like it is something you don't have any idea how to do, like evangelism or something.

Now, let's talk about a "technological" approach. By technological approach, I mean technology tools that will help you maintain and grow your friendships and relationships. (Frankly, many of these can help you build and re-build friendships, as well.)

First, though, an important disclaimer: these are tools, not the relationships themselves. And they are intended to be connection facilitators, not the connections themselves. Don't be fooled into mistaking one for the other.

There are several tools that I have used, and that I think every ministry candidate ought to begin to use, before and during their candidacy process:[4]

- **Plaxo** started off as a tool to help you keep your contact information current, then added a social networking component, and have recently switched their focus back toward contact maintenance. This function is the real benefit of the service. You'll sync your computer's address book with Plaxo, and then you can contact those in your address book who have e-mail addresses (selectively or the whole book) and request that they verify the accuracy of their contact information. You'll probably find that a number of your friends are members of the service, too— which means that their information will always automatically be updated. If you've ever struggled to keep accurate phone numbers for your friends, this is the service for you. Furthermore, Plaxo will (at your request) e-mail you reminders of birthdays, and even provide a service for sending customized eCards via e-mail to them. I've found that an eCard sent to most of my contacts is a great way to maintain a regular connection with those who I don't otherwise have frequent contact with.

- If you're not already a member of **Facebook**, I'm surprised. Whether you are or not, you should begin to turn your attention to this social networking service. While MySpace put the social network on everyone's map, Facebook has emerged as the service to be a part of. Why should you be on Facebook? Because you'll find that you are able to re-connect to people you know, but have lost touch with. Whether it be classmates from seminary, college, and even high school, former co-workers, or a fellow member of a church that you were a member of 10 years ago, chances are good that you'll find dozens, if not hundreds, of people you haven't seen or talked to in years. It's also a fun way to keep up with those who you have seen— watching for changes in status, seeing recent pictures, reading "notes," and

---

4 These are tools that I used during my last candidacy, and they are tools that I still use to maintain my networks. However, this list will inevitably be outdated— maybe even by the time this book reaches publication! But the point remains the same: there are some wonderfully rich tools available online— many of them for free— that will help you build and maintain your networks. You should learn about them and take advantage of them.

If You Build It, They Will Come

writing on their "walls." In fact, it's so fun that it can become an addiction— so be careful that you don't get too sucked in! Facebook has reconnected me with literally hundreds of people that I had lost contact with— some of those re-connection stories are pretty cool.

- While your social networking appetite will find full satisfaction with Facebook, I have to also recommend that you join **LinkedIn**, which is also a social network. This one, though, is focused on networking for professionals. Here's what I really like about LinkedIn: they have built into the system a way for introductions to be made between two others who may not know each other. So, if I find someone I'd like to connect to, but I don't know them directly, I may request an introduction from someone we know in common. Also, because it is focused on "professional" networking, the interface feels more like a resume or CV than a personal website or blog (like Facebook can feel like).

Think of it this way: Plaxo will help you keep your address book current; Facebook will aid you in reconnecting with your friends old and new; and LinkedIn will give you access to new relationships through introductions from the people you already know.

Networking At Work

As I've already discussed, networking quickly emerged as a significant factor in my research on the placement process— indeed, that was the initial reason for including it in my "five factors for effective placement."

Here are some quick stats and results from my research:

- 67% of my survey respondents made initial contact with the ministry they eventually accepted a call from through networking.
- 81% of the respondents said they actively and purposefully utilized a network to some useful extent during their candidacy process.
- In an objective question[5] asking, "What was the best thing you did in your candidacy and placement process?" more than 10% answered something along the lines of, "networking with professors, presbytery or convention, and my church."
- In a different objective question asking, "What would you do differently if you were candidating from seminary again?" 10% replied that they would network more often and/or earlier in the process. (Seminary professors and church/presbytery opportunities were specifically identified as areas they would have networked with more often.)

John's Story (Case Study #1)

One of my survey respondents ended up being an interesting case study in the power of networking in the placement process. This is his story.

---

5 There were no preset answers or multiple choice options, but just a blank, "short answer" style question.

Two seminary students (we'll call them Frank and John) were both going through the candidacy process at the same time; they were good friends, and had resolved not to view the process as a competition between them.

Frank found himself as the lead candidate for a position in a non-traditional ministry (one that was not even on John's radar), and he pursued that position as far as he felt he could. As the process advanced, Frank did not sense a strong call to that position, and he felt that some of those on the search team felt the same way. In the end, Frank declined to accept the position— even though it was offered to him— and instead determined that post-graduate education was where the Lord was leading him.

In declining the position, Frank mentioned John favorably to the search team, and urged them to give him consideration. They contacted John and he quickly advanced to become their prime candidate, and they eventually offered John the position, which he accepted.

In reflecting on this, John said, "I wasn't consciously networking, but through the network the job found me."

Interview Highlights (Case Study #2)

While conducting follow-up interviews with those I have surveyed, I have actually gathered dozens of stories and anecdotes of networking at work in the placement process. Here are a few brief accounts:

- *From "Patrick":* While in seminary, we went on a trip to explore a missions opportunity, and while there connected with a pastor and elder from a church that was seeking an assistant pastor. They brought us up to meet their congregation, and that led to my call to serve this church.
- *From "Eric":* I originally saw my position on one of the lists, but didn't think I would be interested because of the description. One of my classmates was the son of the Headmaster at the school that was affiliated with that church, and the father told his son more about the position, which was then passed along to me. Because of this, I placed a phone call to the senior pastor, and that led to an interview and eventually a call.
- *From "Howard":* A fellow student who graduated with me is friends with the senior pastor at the church I now serve; they were originally talking about him filling the position, and when it became clear that my fellow student would not be a good fit, he returned to the seminary campus and called me— he said he had found the perfect position for me. Then he worked to connect me to the senior pastor, and everything fell into place from there.
- *From "Matthew":* I found my first call out of seminary by simply calling the Stated Clerk of the Presbytery where my church was; he pointed me in the direction of that church. While there, one of my elders (who was also the Headmaster at a local Christian school) encouraged me to consider teaching part-time at his school. That elder later moved to another town to serve as the Headmaster of a different school— and he, in turn, extended a call to me to serve as a full-time teacher at that school, where I am now.
- *From "Mike":* A friend from seminary mentioned a position to me that was being vacated by another friend of his. Another friend— an elder of a

church I had served before seminary— had a brother who was a deacon in that church; this friend also mentioned the same opportunity to me. And the Stated Clerk of a presbytery in which I had been filling pulpits had also served that congregation as their pastor, and he mentioned the opportunity to me as well. From there, I sent my information to them and began making contact, and I worked hard to earn a place on the "short list." At that point, the testimony of these others who knew me encouraged the Search Committee to consider me first.

- *From "Russell":* I was pointed to the church I now serve by one of my seminary professors, who was also one of my mentors. Through his encouragement on both sides of the process, I became their prime candidate. Once I accepted the call, another mentor (who pastors a large church in another city) helped me to connect with a seasoned pastor in my area, who has become a great encourager, a source of wisdom, and a supporter during difficult times.

These are just a few samples of the many stories I have heard. And these don't count the situations where an internship or part-time position during seminary matured into a full-time and permanent pastoral call, or when a church that a seminarian was connected with prior to seminary offered a call once seminary was completed.

The stories bear out the statistics: by far, most seminary graduates find their opportunities through networking in some way.

A Seminary President (Case Study #3)

I've personally had a handful of apparently serendipitous encounters with networking at work. Here is one.

In college, a man named Henry led me through discipleship for several years, and we became good friends. He eventually served as the best man in my wedding, and has remained a source of treasured advice and input over the years.

At one point in my candidacy, I was visiting with Henry during a trip to my hometown. Henry knew that I was seeking pastoral placement, and asked about my progress. After hearing my report, Henry asked, "Would you mind if I made a phone call on your behalf?"

I said, of course not, and Henry pulled out his mobile phone and quickly found a number in his speed-dial.

"Hello— this is Henry."

"We're well, and I hope you are too. Hey, we're going to spend the week after New Years' at the mountain house, and we'd love it if you two would come and burn some firewood with us."

"Great! I'll call you with details next week. Say, I'm sitting here with a friend who is looking for an opening for a position as a pastor. Would you be willing to talk with him, and point him in a helpful direction?"

"That's great— thanks so much, Luder. I'll give him your home number."

And when Henry hung up, he wrote down for me the home number of Luder Whitlock, longtime President of Reformed Theological Seminary and now President of Teleios, Executive Director of Trinity Forum, and probably one of the top 10 most well-connected men in the Reformed and Presbyterian circles.

It turned out that Henry and Dr. Whitlock had been close friends for years, and Dr. Whitlock was glad to be a phone call away for me. He suggested a few leads for me, and also committed to praying for me in my transition and ministry regularly. What a blessing!

A Prominent Pastor (Case Study #4)

Another case study from my own experience is below. This one is almost unbelievable, but it is completely true!

I grew up in a prominent United Methodist church in Columbia, South Carolina. My mother and step-father are still members of that church, and are quite active. Naturally, there are a number of people that my mother sees regularly who knew me well as a child, and who often inquire about how and what I am doing lately.

So it didn't come as a surprise to me one day when mom mentioned, "Our good friends the Harleys in Sunday School asked about you, and I told them you were looking for a position as a pastor. They were very interested in that."

Me: "Were they? That's thoughtful! Please tell them thanks for their interest."

Mom: "Well, they asked about where you were looking, and I mentioned that you were a presbyterian. And they said, 'Oh, our son-in-law is a presbyterian pastor.' I said, well, you were a PCA presbyterian— because I know it's a smaller denomination. And they said, 'He is too! Maybe he could help your son!'"

Me: "Wow – that's great, mom. Where is he a pastor?"

Mom: "They said he was in Mississippi."

Me: "Oh— there are lots of PCA churches in Mississippi. Do you remember his name?"

Mom: "It was sort of a strange name... was it... Ligon?"

Me: "Ligon Duncan?"

Mom: "That's it! Their son-in-law's name is Ligon Duncan!"

And so, that is how I happened to spend a couple of hours in two different conversations with Ligon Duncan, who is certainly one of the most prominent people in the PCA, not to mention his involvement with leadership across the Reformed and evangelical world. Dr. Duncan was very gracious, and took great interest in my placement. In fact, we've stayed in touch, and visit each time we see each other at denominational meetings and other events.

A Denominational Leader (Case Study #5)

Here's the last case study from my own experience, and the one about how I made contact with the position I accepted following seminary.

One of the important parts of my networking in particular, and my placement process in general, was to keep in regular contact with a group of friends who prayed for me, offered me feedback and advice, and generally served as brotherly support through the difficult time that candidacy and placement is.

After seeing the process go to very late stages, then watching it fall apart suddenly, one of these guys— Bryan, a former classmate who graduated a year and a half ahead of me— shot me a quick e-mail:

> *"Sorry that things went south in the end. That stinks, and I'm praying for you about it.*

If You Build It, They Will Come

A guy I work with might be able to help you find some good leads. I was talking to him this morning about how things fell through at this latest position, and he said you should call him. Call me in the next couple of days about it."

When I called, Bryan reminded me that the senior pastor at the church he served had left about a year before, and they had recently called an interim pastor: Dominic Aquila.

If you don't know who he is, here's a quick run-down: he has been involved in leadership at different levels in the PCA for decades, in addition to pastoring several churches, and had also be instrumental in starting New Geneva Theological Seminary in Colorado. At the time that Bryan and I were talking, Dominic was also serving as Moderator of the General Assembly of the PCA— a position that cemented his prominence in the denomination.

Suffice to say, Dominic is also a well-connected contact. I e-mailed him about finding a time to talk, and he also asked to see my resume and Ministerial Data Form, which I sent along. When we talked a few days later, he had studied both of these, and was well-acquainted with what sort of role and position I was seeking. He worked through the "vacant pulpits" list with me, and made some suggestions of which ones to call (and which ones to avoid!).

A couple of months later, I was anticipating the General Assembly in June and hoping for some good networking opportunities then. I e-mailed Dominic and asked if he might have a few moments to meet with me at the Assembly, which he responded that he would. (Remember, he's the outgoing Moderator, so he had his hands full with stuff— but he made time for me, nonetheless.)

When we met up again, he suggested several opportunities, including my current church. Within a few days of returning from General Assembly, I contacted the elder who was leading the search at this church, and mentioned that Dominic had encouraged me to call. We agreed that I would send my resume and Data Form to him. After we talked, he hung up and called Dominic, as well as my friend and former professor Phil Douglass, and asked them about me.

The next thing I knew, I had an invitation to come and interview. No sermon recordings, no phone interview— just the word of two men who had become an important part of my network, and a glimpse of my resume. That was enough.

And there I was. I interviewed, gathered a lot of information, preached and led worship, and enjoyed a covered-dish dinner with them. As we left, Marcie and I were both convinced that this was where the Lord was bringing us— a sentiment that was reciprocated the following Sunday in the congregational meeting.

Final Thoughts On Networking

As you can see from the case studies, networking is a great opportunity for developing strong leads; in fact, as I'll discuss in the next chapter, it is one of the few things you can do to ensure that you will be looked at with serious interest.

I hope you can also see from this chapter that building and maintaining a network isn't unnatural or extremely difficult— it is simply the process of accepting the opportunities for relationships that come your way, and seeking people out who are already accessible to you. Some are better at this than others, and some quickly amass great numbers of contacts while others are doing well to have a few dozen.

But the only "wrong" ways to network are either not to do it, or to do it as if everyone owes you something. If you deny the value of biblical networking, you're functionally saying that the way God's people are described throughout the Scriptures— as a body, as a family, as those who are bound together and connected by Christ and His work— is unimportant. Or at least you're saying that in this one particular aspect— namely, who will be the pastor of a certain congregation— it doesn't matter. Instead, you'd prefer to put your future hopes and ambitions in the hands of lists, job boards, and cold-calls.

God uses His people for each other in many different ways. One of those ways is to place pastors with congregations that are a good fit for each other, and to place people in ministry where they will be able to serve Him and His people the most.

PART 2: FROM KNOWING TO DOING

On Early Birds and Worms

The early bird gets the worm. Or, as I like to say, "Candidate early, candidate often."

The first thing to know about starting the candidacy process is that you must start early. If the thought of finishing seminary doesn't excite you to get started as soon as possible, then your placement work-ethic must. The statistical data supports this, as does my experience and the experiences of dozens of other seminary graduates.

In this chapter, I'll help you better understand why starting early is so important, and tell you what you need to know— both theory and practice— to get started right.

Why Starting Early Is So Important

Why is starting early so important? Why does it take so long? A large part of the equation is what happens on the church's side. One of the churches I candidated with was a good example.

This particular church began developing the position (a new assistant pastor role) in late spring 2006. This development essentially consisted of the elders approving a position in principle, senior pastor drafting a position description, and the elders approving it. While this was a relatively quick procedure (it probably was completed in less than two months), this is exceptional. When a position description is subject to the work of self-studies, committee discussion, and congregational approval, the process obviously would take a lot longer.

Once that was completed, they began listing the position as open (mid-summer) and they formed a search team. By early fall, they had begun gathering a number of candidates, and the search team started the lengthy process of screening and evaluating these candidates.

I contacted them mid-fall; my package of information went into the pile with the others. I don't know how many there were that I was competing with, but if I had to guess it would be over 50 candidates. [Elapsed time since the beginning of the search: six months.]

Remember, these committees are made up of volunteers, meeting as often as they can and doing "homework" (reading documents, listening to sermons, calling references) on their own time. This particular committee met monthly at least; sometimes they were able to meet as often as twice a month, and even on occasion more often than that. Even if they met weekly, the search team had a lot of work to do. They likely eliminated some more quickly than others, but when the time came to make a major cut they probably still had 15 or more to choose from. From there, they cut down to a handful. [Total elapsed time: eight months.]

This handful would next face telephone interviews. Again, if they scheduled them one at a time, each would take 2-3 hours; at least one hour for the interview itself, plus another hour or more for discussion. They planned to meet weekly to conduct these, having a month's worth of work to do. In the end it took almost two months. [Total elapsed time: 10 months.]

By this point they will narrow the candidate pool to one or two candidates. Having done this, they will schedule a visit for the top candidate. In this case, this was simply a matter of bringing the candidate (and his wife, if he's married) to them; however, in other situations (such as when the candidate is a senior or solo pastor, and they must visit him), it may be more complicated. Still, this case-study church needed a few weeks to get this organized. It's reasonable to think that it may usually take a month before the interview weekend actually occurs. [11 months.]

Assuming they still prefer their top candidate, they may begin the process of extending him a call in the week following the interview weekend. (If they vote against him, or if he refused the call, it may take another few weeks before another interview weekend with a different candidate.) It may take a few days, or even a week, for negotiation of the terms of call (that is, if he also believes that this is the call God has for him). Once the negotiations are done, it is likely that the candidate will need a month or six weeks, at minimum, before he is available. However, if he is currently serving another congregation, it may take two or more months to complete the transition from one call to another.

If all of this goes as smoothly as possible, they may have their new assistant pastor approximately one year after they began the process of looking for him. There are any number of things that might complicate it and cause it to be much longer:

- Developing the position description requires broader input than just staff and elders
- Phone interviews are slowed by schedules and take two or three months
- The first "pick" is not the right guy— or he doesn't accept the call— and they have to go another round (or two, three, four...)
- After accepting the call, he needs several months before he can make the transition
- Snags with presbytery slow down the ordination or transfer of credentials process (this is particularly a concern for a solo or senior pastor)

In most cases, a church should expect the process to take a minimum 12-18 months. If a candidate gets in at just the right moment, he may face only the last 2-3 months of it before he knows he has a firm call. In all likelihood, it will be at least four or five months in many candidates' experience. And that's assuming that the first opportunity he contacts is the one he ends up with. In fact, however, almost every respondent to my survey candidated with multiple churches at some level.

Why is starting early so important? If you want to place by graduation, you have to give it the time it takes— and that means six months or more.

Seasons Of Transition

It is peculiar, just a little bit, how much transition happens (or doesn't happen) based on the season.

During most of my transition I regularly (e.g., daily) checked the vacant pulpit listings for my denomination and a few other listings, and I noticed an odd affirmation of this seasonal dependence at one point. Over the summer months, only four new listings were added to the main listing, yet the "last updated" date changed at least twice a week, usually more. In other words, these months saw probably 15 different updates of the list, but only four additions; all of the rest were positions being removed from the list.

Now I would love to see that kind of ratio remain constant— eventually, there would be almost NO churches looking for a pastor! But this is not the way it is; rather, there is an ebb and flow to these kinds of lists that I haven't quite figured out.

I would think, for example, that more pastors would leave churches during the summer; it is a natural time for transition (e.g., it doesn't disrupt the school schedule for the pastor's children, etc.). But what I described above actually shows the opposite: more churches filled pulpits than emptied them, if you will. (It could very well be that some, or even most, of those pastors that filled pulpits left empty ones behind, and those would show up on the list in due time.)

This seasonal effect applies at other times of the year, too. The "holiday season," typically from mid-November until the end of the calendar year, is historically an awful time to be seeking placement. It just doesn't happen much: committees stop meeting, no one brings in a candidate-preacher during that time, and everyone is so busy that even minimal communication is a stretch. As I've talked with December graduates from my seminary, they have all indicated that this is a major obstacle.

The Plight Of The December Graduate

In my discussions with seminary graduates who finish in December, they all tell the same story: December graduation is tough.

Now, placement is not easy for any seminary grad, but I think finishing in December is a lot tougher than in May for most graduates. To introduce my reasons, I'll recap some of what my research in this area has shown:

- 40% of those who started the candidacy process LESS THAN 6 months before graduation were not placed by their graduation date (regardless of when they graduated)
- On the other hand, of those who started candidacy MORE THAN 6 months before graduation, only 11% were not placed by their graduation
- Further, of those who started earlier than 6 months out, less than 3% were not placed within a few months of graduating
- And generally speaking, the earlier the graduates began their search, the more likely they were to be placed by graduation

I would suggest that this research indicates that May is the perfect time to graduate from seminary. Why? Because the school year preceding a May graduation is a full 9 months with only a brief break for Christmas, while the school year preceding a December graduation (generally the only other option) includes the significant summer break. In other words, the 9-month school year for the May graduate is an ideal timeframe for candidacy.

Let me elaborate: the candidacy process, like so many processes, depends on momentum to some degree. While the Christmas break can slow this momentum down somewhat, the length of the summer break will, in most cases, bring it to a halt. Even if the candidate remains diligent during these breaks, there is no guarantee that the churches they are pursuing will keep the momentum up; on the contrary, most search committees I've talked to find summer and the advent season to be the most difficult times to maintain momentum.

This means that things will slow down for both, but May graduates have the entire spring semester to regain momentum. December grads, on the other hand, find that the end of their last semester brings another time for slowing down— because after mid-November, churches lose focus on the search process and get tied up with holiday activities. In other words, May graduates have 4-5 months of strong candidating time in their last semester, while December graduates have only two and a half.

Even the diligent December grads who follow the advice of the statistics and begin their search more than six months before graduation face this, but in my research I have found that few December grads actually begin looking before the summer break. For most December graduates, the timeframe for candidacy begins with a sudden realization that they have only four or five months before they finish, and they hurriedly begin their search in August. Those who wait until their last semester is underway face an even tougher challenge, the statistics say: 50% of graduates who began their search three months or less from graduation were not placed when they graduated.

So is the lesson that December graduates should begin their search in the spring before their last fall semester? Maybe— but this doesn't help them tremendously, because at that point they are in comparison with those May graduates who are just a few weeks from graduation (and therefore available for a position also in a matter of weeks), while they themselves are unavailable for eight months or more.

One lesson to be learned here is simple: if possible, plan to graduate in May. But if you cannot arrange it this way, be prepared for the difficulties it will bring.

What can a December graduate do to be prepared? Here are a few ideas:

- *Still begin early.* Just because you will be "competing" with May graduates doesn't mean that good groundwork cannot be laid. Particularly in the realm of building your network, you can make major headway if you start working on your candidacy in February or March.
- *Be tenacious during the summer.* It is easy— too easy— to let things slip in the summer months. But this can actually be a good time for working on candidacy: attending General Assemblies and other meetings, visiting key churches, pastors, and other friends who will be strong referrals, and making first contact with opportunities whose searches are underway or just beginning.
- *Finish well.* The last semester of seminary is still important. Steel your mind toward doing it right: study hard, write well, be ready to take exams, ask good questions. Attend to the details of field education, final paperwork, and commencement. These are important for May graduates too— but for whatever reason, these details seem to be easier to neglect for December graduates. You haven't graduated yet, which means that your primary calling from God is to remain firmly committed to your studies.
- *Have a contingency plan.* I know several former classmates whose placement fell a month or two after their December graduation. The ones who weathered this the best were the ones who had a contingency plan for what they would do if placement weren't complete. One friend made arrangements to house-sit for a family in his church for the month of January. Another

arranged a lease extension for the seminary housing he occupied. Some took on extra hours at work and saved aggressively during the months before graduation. Your circumstances will vary, but the need for a plan won't. The only ones who have regrets are the ones who don't plan.

Selling Dreams

Christians are called to evangelize the lost— that is, to present the Gospel to unbelievers in a way that is honest, loving, and compelling. Is there a methodology for the presentation of ideas in evangelism that we're missing if we apply it only to the Gospel? Said another way, what if a candidate approached the placement process as the evangelization of himself, if you will, not unlike he might present the Gospel?

I have frequently recommended a great book, *Selling the Dream* by Guy Kawasaki. Kawasaki presents evangelism in exactly this way. He suggests that the best marketing of ideas, whether it be for products or causes, is done through evangelism. This is because anyone can advertise an idea, but no one evangelizes something they don't truly believe in. Thus, Guy defines evangelism as it applies to "marketing" (to use the term in its broadest sense) as "selling the dream"— thus, the title of his book.

Now if you think that Kawasaki is equating products or business ideas with the Gospel, you've misunderstood. Guy, a Christian who is a member of Menlo Park Presbyterian Church in California, uses the idea of evangelism very loosely compared with its biblical sense. But I think he is onto something about marketing, communication, and persuasion that is highly applicable to placement.

If you're with me on the importance of a candidate's sense of calling, hopefully you'll follow me on evangelism as well. Do you believe you are called to ministry? Is it a part of your identity— even similar to your calling as a Christian? Then you should feel compelled to convince others of this calling to ministry, as well. And convincing them out of your own genuine belief, rather than out of a sense of obligation (as advertising might be understood), is all that is meant by evangelism.

Put another way, when you dream of what God will have you doing, what does that look like? Now what if you could do exactly that if you could only convince others to share the same dream— or "sell" them on your dream? See the connection? Selling the dream is exactly what we do when we candidate well. It isn't false advertising or misrepresentation; it is putting ourselves forth as everything we believe ourselves to be. That's good candidacy.

Getting Started

When I've taught classes on candidating and transition into pastoral ministry, one of the questions I'm frequently asked is, "What do I do to get started in the candidacy process?"

This is a great question; it is one of the ideas that motivated me to write this book. I believe that, without helpful guidance at this stage, many seminarians could get stalled and never get the early start that they need in the placement process.

Here are eight steps to starting— and maintaining— your candidacy well:

1. **Make sure your resume, Data Form(s), Reference List, Bio, and Philosophy of Ministry are current.**

These are the documents that I recommend that you offer to send any church you contact, and all of them deserve a review right before you begin the candidacy process. Ask yourself:

- Do I need to add or change any of the titles or descriptions on my resume?
- Does my Data Form accurately reflect what it should?
- Have any of my references moved or changed jobs?
- Should I add anything to my bio?
- Do I still hold to that Philosophy of Ministry?

Since I already have these documents prepared, it might take me a couple of hours to ensure they are current if I were starting candidacy right now. Starting from scratch, however, it could take days or even weeks to get them to "final draft" status. (Getting them to the "final draft" stage is what the next chapter is all about.) This is first priority, since you want to be able to get these out the door (or sent in an e-mail) right away when the time comes.

Now, about that time coming… how do you get that part started?

2. **Contact your "network."**

You should send an e-mail to a trusted group of people and ask them to pray for you as you begin your search and if they know of any positions that would be a good fit. You should also ask them ask their network about any opportunities. I recommend looking for at least 30-50 people for this query. And you should start making intentional individual contact with your network, either by phone or in person, to check in with them in a more personal way.

(2a. Also at this point I suggest you contact your closest 5-10 friends and ask that they be praying regularly and specifically for you; you should begin to send them periodic e-mails that give them updates on your search.)

These people are your best bet for getting a good placement, so you need to take the relationships seriously. Hopefully, you've already taken these relationships seriously, as described in the last chapter. In just a few pages, I'll discuss this in more detail.

3. **Research any opportunities produced by contacting your network.**

You can likely expect that your first round of contact might give you a lead or two— maybe even as many as five or six—and now it is time to look into these opportunities a bit more. Your knee-jerk reaction to a generated lead might be to contact them immediately with a packet of information. DON'T! You need to know more about those opportunities before you contact them.[1]

---

1 A friend of mine who shares my interest in placement has created a helpful tool for gathering and researching information about potential opportunities. With his cooperation, I offer a version of his research tool on the Doulos Resources website. See the appendix on other resources for more information.

On Early Birds And Worms

Here are some questions you'll be asking in this research:
- Have I checked to see if these churches have websites?
- What does a little demographic research tell me about the area and its ministry potential?
- Do I know anyone who is or has been on staff at that church?
- Is this opportunity listed on any of the many websites— and if so, what does that listing tell me about the job description?

You're looking for confirmation that this position would, in fact, be a good fit for you; there's no sense in pursuing something that you won't consider, and you'll protect their time and your own by doing a good job with this step. (I'll walk you through more about gathering research— including how to get the answers to these questions— in the next chapter.)

4. Contact those opportunities that rise to the top after your research is complete.

Chances are, one or two of these leads might be very exciting, even after "vetting" them through good research. If that's the case, you will want to begin contacting them now. (If none of them pass the "vetting" process, return to step #2.)

You'll start by making a phone call. If you've found a contact person listed, try to contact them; this may be through a provided phone number, or by calling the church's number and asking for some help with this. If the opportunity is an assistant or associate pastor role, you might call the senior pastor. When you call, be sure to mention how it was that you came into contact with them— sometimes, the difference between an inhospitable reception and a glowing one will be the mention of a name that they already know.

One opportunity that I explored started exactly like this. I was encouraged to call about this church by an acquaintance, and I called the man whose name had been given to me. He answered with an unenthused, "hello," and despite my best efforts at a winsome self-introduction, he remained deadpan and monosyllabic. That is, until I said, "So-and-so suggested that I call you…" At that, he immediately changed his disposition and the rest of the conversation was animated and enthusiastic.

If all you have is an e-mail address, send a brief (as in, 2-3 short paragraphs) message introducing yourself and asking if you may telephone the contact person; ask them to respond with a number where you may call them. If even this doesn't pan out— if you get no response to this request, or the response simply asks that you "send my data form through e-mail"— you might consider downgrading this opportunity to a last-hope level (unless you later hear something more from them).

Those that you do talk to will get asked the same questions:
- How is the search going (and are you still considering new candidates)?
- What can you tell me about the church?
- Can you tell me anything about what you are seeking for this position?

These questions will tell you much that the paperwork you might receive won't. (We'll talk through phone calls— and why you start with a phone call— later in this chapter.)

5. Send your information to those opportunities that request it.

You shouldn't take for granted that, just because you've done a little ground work and bothered to call, the guy on the other end will automatically want your resume.

He (or she) will probably ask you a few questions to gauge whether they would be interested in you as a candidate. You should begin to get a sense about whether he is interested or not; at this point, it is appropriate to ask if you may send your information— then ask what they would like to receive. I usually offer my resume, Data Form, and bio the first time around. There will be plenty of time to send the rest.

Be sure to ask also if there is a particular format that they would prefer for receiving information. These days, some will want it all to be digital— but be prepared to send paper copies by mail if they would like them.[2] Similarly, many committees will be comfortable working with sermon recordings that are in mp3 format— and even with files that are online. Others, though, would still rather have them on CD; a few may even prefer cassette tapes! It is impossible to know what the preferences of a committee will be, but messing up with something like this is a silly way to give a bad first impression. The safest route is to ask what the preferences of each committee are. (The next chapter will have more advice on how to put together the various options for presentation.)

6. Check the vacancy lists.

There are a surprising number of lists where you can find ministry vacancies, and you'll probably revisit these lists regularly and frequently.[3] This is the first stop for a lot of guys, who will invest most of their candidacy energy in the opportunities listed here— but notice that it is far down in the process for us. After you've worked over all of the opportunities generated by real relationships that you already have— and only then— you'll start to look for new opportunities. The reason is simple: you're far more likely to get your foot in the door with a church that you already have some sort of connection with than you are with a church that you've contacted with no common points of reference.

Those opportunities that look promising will be filtered through #2a (my close friends), #3, and #4: ask your friends if they know anything about this opportunity, do some research about it, then start making phone calls. This part was exhausting for me, because as an introvert I spent an enormous amount of energy trying to build a new relationship on a cold-call. Still, the initial phone call is THE WAY to gain an edge with a church on one of these lists; otherwise, you're just one more resume in a stack of 75 others. When you've gotten to the phone calls, #5 kicks in again, and then you'll start sending out information again.

7. Follow-up in a timely way.

Follow-up is essential.

You don't want to become a pest, and care is required to avoid being one. Nevertheless, You are trying to build a relationship with this person and the search team they are a part of, so you must regularly make follow-up contact with the point person on the search. This may be a quick e-mail, a phone call, or both.

---

2   Some will want it digitally because it will be easy to forward it along to other committee members, while others will be bothered with digital files because they'll have to download and print them. On the other hand, some will like paper copies because it is easy to make photocopies at the church's office, while others will resent the costs of having to make paper duplicates (instead of e-mailing the files around and asking committee members to print them!).

3   There is a collection of links to online lists of ministry opportunities at the Doulos Resources website.

When you contact them, it is a good opportunity to put into practice the idea (from the Attitude Adjustments chapter) that you are actually beginning your ministry to them. For example, every time I made contact in this way, I assured them that I was praying for them and their search; asked how I might be praying more specifically; and I asked if there has been any progress that they can share with me. (By the way, this was not just a tactful way of probing them for updates; I genuinely meant all of this, and would discourage anyone from saying something like this if they don't mean it.) Typically, they were happy to give me an update if there was something to tell, and I slowly got the opportunity to know at least one member of the search team.

Unless you happen to make contact with the church that will end up calling you as one of the first opportunities you contact, you'll eventually find that you must keep a lot of new relationships and information straight as you move through the process. Even if you do contact your future church first, if you fail to follow up well then you'll never make it to that stage in the process!

For almost everyone, then, it will become necessary to have some system of organizing and tracking how frequently you contact an opportunity, what progress you have made with them, and what information you have (and haven't) gathered from them. (I'll walk you through some suggestions for setting up such a system later in this chapter.)

8. Respond promptly to their requests for information.

If things go well, one or more churches may ask you to provide more information— either something you already have prepared, or something that they request, such as a questionnaire that they'd like you to answer. Do they want a CD of some sermons? Would they like your reference list? Could you fill out this profile form they have designed?

Whatever their requests, get your response turned around as quickly as you can, while attending to accuracy and precision. For things that you have already prepared (or should be able to get together quickly)— such as reference lists or sermon recordings— 2-3 days is reasonable; for things like a questionnaire, 7-10 days is fine. If you're unsure, feel free to ask them how quickly they need it; they may be meeting in a week and want to consider your answers at that meeting, if possible. (We'll cover more on this in the next chapter.)

In each of these steps, you must do your utmost to be gracious, tactful, and appreciative. Remember that your ministry to your future church could be starting with this phone call, and work to put their priorities in front of your own if at all possible.

Finding Opportunities

How do you find your dream call? How do you find the leads for opportunities that fit you?

The key starting point, as I've already mentioned, is utilizing your network. Beyond that, you'll have to do some research in some of the growing number of places. We'll talk about those, too— but let's start with your network.

When you first contact your network, you don't want to be presumptuous. Instead, start slow with gracious and appreciative requests for their help. You may need to spend some time introducing them to, or reminding them of, the essentials of what you are looking for. Can you summarize your sense of calling in a sentence or two, or maybe a paragraph? Are you able to succinctly state your notion of what kind of position you seek? Do so in this contact, and accompany it with an open-ended request for their help.

Once you've made an initial contact, follow up with them with more specific questions about opportunities that they might know of, ones that you have encountered that you think they will have some opinion about, or people they may know that you could contact through them. Some of your network will be more forthright about their willingness to help than others; this doesn't mean that the others aren't willing— only that they haven't communicated their willingness as openly. Knowing your network will help you navigate this better. Still, it is usually safe to assume that those who state outright that they want to help are a good starting place.

One thing to remember about finding opportunities through your network is that all information is valuable. They may suggest an opportunity, or they may not; regardless, they might also suggest that you call a friend of theirs for potential leads. (In fact, you should ask them if they know anyone whom you might call for leads.) They may say that they will keep you in mind should something come up, or that they will pray for your search. All of this is vital, as my case studies in the previous chapter illustrate.

Finding opportunities by way of your network also opens the door to opportunities that you otherwise would not have access to: the ones that aren't listed anywhere!

Sometimes The Best Positions Aren't Listed

I was added to the candidate pool for a position at a large, denominational church with a multiple-pastor staff in a major city, that had three or four open positions for ordained ministry (in addition to the five ordained pastors already on staff). **None** of those three or four positions are to be found on any list of available opportunities.

So how did I get word of them? How can you find out about similar positions? You guessed it— through my network.

I learned about it through a telephone call with the former seminary president I mentioned in the last chapter. He told me, "you should call this church," and I did.

The point is this: in a lot of churches, the pastor(s) already have enough contacts in ministry to be choosy about how they recruit candidates. Often, these are churches that people want to work for. The way to get on their radar, if you don't happen to be from that church to begin with, is to use your network.

One of the larger PCA churches in St. Louis hired at least three pastors in this manner. They never solicit resumes or candidates through lists or publications, but prefer to use their existing network.

Finding More Opportunities

There could come a point where you've exhausted the leads that your network has turned up. For some, this point is very far down the line, because their networks are large and well-developed; for others, it might be after a short while. How do you find opportunities beyond your network?

A natural next step is to peruse the many lists of available opportunities. These can be both helpful and harmful to your search— and an uninformed approach won't do you much more good than simply ignoring them altogether. The goal of this book is greater effectiveness in the candidacy process. How do you effectively use opportunity lists?

First, let's talk about how they can be helpful. Some of this is self-evident: they make you aware of vacant pulpits, open positions, and ministry opportunities. The average list might have as few as eight or ten opportunities; it might have 50 or more. Some lists are position-specific; others are denomination-specific. Some break down their listings into categories. Others can be sorted through beneficial use of database tools. In short, if you know what sort of position you're looking for, you can find new leads for it through one or more lists.

But this is also where they can be harmful to your search. The key is that you must know what to look for— and the more you try to keep your options open, the more it seems that the lists are providing too much data! After a short while, it can become overwhelming. Even with some specifics to narrow it down, the sheer quantity of opportunities will exhaust the average candidate-pastor quickly.

Another way that they can be harmful is that they lead to complacency for both the seeking church and the candidating pastor. Using these lists gives a false sense of security regarding how much has been or needs to be done about the search. A candidate might say to himself, "I've checked the lists; I haven't found an opportunity like what I'm seeking. God must be telling me to wait." Maybe— but God also might be waiting for this fellow to get motivated and talk to people, not look at lists! Likewise, it can breed an attitude in churches of, "if you list it, they will come."

Here are some ways that I suggest you make effective use of the opportunity lists:

- *Pick just a few.* If you go to the Doulos Resources website, you'll find links to nearly 200 different websites with placement or opportunity lists. You should choose two or three, or at most four or five, that will be your regular lists, and generally don't bother beyond that. Choose well: decide to review only the denominational lists in those denominations that you want to serve, or the lists from a few like-minded seminaries, or something along these lines. If you're planning to pursue a youth ministry job, there are job-specific lists. Pick a few and don't get distracted by the others.
- *Read the whole listing several times.* Most lists have at least a little more data than simply the church's name and which position is open. Whatever is offered, soak it up— this will be the first steps of researching this opportunity. (I'll cover this more in the next chapter.)
- *Learn what to ignore.* Yes, you read that right— there are some things that you can (at least potentially) ignore in a listing. For example, sometimes a church will list that they seek a candidate in a certain age-range— maybe 50 or older. Does this eliminate you if you're in your 30s? Possibly; but the only way to know is to ask. One interviewee said he learned that some churches will say that mainly because they are an older congregation, and they assume that a younger pastor wouldn't be interested in being their pastor. Discerning this sort of nuance requires that you learn to read between the lines of the listing— and that can only be done after you've gleaned enough experience at researching them that you know how to interpret

them. Not all of these will be things you can truly ignore, but they will be more negotiable than the listing suggests.
- *Seek help.* Solicit input from your network— especially your closest friends and advisors— about the opportunities you find. Do they know of these? Have they known anyone who served these congregations? Who would they recommend that you talk to about evaluating them? One of the most helpful things that happened in my search was to have a denominational leader (who I had come into contact with through my network) sit down with me and work over the entire opportunity list with me. He was familiar with 95% of the churches on that list, and he went straight down, saying things like, "this one would be a good fit for you," or "I'm not sure I could recommend that you pursue that one," or "this opportunity needs someone with a different gift-mix." It was amazing— and helped me eliminate at least a dozen congregations that I had included in my own evaluation of the list.
- *Get good contact information.* This might be offered within the listing; if not, you'll want to research it. Here again, I'll focus on this more in the next chapter— but for now keep in mind that without the right phone number or e-mail address, you won't get off the ground.

The Ground-Breaking Phone Call

This leads us to the all-important first phone call. With it, as I have suggested, you'll break ground on what could be your first (or next) pastoral ministry.

I am firmly convinced that the only way to effectively begin the candidacy process with any church is with a phone call.[4] E-mail is too distant and relationally-ambiguous, and is also somewhat unreliable. Face-to-face meetings are often too intimate for beginning this sort of thing, and require an extraordinary ability for thinking on your feet. Over the phone, however, you are able to be comfortable and confident, yet highly relational; the intonations of your voice and even smiles can be detected, reducing the chance of miscommunication. For introductions in candidacy, phone calls rule.

How should a good introductory phone call go? It starts with consideration: which day, and what time of day, would be best to call? For obvious reasons, you might avoid Sundays; Wednesdays, also, tend to be busy days for most church folks, and many churches also have meetings and events on Tuesday evenings. Mondays, Thursdays, Fridays, and Saturdays are more likely to be better days. And if you're calling on a weekday, for instance, then you'll do best to call in the evening; on the other hand, mid-morning would be preferable. Don't call too early in the mornings or too late in the evenings, and be considerate of mealtimes. Also be sure to take time zone differences into account.

It also starts with having good information in terms of referrals. Who is the person you are calling? What is their position at the church, and/or their role in the search

---

4   The only exception that I can envision is if you have an opportunity to meet someone for the first time at a conference or assembly, and they end up being your primary point of contact with a church you are candidating with. Even in such a circumstance, however, I don't believe this is the most effective way to begin the candidacy process.

process? Who referred you to this opportunity and contact person— and how are they connected to the church? Has your referrer communicated their reference of you with the contact person, or with someone else at the church (in other words, will they be expecting your call)? Ideally, the person referring you will know the church well enough to be at least modestly familiar with the contact person, and would have already communicated with him or her regarding their reference of you to them.

When you call, know who you are calling for by name, and ask for that person (even if you think it is him or her). I would usually introduce myself first: after they said hello, I would say, "Hello, this is Ed Eubanks. I'm calling for Bill Smith; is he available please?"

When your contact is on the line, don't waste time in identifying yourself and why you are calling. Unless you are certain that he knows who you are and why you are calling, he may easily mistake you for a solicitor or some other call that he wouldn't want to take![5] Instead, go right into who you are, why you are calling, and who (if anyone) referred you to them. I might say, "Mr. Smith, this is Ed Eubanks, and John Jones encouraged me to call you about the position of Associate Pastor at First Presbyterian Church."

This should break the ice. Particularly if you have mentioned someone who is acquainted with the church (and with whom the church— and your contact person— is also acquainted), you may expect him to respond enthusiastically. From here, you want to keep three things in mind: continued consideration, a pastoral spirit, and a brief exchange of information.

First, you want to continue to be considerate of the contact person. After saying, "John Jones encouraged me to call you…" then the next sentence out of my mouth might be, "Is now a good time to be calling?" Be prepared for them to say, "no." If they do, ask when might be a good time, and get on their schedule if you can. If you must do this, then try to accommodate their schedule if at all possible— don't make them list off three or four (or more) dates and times to which you have to say, "that won't work." Make it work, if you can.

If now is, indeed, a good time to talk, remember that this might be your first opportunity to exercise your pastoral ministry to a member of your future congregation. Minister to him or her. Ask questions about how they are, how the search team is, how the congregation is doing. Is the search going well— or is it becoming a discouragement to the team and the congregation? How is the congregation as a whole weathering the time of transition? Don't press too hard; there will be plenty of time to learn about their search, and how they are handling it. But inquire enough to establish a pastoral tone in your conversation, and don't rush the conversation if he or she does want to talk.

This will be a good opportunity to begin to pick up details about the position, as well. Listen for cues that suggest what their pastoral needs are; ask questions about the congregation in general, and about the pastoral needs specifically. Don't neglect this chance to glean this information. It is both pastoral to have and express concern

---

5   In fact, I would actually avoid the sort of pleasantries that normally accompany soliciting calls, such as, "how are you today?" or "how is everything today?" since these are almost hallmarks of such a call. You wouldn't want your contact to be looking for ways to hang up with you!

for these matters, and useful for your candidacy and evaluation of whether this opportunity is a good fit for you.

You might look for other points of relational contact, as well: what are things that you have in common, or interests that you share? If the opportunity arises, don't hesitate to strike up a brief conversation with them about something that might become a foundation for future friendship.

Assuming that you remain interested in the opportunity at this point, the last goal is to have a brief exchange of information. Specifically, you want to find out:

- If they would be willing to consider you as a candidate
- What information he would like to have if he will begin to consider you as a candidate
- How should you deliver that information to him
- How you might obtain information about the opportunity
- When would be a good time to follow up with him

You should not presume that they will consider you. There are many reasons why they might not: maybe they already have a strong candidate and want to wait before introducing others, or they have more candidates than they are able to screen at this point. It could be that something you've said has indicated that you might not be the right fit: perhaps your age or experience level raises concerns for the contact person, or something else altogether. These don't have to be deal-breakers. If they don't have room to consider you now, ask if you might follow up with them at a certain point (maybe in a month or two). If they suggest that they are looking for someone with more experience or who is older or younger, ask (politely!) if they would be willing to consider you in spite of these obstacles. I had both circumstances come up in my search, and both were overcome with these requests. (This is another reason why the phone call is so critical for introduction.)

In most cases they will be glad to consider you. By asking, though, you have demonstrated respect and humility, and avoided seeming presumptuous or presenting an air of entitlement. It's always a good idea to simply ask, "Would your search team be willing to consider me as a candidate for this position?"

You'll have a lot of different kinds of information to send, but you won't want to send all of it at once— especially if he or she doesn't request it.[6] You could inquire broadly with an open-ended question such as, "What sort of information would be helpful for your search team to have in order to begin to get to know me?" Or you might prefer a question with specifics: "I have several informational documents I'd be happy to send to you, including a resume, a Ministerial Data Form, a brief biography, a summary of my philosophy of ministry, a list of references, and copies of sample sermons I have preached; would any of those be helpful to your committee?"[7] I recommend the first option, as it allows him to set the pace for how much information he wants/needs.

---

6   Some anecdotal evidence suggests that you will actually hurt your candidacy efforts if you send too much information at first; I'll go over this in detail in the next chapter, along with some discussion about timing and how/when to send more.

7   If you go with the second option, be prepared: he might respond, "send them all" which will put you in jeopardy of the problem mentioned above. That is why I recommend the first.

Once you have established what to send, you should inquire about how to send it. As I mentioned earlier, preferences here may vary greatly. One search team might prefer e-mail for everything, while another would rather get a thick envelope in the mail. Ask, and then accommodate their preferences if at all possible. An ancillary question here might also be: how soon would they like it? It might be the case that their committee will be meeting in a few days, and if you could get the information to them by then you could be introduced at that point. In many ways, this is an ideal situation: your contact person will still have you freshly in mind when he or she attends that meeting, and they will therefore be able to speak of you in a more personal and real manner than if you had simply sent paperwork. Don't hesitate to pay for a next-day shipping of your information packet if it will facilitate this.

You must also begin to gather information about this opportunity, and you should ask your contact person about the best ways to do this. Some will have created a website (or a page on the church's website) with information;[8] Others will have a variety of documents and other information available. Over time, they might begin to send you newsletters, bulletins/worship folders, and other materials from the church, and/or information about the city, county, or region the church is in. This conversation is the time to begin expressing your desire for it, and to start obtaining it. Ask your contact person what information is available that he/she could send you.

Then you'll want to learn when would be a good time to follow up with them. Follow-up will be critical; I'll go into that in the next section of this chapter. There is no better time to schedule a time to follow-up than during this conversation. If they know you're serious about following up, they will take you more seriously as a candidate— and if you do a good job of follow-up, you will establish yourself as attentive, diligent, and responsible in addition to building a good relationship with the search team and contact person. Let one of the last things you do be to ask for some advice about when you should follow up.

Finally: be as brief as possible without being rude. There are several goals here, and none of them require a lengthy conversation. First you want to get your name known to the primary contact person; this was accomplished the minute you got them on the phone. Second, you want to establish a pastoral tone to this new relationship, and begin to get to know the church and its needs; this can be done with even one or two well-placed and well-asked questions, followed by good listening. Third, you want to learn how to get your information to them, and how to get information from them; here again, these don't require much if you are succinct. Five to ten minutes is all that you should need for this conversation; let any amount of time beyond that be because the person on the other end of the line wanted it from you. Again, don't be rudely abrupt, but keep in mind that you have plenty of time to get to know them, and for them to get to know you.

Keeping Track Of Opportunities

Once contact has been made with more than a church or two, it becomes difficult to simply remember what church is what, when you should follow up, etc. In fact,

---

8   If this is the case, you should have already found this website in your initial research! You'll want to follow up on this information and work from there.

I doubt that most people could remember all of the details about even one church from start to finish, given that the process takes as long as it does. So how can a candidate keep track of what they have and haven't done, and what they have and haven't learned, with regard to their candidacy?

The system I used was fairly straightforward, and you could use it too— though it assumes that other things are in place. This system might not be for you, and if not then there are other systems available, or you could develop your own. The important things are that you take follow-up seriously, and that you develop some way to organize your follow-up.

To begin with, I am committed to an organizational system developed by David Allen called *Getting Things Done* (GTD), which is a comprehensive set of principles for keeping tasks and projects managed and running efficiently. I won't give details about the system here, but it has become very popular and there is a lot of good information in print and on the web about it.[9]

One of the key pieces of the puzzle for GTD, however, is what Allen calls a "tickler file" which is essentially a large set of file folders that are in regular use. With Allen's tickler file system, there is a folder designated for every single day of the coming month, plus one for each month itself and a few others. By rotating the folders in a systematic way, it is easy to plan when tasks will be handled, and they can effectively be forgotten about until then (assuming that the tickler file is used and updated consistently).

So my candidacy system worked like this: when I made first contact with a new opportunity, I created a file folder specifically for that opportunity. (Up until first contact, any information I had on a given opportunity was in another folder labeled "Placement Starting Points" from which I tried to pull at least a couple of new opportunities each week for attempted first contact.) I labeled the folder with the church name and its location by city and state. I also began a worksheet for that particular opportunity that helped me keep track of what information had been exchanged.[10]

No big deal so far. Here is where the key pieces fall into place. Because I use my tickler file system regularly, I didn't have to keep track of that opportunity in my mind, in terms of what information I had or when I last contacted them. I put their folder in the appropriate day for follow-up, and I didn't worry about it again until then. (I knew what the appropriate day was for follow-up because I had a commitment to following up regularly, and that predicted the time frame for me. More on this in a moment.)

At one point, for example, I had 16 different opportunities I was exploring, and I probably couldn't have told you what information had passed hands beyond an educated guess. I didn't need to be able to do so— my system kept up with that for me.

A few other notes: my file labeled "Placement Starting Points" always lived in the next day's folder. When the next day came, I'd put it in my inbox with the other work from the day, and at some point in the day I would decide whether I will try to make first contact with any new opportunities. I either did so (and create a new folder for

---

9   I've included a short list of resources on GTD and other systems for follow-up in the appendix and on the Doulos Resources website.

10 A template for these worksheets is on the Doulos Resources website.

it if I was successful) then put the Starting Points folder in the next day's folder, or I would decide not to, and the file went into the next day's folder immediately. Once again, I didn't have to stress out about when I would get in touch with those new opportunities because they were constantly attended to.

I also created a worksheet that helped me keep track of what information I sent to each contact/opportunity. On this worksheet I also noted what I had received from them, as well as details about when I contacted them. I had space for notes, too, so that I could keep track of information I was gathering more informally about the congregation, the city/town/area where they were, and the people I was interacting with. I generated a new copy of my worksheet for each opportunity, and that document also went into the file folder I created for them.[11]

Finally, when I did make first contact with a new opportunity I did one more thing in addition to building a new file for them: I noted the church's name, city, state, and position in my prayer journal. I kept a running list of opportunities I was in communication with there, so that I could be regularly in prayer for them and for their search.

Regular Followup

How frequently should you follow up with your opportunities? I followed up with my active candidacy opportunities by telephone or e-mail about every three weeks.

The goal in this process is to build a relationship with the church you will eventually serve. Your efficacy in placement is and will be measured in direct correlation to how the relationship you build with each opportunity plays out: either one or both of you will figure out it isn't working out, or you'll grow committed to each other. If you're going about this with anything other than your relationships to each church and her members in view, you're approaching it the wrong way.

Thus, you have to do the work of building a relationship with each church. You don't want to become a pest, presumptuous, or over-eager, but you do want and need those relationships to grow and thrive, just like you would when you make new friends (because, after all, that is exactly what you are doing). You can't assume that they will know you from the paperwork you've sent them (because they won't), and you dare not assume that you will understand the circumstances, or know the people, of the church you're considering from the profiles they sent to you (because *you* won't).

So this is how I followed up: when I made first contact with a new opportunity, I generally planned to follow up with them in about three weeks. For any given opportunity, it may have been a little more or a little less, depending on what I learned about the contact person (if weekends were better, for example, or if they told me that Thursdays were usually not good). And I told them that I would be following up.

I preferred for as much communication as possible to be done by telephone; as useful as e-mail is, it doesn't have the personal quality that is needed for truly building these relationships. Sometime my contact person told me that they preferred e-mail, and I was careful to respect that, but if they were willing then I followed up by phone.

---

11 A template of my opportunity worksheet is available online, for free, through the Doulos Resources website in the Transition section.

My follow-up calls were not very dissimilar to my introductory call. I asked them about themselves. Do they have family? How long have they been in that area and/or in that church? Do they work— and what do they do? I also asked about the search: how is it going? How long have they been at it? Is the search team holding up? Are there some specific ways that I can be praying for them?

Of course, I asked questions about where they were in the process and what information, if any, they could give me about my status. I asked this if it was necessary, but it usually wasn't— most of the time they offered this unasked. But I didn't make the whole conversation about this, and I didn't let it become all about this. Those questions wouldn't matter once the search was through, and if that was all that our relationship was founded upon then I would have to start from scratch when my ministry there began.

I tried to keep each phone call to about 15 minutes or so, though I always made sure I could spare 20-30 if they wanted to talk. Sometimes it was as brief as five minutes. At other times, they could be quite chatty or could really open themselves up to me, and I would have to opportunity to get to know them, to shepherd and pastor them, and to build a deeper friendship. After each phone call or e-mail, I updated my notes on my worksheet in the opportunity's folder.

As the process continued with each church, I let where we were in the process and what I had learned from prior conversations determine how often I should continue following up. If I learned that their search team was meeting weekly, I might continue following up every three weeks, or even bump it up to two at some points. If they met less often, I might slow it down to once a month or so. If the search process hit a snag, I might leave them alone for six weeks— or, if the relationship was there, I might have started contacting them more often to check on how they were weathering the difficulties and how I could pray for them. And late in the process, I checked in weekly or even a couple of times a week.

Following up not only keeps you informed about your candidacy efforts, but it also allows key spade work to be done in forming relationships with those whom you will eventually be shepherding. My research has demonstrated with a high degree of certainty that it will also highly increase your chances of moving through the process more smoothly, and to a more advanced level; which is a nice side-effect, even if it is not the primary goal.

Final Thoughts on Getting Started

Starting well is crucial in many aspects of life, and no less so in pastoral candidacy. If you get started well in general— as you begin to solicit help from your network, research opportunities, and formulate a system for tracking the opportunities you pursue— your entire candidacy process will be better and more tolerable. If you begin well with each individual opportunity, your likelihood of finding effective placement increases and you lay a good foundation for the beginning of your ministry to your future congregation. As we continue into the coming chapters to discuss all of the information that you must exchange, as well as how to handle interviews and visits, a good start will be vital.

Paperwork Shuffle

You may not realize yet how much information much change hands, or pass ears, before the process of candidacy and placement is over.

There are many things that you must be ready to present about yourself that describe and summarize who you are, how you are gifted, trained, and prepared for ministry, and what God has called you to do in ministry. There are also many questions that you must answer for any given church before they will know whether you are fit for the ministry opportunity that they might offer you. Likewise, there are many things that you will need to know, and many questions that you must ask, about the churches that might call you to serve them.

This amount of information can be overwhelming. It certainly isn't something that you should wait until the last minute to begin thinking about. If you aren't prepared for it— both in terms of having information ready to present, and knowing what information you are looking for— you will probably not find effective placement.

In this chapter, we'll talk about all of this information. What information do you need to seek? How should you gather and present the information you will need to offer to others? And how should you think about this information exchange in principle? These and other questions will be our focus.

Researching Opportunities— Getting Started

How do you get started researching a specific church? As mentioned in the previous chapter, your work in gathering information about a given opportunity begins well before you make initial contact with them. This is a part of the "information exchange" too. And it is surprisingly easy to gather an extensive amount of information about a church, a community, or a town/city that a church is in— after all, we live in an "information age."

The information age has the Internet as its midwife, and this is a fine place to start. Begin with discovering whether this church has a website, and taking in what information (if any) the website offers. This can be more difficult and/or complicated than it seems at first: many churches have websites that are sparse in information, or woefully out of date in the information they do have.

If there *is* something to their website, however, it can tell you a great deal about the church. Many will have descriptions of current ministries, information about worship, historical data, and statements of belief. Some will have even more information than this. All of these are useful, of course, and will tell you about who they are, or at least how they perceive themselves.[1] But there is a fair amount of information to be

---

[1] One warning about relying on the church's website: often— and perhaps especially in smaller churches— the content of the website comes mostly (if not exclusively) from the pastor. Therefore, what you find there may not be an accurate reflection of the congregation, so much as it is an accurate reflection of their previous pastor. This isn't always the case, and it isn't necessarily bad; after all, he

mined from websites by "reading between the lines," if you know what to look for:

- **Sermons.** If the website has audio or video of sermons or other recordings, give several of these a listen (or at least a partial-listen). From listening to several sermons from past preachers and pastors, you'll be able to determine a good bit about the congregation. How long are the sermons? Do they tend to be topical, or do they work systematically through books of the Bible? Do they include a good amount of exposition and explanation? What is the nature of the application points? Noticing these things will suggest the quality and intensity of the teaching that the congregation is used to, which will help you know whether you might be a good fit or not.
- **"New Media."** The kinds of content that a church's website has suggests a lot about them. Is there a blog from the pastor or staff? Do they offer their audio in "podcast" format? Even the format of the website itself lends information in this way: is it plain with mostly text and an occasional image, or does it contain a lot of well-designed menus and interactive features? Is there a members' section and information for members, or is the content essentially a digital advertisement for the church? These elements will suggest how much the church members use the website, how technologically savvy the congregation (or a portion of it) is, and how much they expect their pastors to be involved in the content creation for the website.
- **Original content.** Is the content of the website mostly reproduced from other sources? It is easy to re-post content on a website without a lot of consideration. For example, many churches will have a section for a statement of faith or beliefs— but frequently these are simply a reproduction of a creed or of a portion of an official statement, like a confession of faith. There is nothing wrong with this, but it may suggest something about the mindset of the church and its leadership about statements of faith. Other churches will post a statement or summary of beliefs that is original, which someone in their congregation (hopefully a pastor or other leader) wrote; such a statement might give more insight into the nuances of that congregation. Neither is "right" or "wrong" but both can be instructive about what the church is like. Other similar content is the same: whether it is pictures, history, or other information, these can be clues that will fit into a bigger picture about the church.
- **Links.** Does the church link to other websites? Which websites does it link to? These can be surprisingly revealing. A church that links to other churches in the area, for example, may do so out of a spirit of connection, fellowship, and partnership in ministry. A church that links only to denominational resources may be cautious about ideas that come from outside of trusted sources. If there are links to ministries and websites that are diverse and varied in nature, however, it may suggest that the church is more focused on the universal church than on divided groups. A church with no links at all may indicate something about itself too! Take a look at

---

was their pastor, so what he thought and believed was probably taught and caught in his ministry to them. But it's worth asking someone, at some point, "where did the information on your website come from?"

their links, and check into a few of the pages they link to— you might be surprised at what they imply about the church.

Moving beyond the church's website, you should know that there is probably a good bit of other information available about the church. What other links did a direct search for the church turn up?[2] Following some of these might turn up some interesting data. You may find links to newspaper articles, obituaries, and other archives that can help you see a bigger picture of the congregation you are researching.

Is the church a part of a denomination? If so, there is likely a wealth of data available if you know the right sources. Some denominations publish a "yearbook" with statistical data about their member congregations. Much like church websites, if you know what to look for you can extrapolate a good bit about a congregation's priorities and ministries. In my denomination, for example, the statistical data includes membership numbers (how many in attendance vs. how many on the roll, how many were added to and taken off of the roll, number of households, etc.) and financial data (including benevolence giving). Taken together, you can get a rough sense of how close to a 10% tithe most households in the congregation give, what percentage of the total church budget is given to missions, and whether there is an active building fund. All of these intimate different things about a congregation, and once again present a piece of the puzzle that will eventually give you an accurate picture of the congregation.

Denominational information will also include facts about who the recent pastor(s) was/were, how long they were there, and possibly even why they left. (You should also be able to find information about where they are now and how to contact them, which may be useful if you continue to have interest in a particular opportunity.) There may be other historical data available, as well— check to see if there is a particular agency or office of church history for the denomination and query them for details, as your interest continues. Also, check the library at your seminary for denominational data; at the seminary I attended, for example, they kept copies of the yearbook for my denomination and several others, for a number of years in the past.

Ministry takes place in a context, and this context can teach you a lot about the church, too. In fact, you probably already have some preferences about context: perhaps you and your wife have decided that you should live in the same general region as your extended family, because of health concerns for an ailing parent. Maybe you feel a particular calling to an urban or inner-city context. It could be that you grew up in a small town community, and sense that your personality would be especially well-suited to that setting. Or you might have worked in a corporate environment before pursuing a call to ministry, and are cautious about ministering to those outside of that demographic that you know so well.

Whatever the case, you will do well to do some research into the context that you are considering. Once again, our information age is your ally in this: the wealth of data available from censuses, surveys, demographical studies, and other research has

---

2   I strongly recommend that you use a search "string" (the collection of words in a search) that includes the church's full name, city/town, and state. For example, you might type in, "New Covenant Community Church Charlotte NC". Searching for less will result spurious results. There are ways to improve and refine your search engine results, as well like using "Boolean" operators; if you don't turn up anything at all, you might consider looking into these methods for searching.

left very few parts of the United States unexamined from a demographic standpoint, and much of this information is available for free.

There are a handful of websites that I have found to be useful in such research, and I continue to look for new ones. Some of these sites offer information about population trends, economy, and housing statistics. Others discuss cost of living and quality of life concerns. Some return specific results about church and religion matters, such as adherents to particular groupings (often quite specifically). Due to the ever-changing nature of the Internet, I am cautious about listing these or discussing particular sites in a book; however, I have linked to them at the Doulos Resources website, and regularly update the list there.

Unless the congregation you are considering is non-denominational, with no website, and literally in the middle of nowhere, you ought to be able to find *something* about the congregation and the community it lives in. By the end of your research efforts, you should have at least a basic idea about them: how long they have been around, a general sense of their congregational ethos, what sort of context they exist in. Using this, you now have a starting point to begin formulating specific questions.

Now you are ready to make some decisions about whether to continue to pursue this opportunity. If so, it will be helpful to think (or re-think) about the candidacy process and what responsibilities and obligations you have, and churches have, in providing information toward one another— before you actually begin exchanging it. That's what is next.

Finding A Balance

As I mentioned in a previous chapter, the candidacy process often favors churches heavily. I'm all for meeting the needs and preferences of churches through the process— anything else would be a sure recipe for failure and burnout, and would leave Christ's bride uncared-for. We need to make sure that churches have the pastor they need: they man who will lead them toward deeper faith and maturity in Christ, who can recognize unhealthy areas of church life and ministry and work to remedy them, who can prepare them for ministry in the long-term and to generation upon generation, and who can help the church become a better part of the larger Church and Kingdom.

That said, I think the candidacy process as it is commonly practiced today focuses almost exclusively on the needs of the church, ignoring or, at best, downplaying the very important needs, preferences, and calling of the candidate-pastor.

When a man sends his "information packet" to a church for their consideration, he provides them with a wealth of information. The information that will, eventually, get into the hands of a search committee during the consideration process includes the following: a resume (detailing education and experience); a "Data Form" (providing details on current position, theological distinctions, ministry emphases, and other ministry-oriented information); a statement of "Ministry Vision" or "Philosophy of Ministry" (often of considerable length— one draft of mine is eight pages long); personal biography (including testimonies of faith and call to ministry); references (I send both personal and professional references); and samples of teaching, such as recordings of sermons or video of a class. This is the information provided *before* the actual interview process begins.

What similar information does a church provide the candidate-pastor? Some churches bother to complete a denominational "Church Profile" which might be similar to the pastor's "Data Form" but sometimes with less information; many, however, don't trouble themselves with this. Some churches have a written history of the church which they will provide, but even if they have it, it can be less than current with the latest (and often most pertinent) information. Many churches have some statement of Ministry Vision, and some even have a developed Philosophy of Ministry— however, the sad truth is that these may be just documents that were developed and never implemented, so they don't truly reflect the true vision or philosophy of that church. Sometimes, it is as embarrassingly little as the last four bulletins, a monthly newsletter or two, and maybe a church directory.

And that's just the early exchange of information. I think that this problem continues through much of the rest of the process, and it poses significant problems for both church and pastor. Considering (and then asking for) what would bring balance might, at best, present churches with the impetus for change, and at worst it will give candidates a heads-up of what is— and isn't— to come.

As a candidate-pastor proceeds through the candidacy process, the interviews will inevitably pose another occasion of unbalanced interaction. A phone interview, for example, will likely be all of the members of the search committee in one room on a speaker phone calling the candidate-pastor. They will take their turns asking questions and following up with more questions. Often, this will take all of the allotted time; it will almost certainly take most of it. Little or no time is afforded for the questions that a candidate-pastor may have of the committee, and when he asks them, the answers are often abridged or awkward. He usually will not get to ask very many questions at this time. My experience has frequently been that search committees are actually surprised at the possibility that a candidate has questions for them.

By the time a candidate-pastor visits the church in person, it is highly possible that the church (or at least the search committee) knows a great deal about him, his experience, and his hopes and ambitions in ministry. In fact, if this were not the case, I would wonder if they have taken their work very seriously. However, it is also quite possible that the candidate-pastor knows very little about the candidate-church at this point. When will he have the chance to learn more about the candidate-church? Hopefully by the end of the visit, although even this is not guaranteed. Will he have an opportunity to ask all of his questions? Will he be able to ask them to different people, even different groups of people? We found that we usually would not have all of our questions answered by the end of a weekend visit, even though we strategically asked our questions to the groups we were with, and we edited our question list heavily. (We did eventually get them answered, but it was only with much perseverance.)

How can these things be remedied?

I think that candidate-pastors can, first and foremost, be confident that they have a right to know what they need to know to make good, thoughtful decisions. In other words, the first remedy to the situation is to act like a candidate-pastor dealing with a candidate-church, not just as an applicant seeking a job. We need to have confidence in the calling God has given us!

Secondly, it can be helpful to let the candidate-church(es) know up-front that you are trying to get to know them just as much as they are trying to get to know you. This may be with bold steps to seek out information from the start. For me, that came in a simple sentence in my cover letter that says as much. I followed that with persistent requests for additional information, such as a Church Profile and a statement of the church's Vision.

Also, it helps to think of creative ways to seek out information about the church. Have you done the research listed above? Gathering extensive profile data about a congregation should be the first step. Are there other churches in the area who are familiar with the ministries of the candidate-church? Asking for a list of "references" and calling the pastors of those churches seems to be a reasonable move. How about within the church itself? Do I know anyone who is or has been there, or who knows a member there? Who were the last two pastors to serve in the position I am seeking— and why did they leave? Who is the pastor now— is he leaving, and why? Have I talked to these men? Do I know others who know them— and what can they tell me about the church and the position I am seeking?

Finally, be prepared with good questions. You don't want to waste the precious time you have with questions that will not get you useful answers, and you don't want to waste the time of those you ask, either. You may have 50 questions you want answers to, but can you condense those into 5 bigger questions that will reveal the answers to the rest? You need to exercise good stewardship of the time and questions you have to make the most of the candidacy process.

Churches Have Obligations Too

What are the specifics that candidate-churches ought to bring to the table? How should a church be prepared for the candidacy process? Or put another way: what sorts of information should a diligent candidate-pastor seek out from the church(es) he candidates with? I have concluded, through research, anecdotal evidence, and personal experience, that pastors leave "early"— before they have served the full-term of their ministry at a particular church— frequently because they did not know key details about the church before they began their ministry there.

Here are some starting points for how a church may begin gathering the information they should present to a candidate-pastor as he goes through the interview process with them.

- *Gather existing documents and information.* Chances are, a candidate-church already has a good bit of information that is useful in the search process. Does the church have a constitution or by-laws? What about Board-approved position papers on various issues over the years? Where are the notes from the Session's "Vision-Casting Retreat" two falls ago? Anything that is already on paper is helpful; some (even most) of it may need updating, but these things are a great starting point right out of the gates.[3]
- *Create a profile of the church.* How would the Search Committee describe it, given unlimited time? How about in five minutes or less? How about in a paragraph— or even a sentence? If the Search Committee can't help

---

3 This is only true if the documents actually represent meaningful information. So, if a "Vision Statement" was developed and adopted two years ago, but nothing has been done with it since then, it is misleading and even ethically questionable for the search team to present it as an accurate statement of the vision of the congregation.

outsiders understand the existing ministries, dynamics, and demographics of the candidate-church, there is no guarantee that the pastor will be anything like what the church needs. My denomination, the PCA, has a church profile form that largely mirrors a candidate-pastor's MDF, so it is easy to compare the two and spot similarities— great idea.

- *Develop a statement of ministry philosophy* (or update it if it already exists). This sounds like a complex, abstract, and boring document, but all it really does is answer this question: "Why are we doing what we are doing?" It addresses the core values, theological emphases, and natural inclinations that exist in the church. Does the church have a special interest in mercy ministries? Are most of her members strong evangelists? Does the prominence of worship resonate as a central aspect of the congregation? These (and others) are the ideas that go into a Philosophy of Ministry statement.

- *Provide a history of the church.* This doesn't have to be a move-by-move account of every Sunday School class that ever existed, but it does need to be honest, and complete enough to present an accurate picture. The obvious milestones should be included: when the church was planted, the first building purchase, any long-term relationships with other churches and organizations, etc. But there are other things a candidate-church might prefer to hide, but shouldn't: have there been any splits? What have the patterns of growth been? How many pastors has the church had— and why did the last few leave? It should give candidate-pastors a fair and true presentation of the church's background.

- *Have a clear sense of what the church is called to do.* Churches have callings just like pastors; some are stronger in evangelism, others in mercy, others in teaching and fellowship. The same five key factors I've identified for candidate-pastors also apply to candidate-churches. How is the church— and especially the Search Committee— attuned to the church's sense of calling, their willingness to follow God (even in new directions), and their submission and humility through the process? If the committee can articulate these, then they're really starting to get somewhere with the search process.

Candidate-pastors should take this list and use it as a check-list, of sorts: do you have this information? Has it been presented to you verbally, if not in writing? Do you have a sense that you "know" this congregation, in any way close to the way that a member or regular attender "knows" it? If you have some familiarity with most or all of the above concepts, even in seed-form, you're off to a good start.

Beyond this, candidate-pastors ought to ask lots of questions. Ask them on the phone, via e-mail, and in person. Ask them during casual conversations, during official interviews, and throughout visits. There will be any number of questions that you will want to have answered, and the "list" will change for every candidate-pastor and with every potential congregation. That said, I have provided a list of 50 questions that I might ask a search committee; you'll find this list in the appendices.

Keep in mind, too, that you're gathering this information over an extended period of time. You shouldn't expect to have all of this information before the first telephone interview, or even by the end of it. It might be that you don't learn all that you need to know until well into the process— perhaps through a couple of phone interviews and a weekend visit. To a degree, the timing of when you gather the information is less important than that you have gathered it. Be patient, and dole out your questions in digestible doses!

Having this information gathered and documented protects everyone, both short-term and long-term. Candidate-pastor(s) get the information they want and need during the interview process, and search committees are not forced to answer questions on the spot or, worse, to try to dodge them. And, both the church and pastor are assured that future problems are less likely, since all of the cards are on the table from the start.

Building Your Resume

One of the vital parts of the "information exchange" that nearly everyone is familiar with is the resume. But what makes a good resume?

There are two common, but different, approaches to developing a resume (also called a "Curriculum Vitae" or C.V.— which, in Latin, literally means "course of life"). One approach is to spill nearly everything you've ever done onto the page, sometimes resulting in a four or five page document. This approach, which is more common in academic and scientific environments, is necessary for those whose employment will be measured (at least to some degree) by the quantity of their work— for example, a college professor is often expected to publish scholarly articles and/or books regularly. In this case, the resume, while organized, can be lengthy and will have some esoteric content.

The other is more of a minimalist approach: provide a basic and brief summary of the most important highlights. More common in the corporate world, these will usually be only a single page and will not try to even approach being exhaustive. The thinking behind this approach is that corporate "HR" types don't have (or won't take) the time to read lengthy resumes, so if you even want to be considered you should keep it short.

So which approach suits ministry candidacy? I'd bet that nine out of 10 readers would guess the long, exhaustive type would be best— but most of the time, they would be wrong.

It seems that nearly every open ministry position gets dozens of applicants. One small church I know of— about 80 members— recently completed a search for a solo pastor. They had over 60 candidates to eliminate at the beginning. Another church I know of, looking for an associate pastor, had over 300 candidates apply. In other words, the quantity of applicants to be considered for an open ministry position is probably more like the corporate world than the academic or scientific world.

As you are preparing your resume, be committed to keeping it brief. You don't need a long, multi-page resume. In fact, if you're just finishing seminary, it is as likely as not that you won't really have enough accomplishments to your credit to make a multi-page resume worthwhile. Most seasoned pastors could summarize the cogent aspects of their careers in one page.

Resume Contents

So what should go onto a pastoral resume? It's pretty simple. (It has to be, if it is going to fit on a single page!)

- **Name, address, phone number, e-mail address** all go at the top of the page. Don't try to get clever with something like putting your name in gigantic letters— you're wasting your time and suggesting that you need to distract the search committee from something else on the page. Put your name on a single line, your address on the next line, and phone number and e-mail on the third line. If you must, make them a few point-sizes larger than the rest of the text.
- **Educational background.** Keep it basic— Put the name of the college you attended, its location (city, state), the year you graduated, and the degree you earned. Same with junior colleges, community colleges, or technical colleges (but only if you earned a degree, such as an Associate of Arts— leave it off if you didn't earn a degree). And the same with seminary and other graduate degrees you've earned. Do not fill up the page with bullets detailing what fraternity you joined, which campus ministry you were vice-president for, or what your GPA was. (The guy who gave us our campus tour when we first visited Covenant Seminary put it best: "If you made straight A's in seminary, they'll call you 'Reverend,' and if you barely passed half of your classes in seminary, they'll still call you 'Reverend.'")
- **Professional experience.** By that I mean, what work experience do you have that is considered career-oriented. If you have enough experience in ministry alone, you might decide to limit this section to only that. If ministry is a second career for you, you'll have significant experience outside of professional ministry to list. The work-study job you had in college and that semester you worked making pizza at Little Caesar's doesn't make this list. (NOTE: don't be afraid to include the internship you did while in seminary and the pulpit supply work you've been doing.)
- **Qualifications for ministry** (OPTIONAL). Include these ONLY if you don't have very much under the professional experience section. If you went to seminary straight from college and/or the only ministry experience you have is an internship at your church while in seminary, you should list the three or four top skills or abilities you have that make you a qualified candidate for the ministry position you're seeking. There should not be more than three or four, and they must be skills or abilities; this is not a place for listing your spiritual gifts or your aspirations in ministry. Hard skills (like "small group leadership" or "strong administrator") and specific abilities (such as "a strong teacher" or "a knack for evangelizing strangers") are what counts here. It's probably best to put them in the order shown above, with the exception of the "Qualifications for ministry" section— if you must include that, put it first. That will give them a reason to read further.

You don't need an objective, even though most resume books will tell you to lead with this. Objectives exist so that Human Resources departments can pull a file of resumes and match them to the 43 different positions they need to fill. Most likely, you're applying at a church where there is a single position open, so they'll know what you are applying for. (On the off-chance that there are multiple positions available— or if you're simply uncomfortable leaving it unsaid— then mention in your cover letter what you are applying for.)

Similarly, don't believe for a minute that the resume is the place for listing your spiritual gifts, the details of your family, your hobbies and interests, your references, or the articles you've published in your favorite ministry journal. There is a place for those, and I'll cover them in another section.

Your resume is a document that gives the frank details of your professional development— and that means education and experience. The other essential information (and there is plenty more essential information that you should prepare) will find a proper place in other documents.

A "Ministerial Data Form"

The second most important part of an information packet for many pastors (and pastors in training) is the denominational "data form." Many denominations have a pre-formatted Data Form that becomes a boilerplate evaluation tool for the search teams. All but one of the denominations that I candidated in used one.[4]

Many people are critical of data forms as redundant, unnecessary, or a distraction from more important issues. While it's true that many denominational data forms need updating (for example, my denomination's data form asks about theological issues that most pastors won't face very much anymore, while it misses some of the current "hot topics"), and often replicate data found on other documents, I believe that they are still valuable tools for early evaluation.

Why? Because, when properly used, data forms give a good snapshot of the essentials for narrowing a field of candidates from dozens— even hundreds— down to a manageable number. In the best cases, churches will fill out a similar form (in my denomination this is called a "Church Profile") that asks identical questions on some sections. The benefit here should be obvious: a side-by-side comparison by either party should immediately reveal whether the "fit" is close enough to continue exploring.

Of course, data forms and church profiles should be appropriately understood as only a part of the picture. It's a problem when either candidate-pastor or candidate-church put too much weight on the content of the data form.

What is a data form, anyway? Nearly all data forms include the following information:

- Personal data (birthdate, marital status, family facts)
- Education and other training
- Ministry experience and other work history
- Personal views on theological issues
- References

---

4   Obviously if you are not a part of a denomination then this will be largely irrelevant. I say "largely" because you would still benefit from putting this sort of information together, and you may wish to prepare one anyway. If you would like a copy of the blank "Data Form" template for my denomination (to use as a starting point), contact me through the Doulos Resources website and I will be happy to provide you with one.

Other points of data that are often requested:
- Questions about "hot topic" theological issues
- Preferences about how a pastor would spend his time and energy
- Information about accomplishments, additional training, personal/professional goals, or key experiences
- Statements about theological views and exceptions to confessional standards

Data forms deserve a lot of thought and time. If you want to make progress in your search, you need to do a good job putting this document together. This will likely mean devoting a number of hour (yes, hours) to writing and editing your information and answers to the questions on a data form. Here are some suggestions about how to go about doing this.

Completing The Data Form

I won't make many suggestions of how you should fill out the "personal information" section on a data form! I assume you know the answers to these basic questions. As for the other points— I certainly don't have the final answer for you in working these out, but I will offer the following brief advice:

Education And Other Training

To a point, this is redundant to your resume. You should fill it out accurately anyway— some will look only at a data form, ignoring resumes altogether. Further, these sections will often allow you to flesh out things that there isn't room for on your resume. For example, if there was a particular emphasis that accompanied one or more of your degrees, here is a good opportunity to mention it. Likewise, if you have received specialized training through conferences or continuing education credits, you should record that training on your data form. If you don't have anything more to say that what is on your resume, that's fine too! But whatever relevant training and education you've had, list it on your data form.

Ministry Experience And Other Work History

As with education, you have probably listed your work history and experience on your resume. Here again, don't neglect this simply because it was covered there.

You may have ministry experience that was voluntary, or that was done through non-traditional or parachurch ministries. You might have work experience that was not directly ministry-related, but still might be understood as relevant to your calling as a pastor. One survey respondent, for example, discussed how his openness about his business experience prior to seminary was invaluable in his pursuit of a position as pastor to young professionals at a large church. This is a good place to "take stock" of what you have done with your life and consider how it fits into your future ministry. List it if you believe it matters.

Personal Views On Theological Issues

My advice here: be concise. Don't neglect to account for the important parts— you should already have a strong sense of what is important for each of these. But don't go on and on; there is no reason why your answers should be lengthy, and it could work against you if they are.

I have seen data forms where each theological issue received a half-page answer. This is too much: the search team will grow weary of it, and the more you offer, the more you may have to explain the nuances of what you wrote. The point to these sections is to check for orthodoxy, not to begin an ordination exam. Answer briefly, touching only the most vital points, and make them ask you follow-up questions if need be.

References

I'll speak more to references in a separate section, but for most data forms there is space for only a few. If you are able, choose one of your seminary professors, a co-worker or supervisor for a ministry position you served (even if it was for an internship), and a friend or classmate. Be sure to list accurate contact information for them, and ask them beforehand if you may use them as a reference!

Questions About "Hot Topic" Theological Issues

Much like the section on personal views, this section is easy to say too much about! Here again, I suggest that you be brief, offering only what is necessary to demonstrate the crucial points of your beliefs.

One piece of advice I have regarding "hot topic" issues, both in documents like a data form and at other times: the processes of candidacy, placement, ordination, and transition are not teaching times! Too many men have come before our presbytery seeking ordination, and have decided that the question they received about a hot topic would be a great opportunity to convince all of the others present of their position. It's not— in fact, it smacks of arrogance and disrespect. It will make it harder for you to get ordained, and it might well tank your candidacy.

If you are called to be the pastor of a particular congregation, you will have ample time to teach them in areas where they need to grow. Likewise, if you are ordained by a body of pastors, there will be plenty of time for dialogue— and you will grow as well as helping others to grow. Be patient, and slow to press your particular views on the "hot topics" onto others.

Preferences About How A Pastor Would Spend His Time And Energy

On the Data Form for my denomination, we are asked to offer an approximate schedule for how we would spend the average week. This is an interesting and telling section. For one thing, it reveals the priorities of a man for his ministry. For another, it represents his self-awareness, and his awareness of external realities, when it comes to how his time will be spent.

The difficulty of this section for a seminary student is that often he doesn't know how to estimate this. You may know your gifts and abilities, desires and passions, and you may be tempted to indicate that these will take up the bulk of your time on a given week. But one of the realities of ministry is that there will be a dozen or more other things competing for our time and attention on any given day. Taking these into account— and still making and prioritizing time for the essentials of prayer and teaching/preaching preparation— can be difficult.

If your Data Form asks for this sort of data, it may be best to simply indicate how you spend your time now: when do you study, when do you spend time with family and/or friends, how much time do you devote to internships or other ministry, etc. This can still give a search team helpful information about where your priorities lie, and more importantly it will suggest to them how well you are able to manage a schedule with competing demands.

Miscellaneous Information
There may be individual sections for topics such as personal accomplishments, additional training, personal/professional goals, or key experiences— or they may fall under one omnibus heading. Regardless, follow the standing advice of being brief, as well as recognizing a couple of nuanced aspects of such thoughts.

For one thing, be careful that your presentation is accurate but not boastful. It can be tempting to highlight— and even embellish— minor accomplishments and present them as more important than they are. On the other hand, I've known men who downplayed how the Lord had used them out of a spirit of humility. You must present yourself honestly, without false humility or vain conceit.

Also, when it comes to goals and ambitions, be sparse. It may be true that, at some point in your life, you hope to write a book or two, complete a Ph.D. or D.Min., sit on the board of your alma-mater seminary, and help to start a Christian school in your community. If you state all of these, however, search teams will get the idea that you won't have any time for ministry to their congregation! Which would probably be true if you were pursuing all of these at once. It's okay to have goals and ambitions that you hope to eventually accomplish, that you don't list on a Data Form; instead, pick the one or maybe two things that you feel will be urgent matters to you—probably the goals you'll pursue first— and list those.

Statements About Theological Views / Exceptions To Confessional Standards
If the denomination you serve in has confessional standards, there may be certain parts that you take exception to; in fact, there probably will be.[5] Some of your thoughts about it won't merit the title of "exception" in your mind— perhaps you think of them as concerns, or linguistic differences, or some idea like that.

This sort of distinction won't really matter: a search team will likely interpret anything that you state as an exception, regardless of how small. This doesn't mean you shouldn't state it— simply that you must keep in mind that they will see it that way.

Thus, the advice of "be brief" holds here as well; you'll do well to say as little as possible. Also, emphasize what you agree with about the section you're taking exception to (this sounds contradictory, but it isn't): there is probably one phrase of a sentence, or one sentence of a paragraph, that you don't fully hold. Affirm the rest even as you are stating your exception to the clause or sentence.

Finally, keep in mind that everyone has slightly different priorities when it comes to which aspects of confessional standards are of vital importance. Some will insist on adherence to a section that others will barely give attention to. I'll talk more about this sort of difference in priorities in the chapter called, "Who? Where? Why?"

---

5 One of my friends and fellow PCA pastors said of our confessional standards, the Westminster Confession of Faith, "If you don't have any exceptions to the Westminster Confession, then you probably haven't read it."

Philosophy Of Ministry

Everyone has one. Just like your worldview and your theology, you have a philosophy of ministry, regardless of whether you know it or can articulate it. Do you know what your philosophy of ministry is?

If you have thought through your philosophy of ministry, can you articulate it? One of the documents that is useful to offer to search teams is a brief statement of your philosophy of ministry. It doesn't have to be long, or exhaustive, but it ought to be descriptive of who you are and what the Lord has called you to do.

In seminary, one of my professors led each of us through a process of self-evaluation where we considered our spiritual gifts; natural skills, talents, and abilities; personality and temperament; communication and evangelism style; core values; goals, dreams, and ambitions; and key influential people. Taking all of these into account, we developed a summary statement of who we are and what we are called to be and do. This 50-word statement provided the foundation for a clear sense of calling and direction. For example, here's mine:

> *I am a pastor-teacher called by God to instruct and shepherd God's Church and her people in the Gospel intellectually, spiritually, and socially as they mature as disciples, with a particular interest in teaching, worship, and training others for leadership and service in the Church and in the world for the vitality of God's church.*[6]

In my case, I took this 50-word statement and broke it down into phrases, then used each phrase as the heading for a one or two-paragraph elaboration on what each means to me. In doing so, I constructed a basic statement of my philosophy of ministry.

Your philosophy of ministry statement won't necessarily be the most popular item in your portfolio of documents to exchange; however, I'd suggest that you offer it any time you are able, since understanding it might clear up a lot of confusion or misconceptions by a search team. If you have been upfront about the content of your philosophy of ministry, they should have a clear understanding of what your ministry among them will be like. It will also help them to know what your ministry will not be.

If you don't know what your philosophy of ministry is, this is a great opportunity to think it through. You might start with some basic reflection on how God has crafted you: what do the things you know about yourself and your ministry abilities suggest to you regarding your future ministry?

Reference List

Your references are crucial. As I mentioned earlier in the book, my first pastoral call out of seminary was brought about because of my references.

Because they are so vital to the process, it is imperative that you choose carefully who will serve as your references. You'll want to include references who have seen you serving in ministry, some that know you very well on a personal basis, and some that have seen you as a student (such as one or more of your seminary professors) and/or as a church member (like a pastor). You should include some references who are

---

6 If you are interested in developing such a statement for yourself, you will find suggested resources in the appendices.

fairly recent, but not all of them must be; you might have a college campus minister, a youth pastor, or even a high school teacher who you would like to offer as a reference, and that is fine— but if all of your references are from several years ago, it may raise questions (or they may simply assume you have something to hide). Likewise, you should include references from at least your last job or two— particularly if one or more of those jobs were ministry positions.

Taking all of this into consideration, you might have a fairly long list of references. Think through where you might consolidate them: there may be a professor who you have gotten to know pretty well, for example, or a pastor with whom you became fairly close friends; so the person who knows you well personally may also be a former professor or pastor. Even then, you may have more than just a few.

This is one of the reasons why I prefer to include the Reference List as a separate document (rather than tagging them onto the end of your resume). I have organized mine onto a single-sided sheet, divided into two categories: Ministerial References (subtitled, "those who I have worked with in ministry") and Personal References (subtitled, "those who can speak to my character, integrity, and quality"). I have four references in the first category, and six in the second— but many of them are interchangeable. For example, three of the four Ministerial References I list are also people who are friends, while four of the six Personal References are people I have worked with in ministry.

It's a good idea to contact everyone you want to put on your reference list and ask them if they are willing to serve you in that capacity. Remind them that you are beginning your candidacy, and ask them if you may list them as a reference. Don't forget that everyone is busy, and they may not be able to be available in that way; don't give them grief about it if they decline.

Be prepared for the fact that a church may track down references that you do not offer them. In a conversation with Dr. Dominic Aquila, he mentioned to me that if a church is doing their duty in evaluating candidates they will check multiple references. "If they get all 'halo' references then they haven't looked hard enough," he said, "because no one is a perfect candidate." This may mean that they ask your references for references, or they might cold-call one of your former places of employment and ask them to find a reference on you.

Still, in my experience a well-developed reference list will solve a lot of problems and answer a lot of questions.

Biography

Probably the most frequently-overlooked aspects of the information packet is some sort of personal biographical sketch. Many assume that the historical information in their resume— their education and work experience— is sufficient; others believe that the content of the Ministerial Data Form covers what the resume lacks.

And, in a sense, it does— if you have an MDF, then much of what you might present in a personal biography is already available. But that doesn't mean that it is effective for the same purpose.

The concept of the personal biography is that you are able to present yourself as a real person, with real experiences, a real family, and real interests and ambitions. A biography accomplishes this in a way that no form or formatted list can: in a descriptive narrative, covering details and aspects that may be irrelevant to what you do or have done, but are essential to understanding who you are.

Thus, the first tip in creating your personal biography is to write it in a narrative form. This means that you're not simply stating the facts of your life and background; you are telling the story of who you are. In your narrative, answer the following questions:

- *Where did you grow up?* Include the name of your hometown, a particular neighborhood if it is a well-known area, whether you moved; be distinctive, if possible, without being cheesy: "Sam was born in the Harbortown community of Hilton Head Island," "I grew up in the mountain town of Everwood…" or, "Fred was raised in the Richmond, the capital city of Virginia."
- *Who were your parents?* Are/were they people that would in some way commend you to your position? No one should be hired just because of who their parents were— but if you are the son of missionaries or the grandson of a pastor, this is good information to include here.[7]
- *What was distinctive about college or undergraduate studies?* At least mention what college or university you attended; however, if there is something more to tell here, then say so. If you were a member of a fraternity, participated in a campus ministry or fellowship, volunteered with a service organization, or worked full-time to put yourself through, then your story includes more than just the facts on your resume.
- *Did you work during/after college before attending seminary?* Usually, your resume will include only the most basic work history— and often it excludes jobs you've held that aren't directly relevant to the one you are seeking. But in ministry, an "irrelevant" job by way of experience is utterly relevant in terms of your capacity to relate to working people. If you held a job for several years between college and seminary— or if you are approaching pastoral ministry as a second career— your biography is a great opportunity to expand on how extensive your work experience is.
- *Have you had any particularly life-shaping experiences?* This is the kind of thing that is vital to a search team's understanding of why you are the right candidate for them, but there usually isn't a natural place for this on a resume or data form. Here is your chance to set yourself apart further, giving them a brief glimpse at how you have become the man you are.[8]
- *Are you involved in other ministries or activities that will contribute or detract from your ministry there?* If you are on the board of an organization, work with a consulting firm part-time, or feel deeply committed to spending part of your week volunteering with a group you have served for years, now is a good time to mention it. Likewise, if you have a special-needs child or an elderly parent who may require a significant amount of your time and

---

7   A seminary classmate of mine was the son of a pastor; furthermore, his mother's side of the family extended his pastoral heritage: both of her grandfathers, her father, her uncle, and her two brothers were all pastors. Needless to say, he was well-familiar with the pastoral life!

8   Brief is all that is necessary; someone on the search team will inevitably read it and ask about it, but if they don't then you can bring it up in a phone interview or in person.

attention, it is only fair to make a search team aware of that— and your biography can offer a tactful way to introduce the subject: "Among other things, Steve delights in the opportunity to serve and care for his mother, who is bed-ridden and lives with Steve and his family."

- [If you're married/family life] *How did you meet your wife?* When did you have your children? Giving a quick sketch of the details will help the search team feel like they know you AND your family— which is crucial, because if you are married then your wife (and children, if you have them) will be a strong factor in whether they connect with you. Introducing your family, if you have one, is a strong use of the personal biography.
- *How do you like to spend your spare time?* You may have offered hobbies or interests somewhere else, but your biography gives you a chance to highlight which ones are dearest to your heart, and give a search team a way to gauge how committed you are to continuing in that interest: "Luke is an avid runner, and enjoys entering 5-K races as often as he is able," or "Chris finds that an evening or two a week tending his garden is a great way to unwind."

There may be other things you'll want to include— after all, it's YOUR story. But here are a few more tips for presenting a good personal biography to a search team:

- *Consider using 3rd-person.* Sometimes it gets awkward to read, "I do this, I am that" over and over. Write it like you were penning your own obituary!
- *Include a photo or several.* It's easy to drop a photo into a document these days, and it makes a biography come to life.
- *Write in your voice.* Don't try to use elaborate language or wordsmith this piece if that's not your natural tendency.
- *Avoid wordiness.* Your biography should be able to tell your story in a single page, front-and-back. Don't talk about yourself too much.
- *Write in complete sentences.* No lists, no short and choppy phrases. Write something that feels like a story.
- *Write something readable.* Ask yourself if you would read it, if it wasn't about you. If the answer is no, you know what you need to do.

Sample Sermons Or Lessons

Make no mistake about it: you *will* be asked to provide some samples of your work.

This may come in any of three forms. The most common will be a request for audio recordings of sermons. These days, such recordings aren't too difficult to come by, assuming you've preached enough to have recordings. Probably, one or more of the churches you've preached for recorded your message, and may have even put it on the Internet!

If not, you might do well to obtain a small recorder that you can make your own recordings with. These days, such recorders are not overly expensive; you can get an acceptable stand-alone digital recorder for less than $100. What is more, you probably can get an adapter to work with a phone, iPod or other device that you already have, converting it into a recording tool. While these won't produce studio-quality results, they will usually provide adequate recordings for this purpose.9 While owning your own digital recorder might be a good idea— I used one frequently to record lectures in class— you may not want to spend that kind of money; in that case, ask around to see if a friend has one, or if it is possible to borrow one elsewhere. At the seminary I attended, for example, the school has purchased a few of these and lends them out to students for exactly this purpose.

Having audio recordings is one thing; getting them to search teams is another. As I've mentioned before, you will want to learn how a search team prefers to receive audio recordings and accommodate them as best as possible. If they want CDs, then send them— you might even ask if it would be helpful to provide multiple copies. Others may prefer to download them from a website, so you might take the time to learn how to set this up as well. It may not be feasible to offer them the cassette tape that they asked for, but if you can meet their requests then it will be helpful to do so.

A second type of sample is video. This isn't common today, but I suspect it will soon be a prominent option. There is less help here, since it is much more inconvenient to carry a video camera and tripod and set it up in a manner that will capture a sermon with acceptable quality. Audio presents a further obstacle here, since you might need to patch your camera into the soundboard or overlay a second audio source (from a recorder you brought with you, for example). And of course editing and finishing video to send out to others is a production in itself— likely more than many guys will have the time or capacity to handle.

Still, video is not a bad option: it can represent you more accurately, and if you are someone who is especially animated or whose speaking style relies on a lot of non-verbal cues, video can be a welcome addition to your information packet. Many seminaries will utilize video as a part of homiletic instruction— your sermon(s) will be recorded for future evaluation. Perhaps you could make use of these copies if video of your preaching is requested of you.

Finally, some will ask for written/printed samples of your work. Whether they want to see your preaching notes, a transcription of one or more sermons, or something else, written work can be another good way to introduce your teaching and preaching to a search team.

I had one church— with which I was candidating for an assistant pastor role— ask for notes from some Sunday School classes I taught. This made sense, as these might give a better idea of how I would fulfill the teaching requirement of the position than a sample sermon might. Another church asked if I could send a copy of my preaching outline or notes along with an audio recording. This, too, had a sensible and useful function to it: for example, they were able to surmise how much structure I had overall, how much I conveyed intentionally, and how much I expected the congregation to intuit.

As you select the various samples of your work, pay attention to the fact that these are called "samples" for a reason. Naturally, you won't send out a poor-quality recording of a sermon that you yourself felt was sub-par. At the same time, cherry-picking

---

9 The truth is, many recordings in churches running directly out of the sound system won't sound like "studio-quality" recordings either. If you're committed to only sending out high-quality recordings, you must either invest a good bit of money into a recorder, or work heavily on editing the audio files in your computer (or both).

your two or three best sermons or lessons and making only those available isn't an accurate portrayal of your work, either. But it doesn't have to be random; you can, and should, select a few examples that you believe accurately represent how well you preach or teach, and know which ones they are. Maybe it would be helpful to have several— or even as many as six or eight— that you are willing and ready to provide to a search team; this way, if they hear two or three and ask for more, you're still prepared to provide them.

Before you set out into candidacy, you might give some thought to what you are able to offer, and in what format. This way, you'll be able to respond to requests with confidence.

Aesthetics In The Information Packet

I had a friend who dabbled in web development for a while; he was a good programmer, and skilled with understanding the behind-the-scenes workings of a website. He couldn't really understand why he wasn't bringing in new business hand-over-fist.

Part of the problem: my friend didn't have much of an aesthetic sense. He didn't really care how things looked— he only cared if they worked. In his view, if a website communicated and/or gathered the information it needed to, then it was a good website.

The rest of the problem: the Internet is now oh, what, about 90% visual? Studies show that most people decide whether they will continue to read a website in 2-5 seconds! Obviously that's not long enough to read anything; this decision is made on aesthetics alone.

My suspicion is that many pastoral candidates view their information packet in the same way my friend viewed his web development: as long as the information is there, it's good enough. Why bother with further editing or tweaking?

That's hyperbole, of course— most will do some formatting or layout adjustment. But I haven't seen many resumes, for example, that visually stand out from others— yet I think we are getting to the point where the information we provide must have such "stand-out" potential to get the attention needed.

This may be a simple adjustment— I recently added photos of myself and my family to the brief biography I send out (more on this in a future post). Or it may be a substantial shift: I met a guy who had formatted his entire information packet— from cover letter to resume to bio to references— into a newsletter-style presentation, printed on 11x17 paper, folded, and stapled.

There are some documents where the aesthetic design is not our choice— as in the Data Form— but even here we can get creative. The fellow who designed a newsletter-style packet tucked his Data Form in the middle, and the folded sheets made a nice case for it.

We're overlooking a major part of the way that people communicate today if we ignore visual communication— and that means a pleasant, well-designed presentation, if we hope to gain favor as candidates.

How Much Information Is Too Much?

I once received an e-mail from a seminary classmate who had joined the staff of a church that recently completed a senior pastor search, and he offered me some fascinating insight into their search process.

First, some background on the church: they are a PCA church, but they aren't hardcore PCA in the way that many seminarians at the denominational seminary are. This is vitally important to realize; they are committed to the PCA because they believe in the importance of associating with a denomination. They are biblically conservative, Reformed in their theology, convinced of the practice of infant baptism, and are essentially presbyterian in their government. So the PCA is a good fit— but to them this means that they affiliate with their regional presbytery and attend General Assembly; they occasionally receive other support from the PCA's denominational offices in Atlanta.

But here's a key take-away: their search team (and, as my friend said, about 98% of their congregation) has very little sense of denominational identity. This means that a candidate tossing around acronyms like MNA, RUF, RUM, and MTW[10] meant little to nothing in that setting. Likewise, although the church sends support dollars to both Covenant College and Covenant Seminary, when my classmate interviewed then his search team (a different one from the senior pastor one) was under the impression that Covenant Seminary was an undergraduate institution.

This is a part of the information exchange that many fail to consider. The key question becomes: What am I assuming about this congregation (in the language of my resume, Ministerial Data Form, etc.) that I ought not? A candidate must realize that a lot of this sort of information is not helpful to their cause of presenting themselves as THE candidate for this position. In some ways, it might hurt them.

It also begs a question of motivation: why are all of these acronyms (or even the names they stand for) cluttering up a resume or data form? In many cases, they may be there for valuable information: if you served for two years as an intern with Reformed University Ministries, then that is directly relevant to your ministry experience.

On the other hand, be careful not to let all of this stuff become what one writer calls "cruft"— which is essentially the literary version of the stuff you scrape off your plate when you're done with a meal.

One scottish pastor said of his sermons, "the last thing I do is go back over my manuscript and cut out all of the cleverness." We might do the same if we want to clear our resumes, data forms, and other documents of cruft.

Probably the most valuable idea that my classmate sent me is a simple truism: There is such a thing as too much information.

Here's what he found as a big-picture observation: The candidates who received the quickest responses submitted only basic information in the first round. My friend said, "it was like they baited the hook just enough to interest the team member responsible for correspondence"— no more, no less. On the other hand, those who sent in a thick, fat packet of information didn't receive

---

10 All of these are "agencies" of the Presbyterian Church in America: MNA= Mission to North America, RUF = Reformed University Fellowship, (which is the local establishment of) RUM = Reformed University Ministries, and MTW = Mission to the World.

responses. There was, as my friend said, "no sense of 'teasing' or 'flirting.'" When you put it all out there, the search team isn't left with anything to wonder about.

So, what does that mean? I admit, the idea of "basic" information vs. a "fat" or "cluttered" packet is a vague distinction. Fortunately, my friend was able to offer more insight:

- **Basic:** a short inquiry, perhaps without even a Ministerial Data Form. Maybe even without a resume. But certainly no more than these.
- **"Cluttered"** packets: included more than a resume and MDF, such as lengthy philosophy of ministry papers, family photos, and other "extras."

At first blush, this seems to fly directly in the face of everything that I've advocated for an information "packet." I don't think so, though; these are still important things to have available.

Here's why: as I've mentioned before, the candidacy process can be sort of like dating; this first exchange is kind of like asking for that first date. A cover letter, along with a resume, may be just the amount of information you want to offer in that first step. Let them know you're interested, and give them enough to get interested as well.

But as the relationship progresses, you'll want to give them more— and that's when things like a brief biography or a very short statement of philosophy of ministry may be helpful. You can almost count on them asking for a recording of a sermon— but it may not be something that they need until later in the process.

Maybe this would be a good way to summarize: your cover letter, resume, data form, and other information will effectively amount to love letters to your future congregation. You don't want to overwhelm them, nor do you want to offer too little. Just enough is difficult to know for sure, but it is always what you strive for.

Phone Tag

We've already discussed how vital phone calls can be for making initial contact. Let's look at how phone interviews go— and what you can do to prepare for them.

To begin with, let's establish some context for a phone interview. A phone interview is not:

- **A random phone-call** for making contact or checking in with a search team. You will make and receive these kinds of phone calls, but they don't constitute a phone interview.
- **A conversation with just one person.** While there may be just one member of the search team you have been getting to know, the phone interview will include more than him. There will be the occasional exception to this, but it will be most exceptional indeed.
- **Just a conversation.** Be careful of the inclination to approach your phone interview casually, as if you're just shooting the breeze with a few people. Important decisions will be made based mainly on this interview; take it seriously!
- **Out of the blue.** Phone interviews don't just happen; you will know and expect that you are approaching the phone interview stage of candidacy.

So what is a phone interview? A phone interview is:

A scheduled interview by phone. This is an appointment, just as you might make to meet with a professor or to see a doctor. It is scheduled, and you are expected to be on-time or early. If you are "late" for this appointment, it may not happen at all— so don't be late! And like any appointment, you need to make sure there is time in your schedule for it. Don't be in a hurry to finish the phone interview; realize that it may take a couple of hours, and be prepared to devote that much time to it.

An interview with a group all at once. It will be conducted ordinarily on speakerphone or perhaps by conference call, and it will usually include the entire search team. Just as in face-to-face discourse, the dynamics change significantly when it is in the context of a group instead of just one or two people and yourself. Be aware of this change, and understand it.

An interview. You will be asked questions about yourself, your family, your background, your experience, your views, your ambitions, and your approach to ministry. Expect them to be particular and pointed at times. Be prepared to be vulnerable with your answers. Also be committed to a degree of formality and orderliness that is appropriate to job interviews (even though this isn't merely a "job").

The next step in the process. No search team conducts phone interviews with every candidate; if you've been invited to interview by phone, that means you've advanced to the "next" stage in the process. While every team will enact a slightly different process, this inevitably means that they see you as a better fit for their congregation than many others who applied. Congratulations!

Tips For More Effective Phone Interviews

With that definition of the "phone interview" in mind, consider what you might do to help it go as well as possible. How can you prepare for it adequately? What can you do during the interview to lend it greater effectiveness? What should you be listening for to better grasp questions of fitness and call from your end?

Good Preparation

Let's start with preparation. What are some things to consider?

Consider time and timing. When you are first contacted about scheduling a phone interview, keep the big picture in mind. When considering what date they suggest, don't simply check your calendar for immediate conflicts; think also of what else will happen that day, and in the days before. Will you be exhausted from a long week? Do you have other mentally-challenging events on the same day? You need to be at your best, so schedule the phone interview at a time that allows you the most opportunity to be fresh and ready.

Also keep time of day in mind. An evening interview may sound fine when you're scheduling it, but what time will it be when you're approaching the end of the second hour? How many of the search team will have spent a full day at work, only now to reach late into the night for an interview? Will they be as fresh and attentive as they need to be? How about time-zone differences— how do those affect your scheduling?

Not all of these must be openly discussed with the search committee chair in order to negotiate. You might simply offer that the best time for you would be on a Saturday morning, perhaps, or earlier in the evening than they initially suggested. And be careful not to be difficult: you don't want to leave a sour taste in the mouth of the one scheduling the interview. If nothing else, do what you need to do to make adjustments in your schedule that day and week, so that you are as alert and ready as you can be.

Ask who will be participating. It's perfectly reasonable for you to know in advance who else will be on the phone with you. Will it be the whole search team, or just a sub-set? Will others from the church be present, like another member of the pastoral staff or some of the officers? Ask for their names, their roles in the church, and how they fit into the search process.

Take notes on this part, if you need to— or better yet, ask the team leader to send the list to you before the interview. If possible, ask them to provide a paragraph or two about each of the search team; chances are good that they already compiled that information for the congregation's sake, especially in a larger church. Begin to get to know who you will be interviewing with days in advance.

I had a classmate who would gather this information beforehand, getting to know the team who would be interviewing him. He then set up chairs around their dining table with names and cartoon pictures taped to each chair, and when the time came for the interview he put his phone on speaker in the middle of the table. It wasn't quite in-person, but it worked for him to make it a bit more personal.

Get ample rest beforehand. This plays into time and timing, as well. Be sure that you get a good night's sleep prior to a phone interview. It almost goes without saying that you need to be well-rested in order to understand and respond to their questions. Make it a priority.

Consider "dressing up" for the phone interview. The morning of a one telephone interview with a candidate-church, I rose from bed, showered, shaved, and put on dress pants and a pressed, starched shirt. No, I didn't have any other appointments that day— I was dressing for my phone interview. How you dress doesn't only affect the way other people see you; it affects how you see yourself.

By dressing up for my phone interview, I felt differently than I would have if I had worn jeans or shorts and a t-shirt. Perhaps I wasn't as comfortable (though I have grown to be quite comfortable in dressier clothes), but I didn't want to be too comfortable. I didn't want to feel too relaxed. Instead, I wanted to feel a level of formality in my attitude and even my physical presence that was appropriate for the situation. "Dressing up" for my interview helped that.

I don't know if this is the right call for everyone. Some guys might be so nervous for their first interview that they need every means available to make them more comfortable. But I would at least encourage you to give it some consideration when you're approaching a telephone interview.

Have a sense of what questions they may ask— and what you would say in response. You need to be prepared for the questions you will get. There will always be one or two that you can't anticipate, and you will have to think on your feet. But there will be plenty of questions that you can expect with a certain degree of confidence. They will basically fall into three categories:

- *Personal questions.* What are the personal issues that will concern them? What do they need to know about you, your family, and your background to give them a level of assurance that you could pastor them effectively? Think back to some of the obstacles to full-term ministry discussed in chapter four; these will get you started in thinking about these questions. Consider also any other data that you've gathered about their congregation; does anything suggest itself as a matter of concern or need? You can anticipate many of these questions fairly easily.

- *Theological questions.* What do you know about this church's history that suggests that certain topics or positions in theology may be "red flags"? What are the difficult theological issues facing this congregation (or their denomination) today? Recognize that, sometimes, those asking the questions may have less familiarity with the core concerns than others, and they may be looking for the "textbook answer" to assuage their worries about orthodoxy. As you anticipate these questions, be ready to forego discussion of nuances and particulars unless you are asked about them.

- *Ministry questions.* How will you conduct your ministry among them? What will your emphases and priorities be? What does this congregation need in their leadership, now and in the future, that they are aware of and looking for? Expect questions that will reveal to the search team how you would lead them were you to be called. Here again, some committees will be looking for particular words or phrases, while others will be less familiar with particular terms or categories. Some will ask about certain circumstances or "case studies" while others will ask more broad questions.

You will find an appendix on "Questions & Answers" that gives concrete examples of some of the questions I have received (in phone interviews and in other contexts), as well as some sample answers to questions that I offered when asked.

Ask for time for your questions. While you are the one being interviewed, it is reasonable for you to take the opportunity to gather information as well. Remember the discussion on the candidacy of churches from chapter three, and request that some time be set aside during the phone interview for your questions, as well.

Alternatively, you may prefer to ask for a chance for a response question after each of the committee's queries. This balances the interview out a good bit, and it can lend itself to providing an abundance of useful information for your decision-making. It is likely, however, that the search team will not realize how much time this approach would take, and the phone interview will go much longer than they expect (or it will be cut short).

Therefore, I recommend a modified version of this approach: have your questions ready, and mark which ones are relevant to the questions you were asked. When the time for your questions comes, focus primarily on these and refer back to the discussion that took place earlier in the interview. The appendix on "Questions & Answers" mentioned above also includes a list of 50 questions about churches I suggest you work toward answering during the candidacy process.

Also, remember this: if they simply refuse to give you any time for your questions, that is telling in itself; it suggests how important your side of the decision is to them, either explicitly or by implication.

During the Interview

With good preparation behind you, what are some ways that you can handle the interview itself more effectively?

Ask their names, and ask them to identify themselves before each question/comment. It will be good to confirm who is present; you may even ask about those whom you were told would be in the interview and are not introduced. It also moves the interview in a more conversational direction[1] if you know who is speaking to you, and an reply directly.

Another benefit of connecting names in the interview is that it can suggest where the priorities lay among the committee members. What you know about the different interviewers (from your earlier reconnaissance) will allow you now to associate people with ideas. Who emphasizes what? How are the questions divided? Are there certain members of the group that never speak— and if so, what group(s) in the congregation might they fit into?

All of this is data that will eventually help you be discerning about your readiness and sense of fitness for a particular congregation.

---

[1] While this seems contrary— we've already discussed that the interview is not just a conversation— it's actually an effort for balance. Your inclination may be to err on the side of conversational tone; you must always push against that, working toward a more formal approach to the interview. The search team's inclination, on the other hand, may be to lean toward a very formal and ill-at-ease discussion; you can help them move more toward the center as well, by giving them conversational cues such as using their names.

Have notes on-hand. Have your list of interviewers in front of you, so that you can refer to it as needed to remind yourself who you are speaking to. If you will ask questions, keep those nearby as well.

You might even think about having some "talking points" prepared. If you've put some time toward anticipating what questions you will be asked, creating a few bullet-pointed reminders of your response should be fairly straightforward. You will need to be careful, of course, that you don't come across as giving a scripted or canned answer; beware of having so much information in your talking points that either, a) you have to read them to get to the idea, or b) you can't adapt the answer to a slightly different form of the question.

Be honest. This seems obvious, and naturally we want to avoid lying outright. But there are several ways that you can be less-than-honest and thereby mislead the search team. When you're giving your answers watch out for these:

- *Embellishing*— it is oh-so-easy to exaggerate about who you are, what you've accomplished, what you know, or how you are gifted. We all fight the desire to look better than we are. Watch out for this temptation.
- *Avoiding the Question*— some of the questions will be hard because they are personal or reveal a weakness. Don't allow your fears of being exposed keep you from honesty by steering you around the question; be vulnerable with them, at least enough to give some disclosure.[2]
- *Knowing It All*— nobody really does, and nobody likes someone who thinks that they do. Yet, our overconfidence and eagerness to appear smart can lead us to answer questions as if we know what we do not. Be careful of a know-it-all attitude.
- *Lack of Accountability*— there will be those questions that there is no way for anyone to verify your answer about. This lack of accountability can tempt you to deny what is true, or to affirm what is really false. Don't let lack of veracity keep you from being honest.

Be humbly confident. I had a friend who was interviewed to join the staff of a ministry we both served as volunteers, and in the first interview they turned him down. Our director, however, knew that this was a mistake, and insisted that they interview him again— and this time, she told him to turn down his humility a notch or two. That did the trick, and he went on to serve that ministry for a decade.

Certainly it is vital that we be humble; no search team should hire the boasting, swaggering candidate for a position in pastoral ministry. You must approach the interview with the humility discussed earlier in the book. "'God opposes the proud but gives grace to the humble.' Humble yourselves, therefore, under God's mighty hand, that he may lift you up in due time."[3]

At the same time, the same humility, without the confidence in how the Lord has gifted and fitted us for ministry, can present an obstacle to effective placement. As with my friend, our humility may stand in the way of our honesty. My friend was gifted for the ministry he was interviewed for, but his humility masked his giftedness

---

2   You don't have to tell every sordid detail of the most painful parts of your life to be vulnerable! Sometimes, a little goes a long way.

3   I Peter 5:5b-6; cf. Luke 14:10, James 4:10.

too much. Had it not been for our wise director, he may not have been effectively placed in ministry.

Therefore, give your answers humbly, but do not let your humility prevent you from also returning an honest answer. If the Lord has blessed your service to Him or prepared you for a particular ministry, say so! You don't have to brag or let your head swell to boast in the Lord and His work.

Be concise. One of the best skills to develop for ministry (and for life, really) is to learn to be concise. This has been a hard one for me, and I still struggle with it; my desire to be understood and to be thorough is often at odds with it!

But you will serve yourself well to be concise in interviews. What do I mean by "concise"? It doesn't mean "blunt"— that describes more the style and tone of your answer than it does its content. Nor does it simply mean "brief"— while shorter answers are preferred, brief ones sometimes come at the expense of important content.

Concise means, "brief but comprehensive;"[4] this is the sort of answer you must give. Don't leave the question unanswered; however, do not feel the need to offer every fact that you know, nuance you can describe, or angle you are familiar with concerning each topic. Offer as much information as they need and have asked for, then stop answering.

It can be wise to give some parts of your answer ambiguously enough that a follow-up question is needed. This will open the door for you to develop the nuance that you may be inclined to give. Wait for the door to be opened— answer concisely.

Keep a record. You will likely forget a lot of what happens in your phone interview. Things will simply vanish from your memory: an important comment, the final answer to a key question you asked, or even the entire discussion surrounding a question.

It will be helpful, therefore, to keep some sort of record of the phone interview. For most of ours, my wife listened on speaker-phone and took notes throughout. This was invaluable; she noted every question asked (on both sides of the discussion) and provided a summary of their answers. Occasionally, she would comment on my answers in her notes, as well.

That may not be an option, or you may prefer to take notes yourself. You may have the technology/equipment needed to record the interview, so that you have an audio record of it.[5] Regardless of how you keep a record, it is vital that you do. It matters in two ways: 1) for the sake of your decision-making about this particular congregation; and 2) for the sake of preparation for future potential opportunities.[6]

Final Thoughts

Handling the phone interview stage is not difficult, but like the rest of the candidacy process, it does require preparation, attention, and diligence. Give some time to get-

---

4   According to the *New American Oxford Dictionary.*
5   For that matter, you may be able to feed the audio through software that will transcribe it completely!
6   Even if you are fairly sure that this congregation is where you will be, don't discount #2— the committee may not agree; something may come up that changes your mind; or you may need the information down the line, when moving to another ministry.

ting ready for your phone interviews before they are on the calendar, and you'll be grateful that you did.

No Vacation

Be assured: while you may be getting on a plane to fly to a never-before visited location, the interview weekend is no vacation.

Rather, it may be one of the hardest trips you will ever take. But it may also be one of the most exciting, emotionally-charging, and invigorating things you have done yet in preparation for sustained vocational ministry. You will meet others who are eager to know if you will be their next pastor. You will encounter those who are spiritually mature and whose faith inspires you, and those who struggle with the barest belief. You will have an opportunity to put your gifts, skills, and experiences to work. Lord willing, you may just meet the people who will become close friends and the flock that you shepherd for the foreseeable future!

You will do well to prepare properly and adequately for the interview weekend.[1] During the trip itself, you will be too focused, too busy, and too tired to be concerned with many of the details and questions that might come your way. If you have prepared for it, however, and have a good understanding of what is to come, it will keep everything from unraveling at the worst moment.

In this chapter, I'll walk through some things to consider about the interview weekend. How do you prepare for it? What should you focus on while there? What will it be like? When does it end? This is a crucial point in the candidacy process, and will be the climactic event before the decision-making time is upon you and the congregation.

Preparing For The Interview Weekend

The first thing to do is focus on getting ready. What preparation do you need to make for the interview weekend?

Spiritual Preparation

The most important preparation you can make— throughout the process, but especially at this point— is spiritual preparation. Because of the nature of the interview weekend, there are two dimensions to this: ministry preparation, and personal/candidacy preparation.

First, remember that you will be in-residence as a minister to the people you are with during your interview weekend. They are sinners in need of God's grace, broken and wounded, growing in their faith and knowledge of God, and being increasingly bound together as His body. Therefore, you must begin beforehand to pray for them— by name, as much as possible. You must prepare well for whatever lessons, sermons, or other preaching/teaching opportunities you will have. You should con-

---

[1] I will refer to this trip as an "interview weekend" although it may not be a full weekend, or it may actually be longer than a weekend.

sider what you know of their circumstances and recent history, and marshall the pastoral knowledge and wisdom that you have for that context.

You also have preparation to do personally, and in terms of your candidacy. Here again, pray for your own discernment and for theirs: that your ministry among them would demonstrate accurately to everyone in what ways He could use you among them; that God would reveal to all whether there is a good "fit;" and that He would begin to bind you together if so. Ask Him to give you the endurance and fortitude to carry you through the whole interview time. Pray that they would also be both aware of and sensitive to the trials that an interview can be.

Mental Preparation

There is also great mental preparation to be made. As you will have learned by the time you set out on an interview weekend, candidacy is a great mental challenge! This doesn't cease when you interview; in fact, it increases.

Be sure that you are prepared for questions that you are able to anticipate. By now you have gained some sense of the priorities and core values of the congregation; they should suggest to you things that you may be asked about. You will be grateful for time spend in advance preparing for these questions. Having a general idea of how you will answer will reap benefits, both in affording you the ability to respond succinctly and clearly, and in easing the mental taxation that will come with being interviewed over the course of a weekend.

Also, understand that part of the mental preparation needed is as much psychological as it is intellectual. The fatigue you will experience from the interview weekend will be physical, mental, and emotional exhaustion. You can prepare for this by understanding both the extent and the limit of the interview weekend; its extent will, potentially, shape the next years of your life and ministry (and those of your family), and it necessarily carries great weight. Since the interview weekend will be one of the biggest factors in a congregation's decision to vote, it can be an enormous encouragement to your ministry to have an interview weekend that is affirming and positive.

However, there is also a limit: you cannot and should not be anything other than yourself, and you mustn't become too stressed or anxious about how you are perceived. Realize this limit, as well: a congregation that meets the real you and votes against calling you has, in the end, protected you from eventual hurt and difficulty.[2] Neither your identity nor your security in Christ are truly threatened by the interview weekend or its result. God already knows the place that He has for you to serve in His Kingdom. Prepare for the interview weekend mentally by recognizing this and going with confidence in God's goodness.

Teaching Preparation

Will you be teaching, preaching, or leading in any way during your interview? The odds are very good that the answer is yes — few churches will hire a man to serve them as pastor without first watching him "in action."

Therefore, you must be ready before you leave for the interview with all of the preparation you will need.

---

[2] See the chapter called "Who? Where? Why?" for more on how God protects candidates through such "rejection."

- **Preaching:** If you are preaching, get ready in such a way that you could preach your sermon in the first hour you are there. Do your exegetical work and prepare your illustrations and application. Gather your notes. Put bookmarks in your Bible. Practice or talk through your sermon, if that is a normal part of your preparation. Don't leave any of the preparation undone.
- **Teaching:** Likewise, if you will be teaching a class or group, make your preparation in advance and get your notes and other resources together. Will you be using some sort of slide presentation, such as PowerPoint™? If so, then get your slides ready, and put the file on the desktop of your computer; it's probably a good idea to carry a copy on a flash-drive or disc, as well. You should also ensure that the church where you are candidating has the technology and equipment to accommodate your needs.[3] If you are using any other visual aids, object lessons, or "props" then get them prepared also.

Do not assume that you will have time to do any preparation on your lesson or sermon while you are there; in fact, assume that you will not have time to think about it! Even if you have some free time scheduled, you may (and probably will) be too tired or focused on other things to concentrate on finishing a sermon or polishing a lesson.

At the same time, you may encounter something or someone that suggests a perfect illustration or point of application during your visit. While you should be very careful about using immediate examples in this way (especially for people), it may also be the key to connecting your points with the people hearing them. Therefore, it may be worthwhile to carry a small notebook and pen or pencil with you to be prepared to make notes when you encounter these (and to make adjustments to your teaching/preaching notes later).

Things to know in advance

Will you be staying with a family from the congregation, or in a hotel? If given the choice, pick the hotel. I know that it seems like staying with a family from the congregation will represent another chance to get to know someone, and that is true; in fact, this is the most compelling reason to stay with a family, and the biggest advantage of it.

But it may be the only advantage that you receive from it.[4] However, if you are with a family from the congregation, that only extends the amount of time that you are "on"— and reduces the time you have to rest. The family will likely want to visit with you during the little bit of time that you have with them; late nights become later still, and breakfast may be an informal interview.

On the other hand, if you are in a hotel then you will have some time to yourself, if only a little. You and your spouse won't worry about keeping your voices down as you talk and debrief with each other. You can decompress as you wish— taking a long shower, watching SportsCenter, surfing the 'net— without concern over your hosts

---

3   The same is true if you plan to use slides in your preaching, as well— but I don't assume that, nor is it as common in preaching (yet!) as in teaching.
4   There is the obvious fact that it costs the congregation money— sometimes a lot of money— to you put in a hotel room, while it costs little or nothing to house you with a family. This IS an advantage, but not one that you will immediately realize.

drawing conclusions from it. The hotel becomes a welcomed break in the midst of an otherwise nonstop weekend.

If they do put you with a family, be ready for it by getting more rest, and by working out plans to keep discussion to a minimum while in the house. Look for an opportunity to take a walk with your spouse (or by yourself), maybe before breakfast. And extend your gratitude to your hosts— they don't realize that their efforts to engage you may take a greater toll on you than otherwise.

Are they expecting your whole family, or just you (and your spouse)? My recommendation is that your family (i.e., your children) stay home, if at all possible. We had one interview weekend where they specifically requested that we bring our children, and it was very difficult. The children were a little confused about what we were doing, and why we were visiting with new people in an unfamiliar place as if we were old friends. My wife (and I) had difficulty giving our undivided attention to the people we were with, and faced many more distractions than we would have had we been alone.

If circumstances allow, leave your children with a family member or close friend. If you accept a call to the congregation you are visiting, there will be plenty of occasion to help your children become familiar with their community and new church family. It will save you some much-needed energy and attention during the interview weekend.

At the same time, definitely take your spouse with you if you are married. As your partner in life and ministry, she will be a second set of eyes and ears, and you will be grateful for the perspective and insight that she offers in evaluating the weekend. Her absence may make some aspects of the interviews awkward, and you will have a more difficult time processing your thoughts and feelings about the weekend after the fact. If they ask you to come alone, press for "permission" for her to come with you.

If you must take your children with you, be proactive about it. Pack games, toys, and activities for them to do, and have something ready for them at a moment's notice. Plan ahead for any times where you may need to hand them off to childcare, including special care information and even snacks. And watch for the unforeseen advantages of having them with you; on our trip that included them, we gained some peculiar insight into the people who kept the nursery and children's Sunday School, based on the reports from our kids!

Would it be wise to visit with a realtor and look at homes while you are there? Don't overlook this opportunity if it emerges for you. If you would be moving far from your current town or city, this may be one of the only chances to get a feel for what housing is available. You may not be ready to put a contract on a house or sign a lease, but at least you will have a sense of where the neighborhoods are, and what you can afford.

For planning purposes, be sure you ask this question in advance of the trip. The search team will need to accommodate this outing in your schedule, which may change your allotted time for interaction with leaders and others substantially. They will also need to connect you with a realtor who will want to get his/her on their calendar.

This may seem like a presumptuous question to ask, but in fact it is a natural one. It communicates to the search team (and to the congregation) that you are serious in your consideration of the call to ministry there. They will appreciate your planning and forward-thinking attitude, and in most cases it will become an advantage for you in more ways than one.

What will your schedule be for your time there? This is one of the most vital questions to get a clear, concrete answer about, as it will impact everything. Has the search team planned a good, helpful schedule for you? If so, they should be happy to share it with you![5]

Be on the lookout for a schedule that seems too full. If there aren't built-in times for meals, it's a problem! Also, look for windows when you will have time for rest, and watch for too much time spent with one group. You want to be exposed to as many segments of the congregation as possible, for your sake and theirs. If there is a key demographic group missing, don't hesitate to ask for some time with them.

What to wear on the Interview Weekend
When you're getting ready to visit a church for an interview weekend, what to wear may not be a high priority in your preparation. But you need to give it attention, if only in the days before you go.

[A disclaimer: in this section I'm assuming a lot about culture. I realize that there are many cultures in which my comments below would not apply— even within the American context. I'm assuming, therefore, that you, the reader, understands that I'm coming from an American, protestant, mostly-white, mostly-suburban Presbyterian context, and that you'll forgive my broad-stroke claims if they don't apply to you.]

For the most part, candidacy is not a casual affair. View it like you do any job interview— only this one lasts two and a half days. You wouldn't wear jeans, flip-flops and a worn-out Van Halen t-shirt to a job interview at a corporation, retail store, or even Starbucks; you would probably wear nice pants (not denim), dark shoes, and a nice shirt— possibly even a tie and sport coat. Why should you view an interview at a church any differently?

A rule of thumb I always taught my Rhetoric students about public speaking is applicable here: you should plan to dress at least as nicely as the other most well-dressed person in the room. You are not a mere participant in these situations— you are the object of everyone's attention, and the way you present yourself communicates a lot to them about how much you respect them and the situation.

So here's a list of what I usually took on my interview weekends:
- 1-2 two-piece suits
- 1-2 sport jackets (2 if I only take 1 suit)
- 2-3 pairs of nice pants (probably 1 pair of "dress slacks" and 2 pairs of "chino" pants)
- 1 pair of black dress shoes
- 2 pair of brown shoes— one casual and one dress
- 2 oxford dress shirts
- 2-3 other shirts (either Polo-style golf shirts or casual button-down shirts)
- 3 neckties
- Appropriate accessories (belts, socks, etc.)

---

5 And if not, this communicates a strong subconscious message about the type of congregation you are considering.

Here's what I did ***not*** take: blue jeans, shorts, printed t-shirts, sneakers, or a swim suit. I didn't go swimming or play sports while on the interview weekend, and you probably won't either (the lone exception to this *might* be a youth pastor). Even if one of my opportunities was in a beach town in Florida, and even if I were going there in mid-July, I knew I would not be swimming or even wearing shorts in 95% of the circumstances.

Along these lines— guys: wear a sleeved, plain white undershirt. All the time. (Yes, it does look different.)

One more thing: the suits, jackets, pants, and shirts should all go to the dry cleaner's a week before the trip. That will cost money (probably about $20, if my experience with dry cleaners is accurate), but you're guaranteed to have cleaned, pressed clothes that look neat for the whole trip.

Here's a fact to take to the bank: in even the most casual American church, you will never be too over-dressed in a tie and blazer. You could wear a suit to 80% of the churches in any given town and not stand out. So remember this as you're packing for your interview weekend.

The Interview Weekend

I don't know if there is a "typical" interview weekend, but almost all of the interview trips I've taken have been packed as full as they could be. (The anecdotal evidence of my friends and classmates affirms this.) I have had some that were more intense than others, but they often are surprisingly busy events.

Schedule

Your experiences will be different from mine; in fact, each experience you have will be different from the others. But some things will certainly be true:
- You will meet with as many people as possible
- You will be asked many of the same questions over and over
- There will be very little awareness of how full your schedule is by most of the people you meet
- You will have at least one formal interview, and it will last several hours
- There may be more than one interview, and they may seem quite redundant to you
- You will probably be asked to teach and/or preach on at least one occasion
- You will eat a lot of meals out!

For example, this was my experience on one of my interview trips (it was a preliminary interview for a ministry staff position):

Day one: I left my house at 4:30am to get on a 7am plane, which landed at 9:15 local time. I was met by an associate pastor (I'll call him Jeff), who drove me from the airport to the church grounds (asking questions all the way). I was given a tour of the grounds, and I met three other staff members and the principal of the school hosted by the church, with whom I sat down and answered questions for about 45 minutes. From there, we left to meet two elders for lunch, and spent almost two hours with them. Then back to the church grounds, where I met the senior pastor and talked with him for about two hours. Jeff and I went back to his house, where I had supper with he and his family, then back to the senior pastor's study for an interview with the whole Session. That interview lasted about two hours, after which I returned to Jeff's house (where I was staying) and visited with he and his wife until about midnight (which was actually 2am my time).

Day two: The next morning, I rose at 6am to shower and dress for breakfast with the senior pastor at 7:30. Then Jeff gave me a driving tour of the community before going back to the church, where he went through some of the church's policies and long-range plans with me. We met with two couples from the congregation for lunch at noon, then I met with the Diaconate from 2pm to about 3:30. Jeff took me back to the airport by 4:30, for my 6pm flight to leave. After missing my connection, I finally boarded a flight home at 10:30, and got in the car to go home at midnight.

That was a whirlwind— and, needless to say, exhausting. I slept through the last connection flight on the way home, and probably half the day after. Here is another example, when I was interviewing to be the solo pastor of a small church:

Days one & two: my wife and I flew to the closest city, picked up a rental car, and went to a hotel to stay the night before driving almost three hours to the small town where the church was located. We arrived at the church's property by late morning, and were met with an elder who took us to lunch. After that, he drove us on a tour of the area, then back to the church property for a tour of the facilities. We then went to the hotel where we would be staying, got a few minutes' rest, then dressed for the evening. The congregation had a dinner in the fellowship hall, and we met most of the members. Then we returned to the hotel.

Day three: we rose for an early breakfast the next morning with another of the elders and his wife, and afterwards he drove us around the area to show us where each family lived. After that, we had some free time, and met some of our family (who lived nearby) for a quick lunch. After lunch we met a realtor, who showed us about eight homes that would be suitable for us; then it was back to the hotel to freshen up and dress for the evening. My wife visited with all of the elders' wives and a few other women in the church while I was interviewed by the Session and the search committee together for almost three hours. After that, I picked up my wife and we returned to the hotel.

Days four & five: we rose and dressed, checked out of the hotel, and left for the church. I taught a lesson during the Sunday School hour, then prayed with the elders before worship. I led worship, preached, and greeted the congregation on their way out. We then went to lunch with one of the elders and his wife before driving three hours back to the city where we would fly out the next morning. We had supper, checked into the same hotel as before, and returned to the airport the next morning to fly home.

When It Starts

Like it or not, your interview begins the minute your plane touches down, or your car drives into the city limits. From that point on, you're "on" in terms of being interviewed.

This may sound like an exaggeration, but consider this: you don't know when you will meet the party that has been sent to meet you at the airport. You don't know who you will pass on the drive into town. One classmate of mine was surprised to learn that one of the members of the search team had been on the plane with him on the way there!

What To Ask

There are so many things to learn and find out about a congregation. By this point, if you have been doing diligent work to research the potential congregation and ask questions during interviews, you probably already know a great deal. But sometimes it can seem like every answer suggests two more questions!

As I mentioned in the previous chapter, I have provided a list of questions that I recommend seeking answers for in the appendix, "Questions & Answers." This list may prove a valuable resource as you continue to gather information and determine what you don't yet know. Ironically, however, the interview weekend can be a difficult time to get your questions answered. This is because you are not usually spending extended time with any one person or group of people, but are with different people all weekend. Therefore, you may barely get a handful of questions answered by one group before another, with another perspective and a different set of priorities, takes its place.

Therefore, this is my recommendation for questions on the interview weekend: have three to five big-picture questions that you will ask of everyone. These will be summary questions, that get at key concepts about core values, philosophy of ministry, and the practices of church life. You might even simply say to folks, "I'm asking these questions of everyone I meet this weekend…"

Then, have another (very) small handful of more particular questions that you will ask directly to those who are in the best position to answer them fully. When you meet with the leadership, you ask them a direct question about leadership; when you spend time with the young families, ask a specific question about children's or family ministry; and so on. Don't count on getting more than one of these in for each group, and realize that some groups won't get that far.

Remember, you can still ask questions after the interview weekend! This is not a "last-chance" moment for information-gathering; it is vital, however, that you have been diligent in gathering information up to this point, and that you be close to having all of the most crucial information in-hand.

How To Survive

Debrief with your spouse (or by yourself) regularly. Make sure you note important things, if only in short-hand in a notebook or in your computer. You won't remember it all when you get home— and you'll wish that you had better notes, even if you do take some! The more communication you have with your spouse (if you're married), the better the chances that you will remember what you need to know to begin making decisions.

Take every opportunity for rest. Look for breaks and take them. Even if you aren't that tired yet, you will be; don't miss the five or ten minutes here and there to catch your breath. It won't keep you from the inevitable exhaustion, but it may stave off early-onset of fatigue that will keep you from being sharp when you need it.

Pray. Be always asking for God's guidance through the trip. Pray silently by yourself, and pray with others. Ask regularly for time to pray with those you are meeting and interviewing with.

Be Careful Of The "Hard Sell"

For my first five years in ministry, I also worked in retail; at first it was when I was volunteering for a church youth group and Young Life, then when I needed full-time employment but the church I served could only pay part-time. I worked briefly for a clothing store, then a toy store, then two different camera stores. I learned a lot of lessons in those jobs that have served me well in ministry.

One of the best things I learned from retail sales was how to simultaneously make a sale and satisfy a customer. It works like this: figure out what the customer really wants and needs, then sell them that. Pretty simple, right? Not so fast...

First of all, the customer often does not know what they want or need. They usually think they do; it requires a greater-than-average level of humility to admit that they don't understand their own needs or desires. Nevertheless, most of the time they don't have any clear idea of what they are shopping for. They have some ideas— for example, a customer at a camera store knows what kind of pictures they usually take now, or would if they had a camera. But when it comes to camera models, features and functions, or technical specifications and capabilities, they rarely even have a clue, let alone the language to articulate it.

This presents a second obstacle: since they don't really know which products meet their needs and which do not, it is often possible to sell them whatever you want them to buy. In fact, I had co-workers who employed this tactic: they pushed whatever product offered them the best commission, whether or not that was what their customers were looking for.

It is because customers don't know what they need or want, however, that they have come to a retail store in first place. They need someone who can ask the right questions, who knows the available product lines, and who can take answers and products together for the right recommendation. That's why they would come to me. When I worked at a camera store, for instance, I knew the specs and abilities of every camera, lens, and flash unit we sold. I also learned the right questions to ask to determine which products would best fit a customer, and could make recommendations based on what they want and need, even if they couldn't specify this themselves.

My co-workers in the camera store may have earned a fast buck through a commission on, say, a camera body and lens. But if that camera did not meet the needs or desires of the customer, you can bet that customer would not return to buy another camera from them; in fact, they may not return to our store at all (after all, they believed they were getting what they needed, but were deceived). In the long run, determining what met their needs and selling them that product would produce a trusting relationship that would result, in time, in far greater amounts of sales and commissions. Pushing the wrong product may satisfy for now, but it will leave a salesman wanting in the future.

It works in a similar way in pastoral placement: churches often don't know how to articulate what they are looking for in a pastor, but they will know if they get it or not. A candidate who "sells himself" to a search committee— he tells them what he thinks they want to hear so that they will offer him the position— will mirror my commission-minded co-workers. It may produce a short-term satisfaction on both sides: the candidate-church thinks it is getting what it desires, and the candidate-pastor gets a placement (and therefore a paycheck). Long-term, however, both will be found wanting. The pastor will likely be unfulfilled in his work, since he had to misrepresent his own sense of calling to get the position. The church will realize quickly that they were taken by a fast-talker, and become even more difficult to shepherd. Everyone loses.

On the other hand, if a candidate-pastor follows my lesson from retail— figure out what the church really wants and needs, then offer them that (if he can)— then everyone wins. To do this, a candidate-pastor has to figure out what questions will reveal whether a church is looking for someone like him. Ask the right questions, and he will know if he is the man for the job. If not, then his integrity should lead him to say so. If he is the one, it is far from a "sales job" or "selling himself" to help them understand that it is a good fit.

This comes back to the basic assumption that you know what you're called to do. You must be the expert on you— in retail terms, you have to know what kind of "product" you are, and what needs and desires you can and cannot satisfy. If you know this and learn to articulate it, what you present is no sales pitch— it's the truth.

When Does The Interview End?

I've already talked briefly about how the interview begins the moment the plane touches down. But when does it end?

I sometimes read the blog of a Silicon Valley manager who calls himself "Rands." He suggests that the interview really lasts for 90 days past your first day on the job. I think he's right— and that this applies in some ways to the pastoral candidacy process, too.

Folks can't evaluate you accurately by just your information packet— and neither can they really assess your value during an interview weekend. While you probably won't get fired for not handling the first ninety days (or the first six months) well, it will definitely set the tone for how your ministry will go. And since the goal is always effective ministry for the full-term of service God has called you to, starting well may be the key to finishing well (or at all).

In addition to the eight principles I've already laid out, Rands has some good ideas, including showing up early and staying late, accepting every lunch invitation you get, and saying something stupid. Rands says it well:

> *It's not just that you forgot to ask key questions during your initial interview process; it's that the person that you were walking into that interview isn't who you are. You're a resume, you're a referral, and you're a reputation.*

In other words, as Rands says, "Your job interview isn't over until you've asked all the questions and heard all of the stories."

Who? Where? Why?

What Happens Now

Once you have exchanged an extraordinary amount of information, talked by phone (probably several times), and likely made a trip or two to visit a potential congregation, the candidacy process reaches something of a climax.

There are decisions to be made.

Some of the decisions will be out of your hands. After you have been presented to a congregation as a candidate, in most cases it is up to the congregation (or some representation thereof) to decide whether you are the right candidate for the position they seek to fill. This may entail a simple vote of a board or leadership team, or it may require a meeting and vote of the whole congregation. This part will be out of your hands— and it will probably be the cause of no small amount of curiosity and nervous energy for you!

Some aspects of the decision will fall to you. How will you make these decisions? What are you looking to, and looking for, in terms of guidance for your discernment?

In this chapter, I want to consider some ways to think about the decision-making part of the candidacy process. In the first section, I'll discuss some strategies and approaches to your side of the decision-making; this will include a "rubric" for making the decision, and earnest discussion about priorities and convictions about what you are looking for in relation to what you are offered. In the second part of the chapter, I'll cover some of the more interactive aspects, including how to think about rejection and the vulnerability required to move ahead with the commitment of a ministry call.

A "Decision-Making" Rubric

When it comes down to that time, how do you actually make the decision?

Many folks will rely on their "gut instinct" trusting that the Lord is leading. This can be presented in an appeal to the work of the Holy Spirit: "I'll wait for the Spirit's prompting in me to know what is right." While that sounds very spiritual and righteous, it leaves some things a bit too open-ended. How do we know when it is the Holy Spirit "prompting" us? How does that manifest itself? Some will claim it is simply the inspiration of an idea. Others will call it a "still, small, voice." Some will look for the Holy Spirit in a seeming "coincidence" that they take for profound meaning. But is this truly the Holy Spirit? Could it be instead that Satan, the Deceiver, is whispering lies to us? Or could it be the beans we ate at supper last night? Trusting our "gut" in this way can lead to problems.

Others will leave the decision up to the congregation: if a call is offered, they will take it. Here again, this may initially seem like the ultimate trusting in God: a completely passive submission to His working through the local congregation. But this too has problems. For one, it ignores the fact that congregations are made up of fallen sinners! It may be that they have applied the wrong criteria, allowed poor motives or goals to steer the process, or simply erred in their decision. They may have overlooked something that you took notice of, and that factor is a vital part of the decision.[1] For another thing, they are likely expecting you to be exercising wisdom and discernment in the process, too. In fact, it may be the case that your failure to engage actively in the decision-making would itself be a signal to them of a lack of leadership ability. Be very cautious about handing a decision to others in this way.

Still others will work from a "pros" and "cons" list. They will line up all of the factors as favorable or not, and see which column has more items listed. This is the ultra-practical approach, and may appear to be the perfect counter-balance to an over-spiritualization that may be found in one of the first two approaches named above. But watch out! Simple pros vs. cons lists can frequently miss the mark. They almost never include a truly exhaustive list of factors It is alway easy to have one side skew more favorably: for an opportunity that you are hopeful about, you will inevitably remember more things on the favorable side, whereas a position that you are more skeptical about may evoke recollection of the negatives more freely. It also ignores the reality that some factors are weightier than others; how will different factors' priorities play into a pro/con list?

Clearly, some guidance is needed in decision-making. That's what this chapter is all about— but be forewarned! Decision-making itself is a difficult topic, and I certainly don't claim to be an expert on the subject. This chapter, therefore, is highly-subjective. I'll provide some anecdotal evidence supporting what I suggest here, but please take it as exactly that: suggestions. As the saying goes, "your mileage may vary."

The Starting Point: Prayer

Begin with prayer. Pray for the wisdom of the congregation, and pray for the Lord to give you (and your spouse, if you're married) wisdom about your future ministry. I discussed ways to pray for transition in chapter II; now add to your prayers the decision(s) before you. You have a matter of great consideration and discernment before you. That decision must be bathed in prayer.

What prayer does matters most in times like this— weighty, substantial times. Times of whole-life importance. Prayer changes you. It changes how you think, what your priorities are, and why you do what you do. It changes whether you are afraid or nervous or anxious or worried— or not. It alters your orientation to what is before you.

How does prayer do all of this? By reminding you that God is in control, and you are not. That God knows what will happen, and you do not. That God has a perfect and complete plan for your life and service to Him, and you do not. Prayer is a means by which God infuses you with His grace, administering to you a life-giving dependence upon Him and freedom from yourself.

In prayer, God grants wisdom and discernment. He also grants contentment and peace, freedom from cares and worry, and readiness to follow him. Fill your decision-making with prayerfulness.

---

[1] See the section of this chapter called "Making Decisions For Them" for more on this.

"God's Will?"

How do we know God's will? Can we discern God's will for our lives?

It is significant to recognize that speaking of "God's will" may mean a variety of things. In one sense, God's will is obvious: whatever has happened up to this point has clearly been God's will! But in another sense, God's will can be mysterious and elusive. We distinguish theologically between different kinds of "will" when we speak of the will of God: the decretive and the preceptive will of God; the secret and the revealed will of God; the will of that which shall certainly be accomplished vs. that which it pleases God for His creatures to do; and so on. Louis Berkhof describes these variations effectively:

"The word 'will' as applied to God does not always have the same connotation in Scripture. It may denote (1) the whole moral nature of God, including such attributes as love, holiness, righteousness, etc.; (2) the faculty of self – determination, I.e. The power to determine self to a course of action or to form a plan; (3) the product of this activity, that is, the predetermined plan or purpose; (4) the power to execute this plan and to realize this purpose (the will in action or omnipotence); and (5) the rule of life laid down for rational creatures."[2]

We see these differences in Scripture clearly: God is sovereign, and doubtless nothing escapes His control. Yet, when we read that He does not will for "anyone to perish, but everyone to come to repentance" (2 Peter 3:9) then we must conclude one of three things:

1. God is, in fact, not sovereign, because not everyone has come to repentance.
2. Peter's teaching is a form of universalism that is incompatible with other clear teachings from Scripture that deny such universalism (such as Matthew 7:21).
3. The "will of God" as described by Peter means something other than a declaration of what God will surely cause to come to pass.

When it comes to discernment and decision-making with regard to calling and ministry candidacy, therefore, we must go in with an awareness that there is much of what is "God's will" that we cannot know— we will never be absolutely certain of it. Our understanding of God's will is always veiled with a certain amount of ignorance, at least in the way that we often wish to know God's will.

In what way can we know God's will? There is one way that we definitely know God's will: that which He has revealed to us in Scripture. God's will is displayed clearly to us in the Bible, and if we are obedient to the prescriptions of the Word of God then we need not fear that we are out of accord with God's will. This fact is what led Saint Augustine to proclaim, "Love, and do what you will"[3]— in other words, obey God's command to love, and whatever you may wish to do beyond that will still be permitted within God's will. God has revealed to us in Scripture His ultimate purposes for us, His creatures, and His Word reveals those purposes to us as His will.[4]

---

2   Louis Berkhof, *Systematic Theology* (Edinburgh: The Banner of Truth Trust, 2000), p. 76.

3   Augustine of Hippo, *Tractatus* VII, 8.

4   Sinclair Ferguson's brief book, *Discovering God's Will* (Edinburgh: The Banner of Truth Trust, 1993) is an excellent introduction to this idea.

Consequently, much of what falls into the category of decision-making with regard to pastoral candidacy and transition may actually fall into a category called adiaphora: those things which are outside of the categories of "right" or "wrong"— they are permissible regardless of the choice. There is not a "right choice" or a wrong one in many cases; it's simply a matter of which will best suit your preferences and those of others involved.

What you will have for supper tonight is largely an adiaphoron; it will not matter whether you choose fish or steak (unless your doctor has forbidden one!). Whether you invest your savings in a mutual fund or a certificate of deposit is an adiaphoron. The apostle Paul goes as far as to suggest that eating food that had been sacrificed to idols is essentially an adiaphoron: "Food will not commend us to God. We are no worse off if we do not eat, and no better off if we do" (I Corinthians 8:8, ESV). This is not to say that adiaphora are morally or theologically indifferent; rather, that their acceptability is based upon motive, goals, and other factors beyond the decision itself.

Therefore, we must be careful that we approach decision-making in the candidacy process without over-spiritualizing, and without expectation that we can or will know and understand more of God's will than is truly the case. We must go into our evaluation and decision with a biblically-complete theology of the will of God.

Evaluation

It is important that we evauate all of the factors involved in a decision as carefully and objectively as possible. As I've already mentioned, I believe the "Pros & Cons" approach lends itself to subjectivity too much to be useful. Rather, I prefer something more like a "traffic light" approach.[5] It works like this: brainstorm all of the things that you know about this opportunity, whether it be related to ministry, personal and family factors, cultural elements, or other things (even if they are incidental). Then place each of those into one of three categories:

- **Red Light**— those indicators that certainly tell you to stop. These are huge barriers to effective life and ministry in this particular opportunity. You might be able to live with one or even two of these, but three or more should cause you to seriously reconsider whether you should accept this call.
- **Yellow Light**— those factors that cause you to slow down and think. These are not barriers as much as speed bumps— they force you to look around, prevent you from rushing into the decision, and encourage you to count the cost of accepting a call. No single "yellow light" is a substantial threat to effective ministry, and you can probably abide a handful of these without much problem. But if they start mounting up into a substantial number, it may be worth questioning whether you can ever get up to speed in that particular work.
- **Green Light**— the things that get your engine revving and your heart pumping. These are the factors that will thrust you toward being excited about an opportunity, and represent lasting possibilities for thriving and

---

5 You may download a free, printable copy of an "Opportunity Evaluation Worksheet" at the Doulos Resources website: www.doulosresources.org— under "Transition Tools".

effective ministry. A few of these will take you a long way, and a significant number of "green lights" can balance out a few "yellow lights" or even a "red light."

It's important to remember, too, that these factors and indicators need not be limited to aspects that are directly related to ministry. Because you (and your family) will almost certainly live daily life in the context where you will minister, many other factors are at play here, as well. For example, you may be a fan of pro football, but the city where you're moving doesn't have a team; that's probably not a red light, but it may be a yellow light. (On the other hand, if you're considering a move to the city where your favorite team is, that may be an easy green light!) Likewise, if your wife's parents are seeing their health decline, then an opportunity that is closer to them may represent a strong green light, while a call to a church many hours away may qualify as a yellow or even a red light.

It's also vital to remember that different factors have different priorities. This is true for any type of factor, be it personal, cultural, ministry-related, or otherwise. It is especially true for factors like theological and ministry-related aspects of an opportunity, because these speak not only to your comfort and ease of ministry, but to the integrity with which you are able to minister and serve both God and your congregation. Therefore, let's consider how we understand priorities in terms of such convictions.

Convictions Are Important
At one point during candidacy, I knew of a church that was without a pastor; in many ways, this church fit a lot of the criteria of my preferences:
- They were looking for a preaching/teaching pastor
- They wanted a vision-caster and leadership-equipper
- They were in a strong area for growth and ministry opportunity
- They were in need of revitalization, and were aware of that (and desired it)

It sounded like the perfect fit. Add to this that I already knew several of the leaders in this church, and had (and still have) great respect for them. I believed they were favorable to me, as well. And in my prayers for them as they were seeking a pastor, many times I felt led to submit my name as a candidate. I even had others suggest that I do so. They were in St. Louis, so we wouldn't even have had to move.

At a certain point, however, I determined that I could not, in good conscience, be considered as a candidate for this church. Why not? Because this church is in a different denomination, and there are a few fundamental differences in that denomination's distinctives that I cannot agree with. There are reasons that I am presbyterian, and those reasons matter in decisions like these.

In this case, the differences were matters of eschatology (the study of the "last things" or the end—times) and matters of church government. For some, admittedly, neither of these would be perceived as significant enough to matter. For me, however, they are and were substantial.

My eschatology is rooted in some of my most fundamental views of scripture itself, and it affects how I understand God's ongoing interaction with this present world, His intentions for the Church's place in the world, and what the hope of the future and the promise of eternity truly hold. A difference in eschatological views could indirectly result in entirely different worldviews.

My understanding of church government shapes how I interact with the immediate leaders within my church, how I view the authority and autonomy of the pastoral office, how one church is connected to others, and how churches submit to one another in accountability and service. Differences in views of church government can completely change the way that a pastor relates (and is expected to relate) to his congregation, and how that congregation and its leadership relates to other churches. In this particular instance, the church in question had some struggles with leadership in its past, and I believe that a different view of church government (on their part) may have contributed to the difficulties that followed those struggles. (I'm not saying that if they had been presbyterian it would have made it all better— but I do believe that they had to deal with the repercussions of their congregational government in ways that presbyterians usually don't.)

I don't think a pastor must agree utterly with every position or theological conviction of his congregation or even his denomination. He must, however, understand what matters are of primary consideration and which ones are more preferential.

These issues need to be weighed carefully in the candidacy process (or before). I think part of the reason why many pastors are not more effectively placed is because some of these subtle concerns have not been attended to, and their implications are unexpected.

Primary Convictions Vs. Incidental Preferences

Let me expand on the decisions surrounding the concept of convictions versus preferences, using a graphical representation that I have found helpful.

The diagram that has helped me— and scores of other students at Covenant Seminary— understand this concept was developed in 2002 by Bryan Clark, and the foundation of it looks like the one at the bottom of this page.

Obviously, the premise is that the issues we face in ministry— those things which we may disagree about to one degree or another— should be broken down into three categories. And the key to the whole thing is how those categories are understood. What is a primary issue? How do you handle it? When must you agree— or put another way, when may you disagree?

It's easiest to understand the primary issues as those that define orthodoxy in Christianity (think Apostles' Creed)— these are doctrines that are essential to Christian life and faith. On the other hand, secondary issues are those which may typically divide one denomination from another (think Westminster Confession). These are doctrines for which there may be a large amount of biblical data, but that data can be construed in more than one way.

Tertiary issues are much more personal, and obviously have a great deal more variance than the other two. They may not be doctrines at all, but simply matters of preference or a conviction about the application or result of a doctrine. If they are doctrinal, they have limited biblical data supporting them— in other words, they are more inferential than clear, evident doctrines. Tertiary issues are typically understood to be matters of conscience rather than dogma.

The biblical basis for dividing out issues into these categories can be seen in three verses:

- **Galatians 1:9:** If anybody is preaching to you a gospel other than what you accepted, let him be eternally condemned.
- **Titus 1:9:** He must hold firmly to the trustworthy message as it has been taught, so that he can encourage others by sound doctrine and refute those who oppose it.
- **Romans 14:5** One man considers one day more sacred than another; another man considers every day alike. Each one should be fully convinced in his own mind.

Clearly, the scriptures themselves delineate different levels of issues or matters of division, and some are more severe than others. It may be helpful to think of them in this way: primary issues are matters you should be willing to die for. Secondary issues are matters worth sacrificing unity about, and you may divide over them. Tertiary issues should be those which you dialog about, but should not break fellowship because of them.

Examples are numerous, but just a few that come to mind are here. There are those matters that are non-negotiable, such as the nature of Jesus Christ as both fully God and fully man, and the theology of God as trinity. These are clearly primary issues. Secondary issues might include matters of church polity, views on the Sacraments, and whether woman may be ordained to any of the church's offices. Tertiary matters encompass questions such as worship style preferences, political perspectives (in the secular/civic sense), matters of "Christian liberty," and in some cases eschatology. (However, some traditions will categorize eschatology in the category of secondary issues.)

What should you do when these— and many others like them— present themselves? How should you handle them?

Clearly, deviation of primary issues requires church discipline, and persistence in such deviation should result in excommunication. The only way for the church to keep herself pure is to insist upon this. (This idea is latent in Galatians 1:9, above.)

Deviation on secondary issues generally does not require formal discipline. However, if the differences here threaten the peace and unity of the congregation, discipline may be necessary. Excommunication, however, is seldom appropriate at this level.

For tertiary issues, deviation requires humility, acceptance, and dialog. We should seek to understand each other at this level, and even be open-minded to the perspectives of others. However, it is perfectly normal— even expected— that there will be many points of disagreement at this level.

One caveat to remember: while there is room for honest differences in categorization (such as eschatological matters being secondard for some and tertiary for others), sometimes issues that are objectively tertiary matters are misplaced into the category of secondary matters. I've noted groups that consider school choice (homeschooling vs. private Christian school vs. public school) as a *secondary* issue; biblically – speaking, it should be a tertiary matter.[6] When that happens, real problems can arise, and a wise pastor will recognize what has happened and work to clarify the misunderstanding.

Convictions and Preferences in Candidacy

Let's think about how this matters in pastoral candidacy.

One of the first things that candidates must understand is that they do not get the same flexibility with these issues that others get. Only primary issues are matters that should be required for church membership. Agreement on secondary issues, however, must be present for church leadership; a ruling elder in the Presbyterian Church in America, for example, should not have a significant dispute with the Westminster Confession, because that is the doctrinal standard of the PCA.

This, for example, is why it is crucial for a candidate to understand the core doctrines of a denomination he is considering, and whether he agrees with them or not. A pastoral candidate has an obligation to state his exceptions to doctrinal standards, and if he is not approved for ordination in that denomination— or is not offered a a call to a particular church— because of those exceptions, he should accept that graciously. Responding otherwise will only extend the division.

---

6 You may ask, "Why must this be a tertiary issue instead of a secondary one?" The answer, in my view, is that, while there is room for difference, secondary matters are still matters of essence to Gospel identity, whereas tertiary matters are more the outcropping of biblical conviction. One way to evaluate this might be to ask, "If this issue were all that an unchurched person knew about me, would they be able to draw a direct line to the Gospel from it?" If the answer is no, then the issue is a tertiary one— regardless of how important it is to you or how strongly you hold that conviction.

But pastoral candidates should be aware that they are being evaluated at the tertiary level, as well. While there is greater room for disagreement here— just as there is more room at the secondary level than at the primary one— there still needs to be a broad amount of agreement for the ministry to work. A pastoral candidate should find out what the key tertiary issues are, and determine if he is in agreement with them.

For example, a pastor that chooses to homeschool his children will find that some churches want their congregation to be involved as a witness in the public schools, and therefore the pastor will lose the trust of some of his congregation. Similarly, a pastor who introduces guitar, praise choruses, and new melodies for familiar hymns will not find a congregation that prefers a strictly "traditional" musical style in its worship service to be very open to his changes.

This brings me to the second point about how the distinction of issues matters in candidacy. Both candidate-pastor and candidate-church must take care to ensure that the issues are properly categorized. It is too easy for those issues that are particularly dear to us to migrate up the scale of importance.

In many cases, those issues that are important personally will shift from tertiary to secondary— or even, in some cases, from secondary to primary. In my experience, this happens in churches when there is little, if any, disagreement about the issue in question; because everyone shares the same perspective on an issue, the importance of that perspective elevates.

On the other hand, when this happens for a pastor or pastoral candidate, it is more likely the result of one or more of the following:
- He has spent a significant amount of study on a particular issue
- He has been heavily influenced by one or two mentors/pastors/professors who shaped his life in many ways, including his perspective on that issue
- He has met a substantial amount of resistance about his view on that issue, and this has made him defensive

The antidote to this "Creeping Priority Syndrome" is, on both sides, a good dose of humility. Proper perspective through humbling oneself is always appropriate, but never more so than when dealing with issues upon which others disagree.

At the risk of seeming cynical, however, I presume that the more ready (and more frequently applied) salve for this "Syndrome" is simply looking elsewhere. While the long-term problems of mis-categorized issues are not solved by this, in the short-term it is obviously easier to avoid facing them, instead seeking for a pastor or church that is more directly compatible with your view.

When You're Ready To "Commit"

Someone has to be the first one to say, "I love you."

When Marcie and I were dating, we came to that point— like so many other couples— in which one of us had made up his mind about where all of this was headed.

In our case, I was the one who had arrived there first, and it would take Marcie some time to get there with me. I knew it would take her awhile, that she wasn't ready. In spite of that, I put my heart out there and told her how I felt: that I loved her, that I thought I wanted to marry her, and that I was willing to wait for her to decide how she felt.

It took more than six months.

Still, I wouldn't have changed anything if I could do it again. The anguish, the tears, the wondering were all worth it. I could live with the lack of immediate response. The vulnerability that defined our relationship at that time has set a pace for a safe, committed marriage of (as of this writing) more than thirteen years. I would do it again.

If you have to wonder why, then you've never had a love for which you're willing to be disappointed— nay, devastated. I loved Marcie then, as now, so strongly that I had to try— no pain was too much.

A friend of mine (I'll call him Fred) was going through that while we were in seminary; he knew the kind of love I'm talking about. The thing is, though, Fred was already married, happily, with children. The love that he was feeling was love for a church— not THE Church, or just any church, but a particular church. Fred was a candidate to be pastor of this flock, and he had fallen in love with them.

Fred had a peculiar opportunity, in that he had gotten to know this congregation more than most candidate-pastors can. Since Fred was still in seminary, he was without a call, and the church was not far from his seminary. He preached there, met with the Search Committee and the Session, and helped with Vacation Bible School.

Talking with Fred one day, he reminded me of a man searching for a way to tell his girlfriend that he loves her for the first time. He reminded himself of that, too; he spoke of this feeling like the time he was courting his wife— uncertain of how she felt, second-guessing whether it was the right time, but wanting so badly to say it.

"Say it," I told him. "Don't hold back. Find a way and tell them how you feel— that you're ready to commit if they are."

Candidate-pastors (and their families) get to a point in the process when they begin to hold back. They want to guard themselves against the emotional devastation that will befall them if they don't get the call. Frankly, many are glad they did, because they didn't get that call. And they go through this cycle time and time again, getting close and then guarding, withholding the best of themselves from a church that could be the one for them— and then disappointment mixed with relief when they don't get it.

But if this relationship really is like a marriage, why hold back? Maybe the committee needs to see that little piece of a candidate-pastor that he's withholding to know that he's the one for them. Maybe that "best of himself" that he's clinging to, protecting, is the part of a pastor that is the most important. How will they ever know it is there? How can they be sure that they will ever see it?

On the other hand, a candidate-pastor who abandons himself to the calling, forget the pain, will show himself to be every bit of who he is. They won't wonder about what they haven't seen. My hunch is that most committees can tell when a candidate is giving them everything, and if it came down to a candidate who held back and one who did not, which would you choose?

Maybe this approach is threatening to some of us. It's too personal, too vulnerable, too relational. Then again, maybe personal, vulnerable, and relational are what life, church, and ministry are all about. Maybe the self-denial and service that Christ calls all Christians to embody— and pastors to model— involves exactly this kind of relational vulnerability.

Giving yourself completely is risky, but it might just result in a wonderful relationship. Mine did— I love Marcie more today than ever, even if I didn't know then whether she would love me back. Candidates can't predict how committees will respond to such self-denial, but the possibilities are beautiful.

Making Decisions FOR Them

Sometimes a church faces decisions that it isn't aware of.

As a candidate, you might see things that the church itself is unaware are factors in the calling of their new pastor. Or they may be aware of the factors, but unaware of the implications they have for their search and decision.

A case in point is a church I was once in discussion with. They had been a small, rural church for over 100 years. Everyone in the church had been in that area all their lives, or had ties (such as marriage) to some who had. Yet the area where the church is— and the small towns around it— were increasing in population by huge percentages, and that region was the fastest growing area in the state, having become a preferred area for bedroom communities for the large city that is 20 miles away.

This church is facing a situation where they will rapidly change from a rural church to a "rurban," then suburban church over the coming 5-10 years. The implications of this are huge; they recognize that the potential for growth is substantial, and they are capitalizing on that in their search. But I wasn't sure they saw the whole picture at first— and if they hadn't it would have implied a need for me to step up.

When it came to their next pastor, they needed someone who would understand small town/rural people, and could comfortably minister to them as such. This is what they were looking for. But they also needed someone who could capably lead them through the vast changes they would face over the next few years, and help them to lay solid foundations for future growth, leadership, and outreach needs.

So as a candidate it fell to me, in a sense, to make some decisions for them: I needed to assess myself, and determine whether I was/am the sort of leader they would need in their circumstances. If not, I should have declined the position, and explained why— in hopes that they would gain some discernment about the issue in the process.

It may be that a church you are considering faces a similar need: they have circumstances that require a particular kind of leader, or a particular kind of leadership, to see them through the coming years in a healthy way. And it may also be that they aren't considering that as a factor in their decision.[7] Maybe because they just don't see the implications. Or, frankly, maybe because they have reached a point where they are too eager to find a pastor to be properly address such factors.

Thus, there is a sense that the decisions fall to you, as the candidate. In a way, this is right— after all, part of a pastor's role is to see the things that others don't see, and appropriately minister to them in it.

---

[7] Or that they are placing less emphasis or "weight" on that factor in their consideration.

But it also requires a warning to be very diligent: don't get so focused on simply finding a call— any call— that you overlook the decisions that are placed before you, even if they are really other people's decisions. Having a paycheck is not more important than a good fit.

Of course, in the end it is the Holy Spirit who guides all of these decisions. He alone will bring you to awareness of what factors you must take into consideration, and will lead your heart in the final decision-making. But as a pastor, you will be a spiritual leader for your congregation— and that will sometimes require that your discernment of the Spirit's leading spill over to your flock. This begins with candidacy.

Place Vs. Timing

A friend and classmate from seminary reminded me of an important set of priorities at one point. He said: "Remember that place is more important than timing."

This is good advice, and important to keep in focus. When you're in the midst of transition (as I was then), it is natural to want to place as quickly as possible— and when you have an opportunity near at-hand, the temptation to be ready to jump at accepting an offer is great.

I've known men whose desire for the "right timing" caused them to accept a call that they were not sure of; more than a few of those who responded to my survey reported this. I've also known those who have chosen to wait (even turning down offers) until the right "place" came available; again, a number of my survey respondents described their circumstances in this way. Invariably, those who have waited for the right place have had a better, longer, more fulfilling ministry than those who were in a hurry.

This may be the most difficult part of placement. But, as I pointed out in chapter four, it is also one of the key factors to effective placement.

Rejection=Protection

My friend Mark Long offered this equation to me about candidacy today. I think it works.

When a church finds a reason to go a different direction, you should be glad for it. It doesn't matter how small or insignificant you believe their reason is— because if it was significant enough for them to eliminate you now, it may turn up as significant enough to spoil an otherwise strong ministry later. They are simply saving you— and the congregation— the pain of that spoiling.

More than one of the churches I corresponded with did this with me. I had submitted my name as a candidate, and felt like I was a very good match for what each claimed to be seeking. Several people within those churches echoed my confidence, and at some point we (Marcie and I) thought I might be the strongest candidate for each. I was not out of the running entirely, reported one senior pastor, but they had several candidates that were a better fit in one way or another. Thus, while I remained open about the pursuit of that position if they had asked me to, I wasn't going to pin a lot of hope on it— nor did I give it much attention from that point forward.[8]

---

8 Had the situation changed— and I had returned to a more prominent position of candidacy— then naturally I would have given it more attention.

In my view, they did me a great service: they helped us see more clearly where the Lord was (and wasn't) leading us. They also did their congregation a great service, by maintaining a firm stance on what they needed and wanted in an assistant pastor.

It is short-sighted, therefore, to think of this as "rejection." In the Lord's great plans, it is actually "protection."

What's Next?

By the end of the "decision-making" season of the candidacy process, you will either be ready to accept the call offered and begin the next steps of making an effective transition, or you will be facing the difficult and complex point of either having turned down an offer or having been passed over.

If you find yourself in the second category, you will feel a wash of many emotions. Disappointment. Relief. Loneliness. Discouragement. Uncertainty and doubt. Ambivalence about moving forward with other opportunities. Inclination to guard your heart and avoid honest vulnerability in future candidacy encounters.

This is a hard point to reach, yet it is a point that almost every pastor and candidate-pastor will eventually face. If my research is any indication, very few seminary graduates landed a call to a particular ministry the first time through; even rarer is the case when a man might do so and remain there for the duration of his ministry. In other words, you may feel very alone, but you are not alone. You are in the company of 99% of all pastors and seminary graduates around you.

Don't be afraid to simply live in these emotions for a little while— maybe a day or two, or even a week or two. Spend that time in spiritual refreshment and in relationships that are renewing to you. Engage your heart in soul-nourishing spiritual disciplines. Get extra rest. Do something fun.

A few more concrete suggestions for this hard season come to mind:

Speak frequently and openly with your spouse and/or a few close friends. If you are married, the conversations with your wife (or husband) are vital. Open your heart to them and let them open theirs to you. Lean heavily on your friends, as well. After one particularly discouraging rejection, I may not have been able to continue pursuit of candidacy had it not been for the prayerful support of a few good friends; I simply sent out an e-mail plea for their prayers, and the following days were filled with e-mails, phone calls, and visits from those who bore my burdens with me.

Ask for your pastor's counsel and support. There may be no one better to understand what you are going through than your pastor: he has been through the process, and also knows you individually. He can offer you a unique type of care and encouragement.

Find renewal in Word, prayer, and worship. I found corporate worship especially poignant during my last season of candidacy, especially during the hardest times (like when I was processing a recent rejection). Longer seasons of Bible reading and prayer were also great times of soul-searching for me.

Take stock of the calling God has given to you. Remember how He has particularly gifted you, prepared you, and strengthened you for ministry. Our Lord does not labor in vain; His calling for you will be fulfilled in a way that will be satisfying and beyond your dreams or expectations. In His timing, He will place you in an opportunity that will be even better than recently ceased to be before you.

Remember God's protection. The ideas that I named above, regarding "place vs. timing" and "rejection=protection," aren't meant as mere platitudes; they are biblical truths that you are feeling the reality of in a hard way. But the other side of the equation is just as real and true for you: God is protecting you from what is a bad fit, and making you all the more ready for His service elsewhere.

Getting Ready For Transition

If you have found yourself on the *first* side of my description at the beginning of this part of the chapter— you are ready to accept an offer and begin transition— then the next section of this book is for you. Congratulations! Now the real work of starting your new ministry begins.

PART 3: TRANSITION STEPS

Beyond Minimum Wage

There are a lot of factors that go into the successful negotiation of the "terms of call" when a pastor is in transition.

When I say "terms of call" I mean those things which would, in other fields, be included in the contract. For the most part, however, there is no "contract" in the pastorate. (In my denomination, there is typically a letter, stating the agreed-upon terms, which is sent to the presbytery for approval.) This list includes things like:

- Cash salary
- Housing allowance
- Salary-related benefits (including health insurance, life insurance, retirement savings, etc.)
- Other benefits (including continuing education or book allowances, ministry-related expense accounts, other similar benefits)
- Vacation and/or other paid time off
- Other quirky terms

What follows is loose advice on how to think about each of these categories. First, though, let me make a clear and bold disclaimer up-front: I am ***not*** an accountant, tax-preparer, financial advisor, or in any other way a financial professional. I don't offer this advice on any authority other than my anecdotal experience and discussions with others. At times in compiling this chapter I have consulted those who are professionals— however, I don't presume to represent them here. 95% of this advice is simply hard-won experience, and it is my experience. Yours may be quite different.

In other words, take all of this with a huge grain of salt. If you have any question or doubt about a decision you are making, seek the advice of someone who IS a professional. Also, you are surely already aware that there are dozens of very good books on personal finance, money management, and how to draft a budget (and how to stay on it). In the appendix on recommended reading, I've included a few titles in this category.

Cash Salary: The Foundation

A friend of mine accepted a position with Covenant Seminary, but remained in seminary housing as a part of his job. He subsequently had conversation with a (then) current seminarian, a neighbor in seminary housing, in which the other person assumed that my friend was making "the big bucks" since he had graduated and found placement. Of course, this is fallacious— at best, my friend is making the "medium bucks." But those medium bucks go only so far, and in some ways not as far as the "small bucks" of seminary went.

Take-home pay, or cash salary, is obviously of foundational importance in negotiating terms of call. How should a new seminary graduate (or one nearing graduation) approach it? How might a pastor seeking a change of call approach it?

For new graduates, there are two difficulties to overcome: first, your budget in seminary does not approximate what you will need after seminary. Do not be fooled.: what you are spending now is, in so many ways, nothing like what you will spend once you are placed.

Consider the following "perks" or money-savers that carried Marcie and me through our seminary years:

- The seminary's "free store"— where any seminary student (or their family) could go to get free clothes, toys, even books and household items.
- "Free bread"— our seminary had a deal with the local Panera Bread Company store to make day-old bread available to seminarians.
- The "Gulf Drive Exchange"— basically a road-side trash pile, but there was an understanding that folks in our apartment complex would put things out on the street that they didn't want (whether it was broken or not) and others could feel free to take it.
- Low rent— seminary housing is not free, but it certainly undercut the rest of the market in St. Louis by a long shot.
- Cheap groceries— we lived in a area of town where several "low end" grocery stores were nearby, affording us very low prices.

While we didn't always make full use of these, they probably saved us thousands of dollars during our nearly five years in seminary. This is alongside the support of friends, family, and our church: we received regular and one-time cash gifts to the tune of additional thousands during seminary. Now, (nearly) all of these are gone— and rightly so. Their departures make for a substantial increase in costs. Add to that a handful of familial, social, psychological, and professional mindset changes. You're not in seminary anymore, so...

>...*You really need to buy some grown-up furniture.* That futon and papasan chair will hardly do for hosting elders and other folks from your church. (This is only partly true: while it is reasonable to want better furniture for "entertaining", you don't have to do it all at once— and it doesn't have to be straight out of *House Beautiful*.)
>
>...*It's no longer okay to wear threadbare clothes all the time.* (This one is mostly true— though, if you've followed my earlier advice, you will already have some decent clothes in the closet.)
>
>...*That two-bedroom, 800 square-foot apartment that the two of you moved into four years ago* was fine for then, but it doesn't bode well for the long-term health of your growing family of four or five. (Inevitably, you will need more space after seminary if you've gotten married, had children, or had more children. Maybe you've worked this out already, but it will still effect the size of your housing.)
>
>...*You can't count on the regular pooling of food* with neighbors, the food co-op, or the frequent invites from wealthy fellow church members. (Again, only partly true: you might be able to count on all of these, especially if you are pro-active in organizing them— but probably not always, and not right away.)

In short, your time in seminary has affected the way you view your finances more than you realize. It is easy (or at least easier) to be poor when all of your friends and neighbors are poor as well.[1]

But once you are a "ministry professional" then it becomes a lot harder to be "poor." There are expectations, requests, and demands involved in a pastor or ministry professional's life— some unreasonable, others quite reasonable— that require additional expense. And there are life choices that you made during seminary that were simply bad choices— how many, after all, carry life insurance throughout seminary? (As if somehow, because we were seminary students, we were suddenly under Divine protection.)

Cash salary is about providing for the needs of your family— and as difficult as it is to admit or accept, that provision falls more squarely on your shoulders after seminary than it does during it. There are not as many people around you who understand or care. It is more individualized and less communal. Those approaching (or in the midst of) the negotiation of terms of call should be attentive to the needs of their family as they negotiate the cash salary portion. This is the prime goal.

Key Factors
Beyond these changes of lifestyle, life-patterns, and life-needs, there are some objective factors at play in determining what your cash salary must be. If you are in the process of negotiating terms of call, you have all of the information that you will need to assess these objective factors— even if you will be moving far from where you are.

How do you estimate what your cash salary needs to be, when you may be in an entirely different part of the country? These are the factors that go into the difference:

- **Household cost-of-living changes.** How much has your life changed since you began seminary? Have you gotten married? Did you have a baby (or another one)? What changes are coming your way (that you might anticipate)? Will your ailing parent come to live with your family? Might you have another baby?[2] All of these changes impact your household budget, of course— costs for groceries, staples, clothes, and gas are probably higher now than before. So they should impact the negotiation of the cash salary in your terms of call, as well.
- **Housing changes.** If you had any changes in the household cost of living— or if you are expecting any— you probably need a larger housing situation, as well. Maybe you've been able to manage in a small apartment, but now that you're married you've felt a bit cramped. Maybe the condo that suited your new marriage in the city won't quite serve your family of four in the suburbs. These will almost completely come under the heading

---

[1] An aside: when I say that seminarians are "poor" I do not mean to belittle the issue of poverty in our world; "poor" is a relative term, and for many seminarians it means, as it did for us, that income is substantially less than it was previously. Nevertheless, our family found ourselves as the beneficiaries of Medicaid and the WIC (Women, Infants, and Children) food programs— and I knew other seminary families that were in much worse financial shape than us. "Poor" often applies more readily to seminary families than some would like to admit.

[2] In our case, we moved into a smaller but comfortable home with the expectation that we would not have more children. Six months later, we learned that we were expecting twins!

of "Housing Allowance" but there are a very few things that won't. For example, if you are moving into a church-owned house, repairs you make to the house won't be covered under "Housing Allowance." (When I discuss "Housing Allowances" I'll go into more detail about this.)
- **Ministry-cost adjustments.** Depending on what type of change you are making ministry-wise, your personally-born ministry costs may change. Have you been in ministry while in seminary? If so you may have some baseline to work from. Are you moving from a city or larger town to a smaller town or rural area? Then your mileage and vehicle costs will change. Are you moving into a solo pastorate, or into an assistant or associate pastor role? You will find that ministry expenses vary (sometimes substantially) from one kind of ministry job to another. This is a pretty subjective adjustment, and will require experience, thought, and a heavy amount of guessing!
- **Cost-of-living adjustments.** Whenever you move from one town to another (or even from one area of a large city to another), there will be cost of living adjustments. These are the differences between the prices of gas, housing, groceries, taxes, and a lot of other things. The government maintains a cost of living index, and every city (and sometimes townships within a city) are measured against this index. Do some research to find out what the cost of living adjustments will be when you move from your current residence to a new place.

Figuring It Out
So now we've talked about some factors to keep in mind. How do you calculate the actual amount you need to ask for?

All of this forms a sort of calculus for establishing the cash salary that you need. Here are some suggested steps for determining the best numbers for you:
1. *Re-evaluate your budget history.* If you're good with this sort of thing, this step will probably take very little time. However, many will have to do some heavy processing to get this accurate. Don't fudge on this step— this will become the cornerstone for the rest of this process, and the care you put into this part will determine the accuracy of your final numbers. Here's the key: the best way to re-evaluate your budget history is to simply determine whether it accurately reflects current practice. If it doesn't, then put in the numbers that do reflect it. This is no time to be timid, humble, or hopeful; don't state what you wish the numbers were, but what they actually are. And be sure to include EVERY aspect of income and expense you have— even if you haven't budgeted for them in the past.
2. *Calculate the effects of the changes and adjustments.* The cost of living, ministry costs, and some housing costs discussed above affect this calculation. How will your spending patterns change between now and then? What will you add to your budget that you aren't paying for now? What will drop off of your budget entirely? You should go through your budget history line-by-line and calculate what should be adjusted.

3. *Spend some time considering the future.* What will likely change over the coming year or two? Will any household changes take place— will you get married, have children, or take in a dependent relative? Will your car(s) survive the coming years— and will they require any major repairs or maintenance? Will your children begin school or college? Will you begin another degree or educational program? Will your spouse start working, change jobs, or leave work? Now— here's the key— estimate how these changes will effect your needs in terms of cash salary.
4. *Do the math.* Take your budget history (step 1), adjust the numbers to accommodate the changes due to a move to a new ministry (step 2), and add in the projected changes for the next few years (step 3). The result should be a good starting point for a budget in your new ministry position.
5. *Add in 1-3%.* No matter how careful you've been, you have probably been off a little bit. Estimations are like that— it's why they're called "estimations". To account for this, I recommend that you put in a fudge-factor of 1-3% additional in your budget. If you don't need it, you can always put it in savings.
6. *Estimate your tax burden.* You can roughly calculate take-home pay through a handful of calculators online,[3] and you can also reverse them to see what your income must be to support a certain dollar-figure of take-home pay. It is worth the time fiddling with these, even though they can only give you rough amounts (remember, your tax status is probably different because of your status as a pastor— more on this in another post). If you can estimate what total pay it requires to make budget from step 4, you're much closer to having a real number to present to the church you're negotiating with.
7. *Don't forget to save.* Probably the easiest part of the budget to cut— or forget to add in to begin with— is savings. When budgets are tight, it's hard to be disciplined about saving. But it is when budgets are tight that savings become the most important. I suggest that you set up an account with a bank like ING Direct, where you can set up an automatic draft into savings. It will pull out a pre-determined amount on a pre-defined schedule, and all you have to do is record the transaction. When you need your savings, it will be there for you.
8. *Do the math—again.* Total up all of these, and you're done. Congratulations— you now have a functional and accurate budget.

Now you have the number you should take back to the church you're negotiating with. That's the amount you should ask for.

I know—actually asking for this amount is another thing altogether. You probably aren't certain if you even have a right to simply ask for whatever amount you believe you need. At the end of the series on "Negotiating your terms of call" I'll talk about how to muster up the courage to ask for what you need.

For now, just get the numbers on paper and move ahead. We'll get to the actual negotiation in time.

---

3   There are links to a few such calculators at the Doulos Resources website: www.doulosresources.org (look in the "Transition Tools" section).

Housing Allowance

When it comes to the housing allowance, the first thing to know is this: if you're not ordained, everything you're about to read is irrelevant.

Since your tax status and employment status are different when you are ordained, you're able to designate a portion of your salary package as your "Housing Allowance" (according to IRS Code Section 107). If you don't know already, this should be one of the most exciting aspects of the terms of call— maybe even more than the cash salary.

Why? Because, the housing allowance is tax-sheltered. The housing allowance is considered an "exclusion" for tax purposes (not a deduction), so it never enters the equation for computing gross income. So you will never pay income tax on your housing allowance. Further, if you own your home, you are still allowed (through itemized deductions) to deduct interest paid on your mortgage and property taxes when you file your federal income taxes— even though the interest was paid through the tax-sheltered housing allowance. In this way, the housing allowance represents a legal "double-dip" into a reduction of tax burden.

Still further, there is more to the housing allowance than just the money paid for mortgage or rent. A housing allowance includes a lot of aspects related to the house, all of which are legitimately tax-sheltered as well. Here is what is legally included in the housing allowance:

- The principle + interest on a home mortgage, OR rent on a leased home (including apartments, condos, or houses)
- Real estate taxes
- Costs of maintenance and repairs
- Insurance on the home and/or the contents of the home (i.e., renter's insurance or homeowner's insurance)
- Cost of all utilities, including electric, gas, local telephone, water, basic cable TV, and trash pickup
- Home furnishings and appliances (both the purchase and repair of them)
- Maintenance items, such as cleaning supplies, pest control, and light bulbs
- Yard maintenance and improvement costs
- Neighborhood or homeowner's association dues

As you can see, the scope of the housing allowance includes a lot of things that you wouldn't necessarily assume are part of the cost of housing. Nevertheless, all of these are legitimate inclusions.

Another important thing to know is that this is no limit of percentage when it comes to a housing allowance. In other words, it is possible for a housing allowance to be most or all of the amount of compensation, as long as the costs do not exceed the legal limits of what may be included (see the list above). The limit, however, comes with the costs themselves. (I'll discuss that in a few paragraphs.)

Now that you know what a housing allowance is, next time I'll talk about how to calculate and negotiate it with your new church.

Determining What You Need

We've defined the Housing Allowance, so now let's talk a bit about how to determine what you need.

First of all, there are some limits to what can qualify as legitimate Housing Allowance. According to IRS code, a Housing Allowance cannot be more than the smaller of any of the following:

- The fair market rental value of the home, including furnishings, repair, etc.
- The amount officially designated (in advance) as rental or housing allowance
- The actual amount spent to provide a home

What this means is that in the end, you are not allowed to claim as Housing Allowance more than the actual cost of owning or renting your home. Even if you are getting a deal— for example, you are renting for 75% of the market value of your home— you can't claim the difference as Housing Allowance. And if you're paying too much in rent, you can only claim the market value. In other words, the IRS doesn't want you to claim more as Housing Allowance than you should actually require.

When you set up your terms of call, you must designate in advance what will be construed as Housing Allowance. If you fail to do this at the beginning, you will lose the right to claim what you spend in the ensuing months until you do designate. That designation must be stated in writing in the terms of call (and subsequent annual changes must also be reflected in writing).

This is the reason behind the second limit: until the year is out, the amount designated in advance is automatically the smallest of the three. You won't know if the actual costs are more or less than the designation until you've paid them all; thus, you won't know how accurate your designation has been until you can't do much about it.

This represents a double-edged sword that can frustrate new pastors: on the one hand, if you designate too few dollars for Housing Allowance, you'll be taxed on money spent for housing when you didn't have to be. On the other hand, if you designate too much, you will be taxed for the difference (per the limits listed above), which may mean a significant tax burden next April 15.

(I'd like to point out that, after the first year or two, you should be able to determine fairly accurately what your costs will be for the coming year— even with the substantial list of inclusions. If you've remained in the same home this is especially true. The only true variables, ordinarily, would be the replacement of furnishings, major repairs, or improvements such as additions or remodels.)

The key is to target your Housing Allowance to be just above what the actual amount will be; then you will cover all of your housing expenses, but your tax burden will not be substantially increased.

To do this, work through the list of inclusions for a Housing Allowance as carefully as possible, estimating each item based on your budget history (remember doing that exercise from the cash salary section above?). Make adjustments where you know they will exist: perhaps your seminary housing was less expensive than the house you're buying, so the base costs will go up; if you have more square footage in your new place, calculate that your utility costs will increase; and so on. Total these numbers, then add 3-4% to the bottom line.

Don't forget to account for larger variables. If you know that you're going to add on a room, paint the whole house inside and out, and replace the gutters, get professional estimates for these jobs before you designate your Housing Allowance. (Even if you do the work yourself, you're allowed to claim full market value— but only if you have a written estimate.) If you're going to re-finance your existing home (and thereby lower your payments), include that in your calculations.

Once you've computed what your Housing Allowance will be, you've largely determined your compensation package. Often, churches will view cash salary and Housing as the "payment" and the rest— insurance, continuing education, expense account, etc.— as benefits. We'll get to those in a bit, but you should feel great about getting this far.

What About a Manse?

When churches provide housing for their pastor— usually called a "manse" or "parsonage"— it creates a peculiar situation for the pastor, as far as his salary package goes.

To begin with, this is technically income: a material benefit, in this case free housing, is offered as a part of his payment. However, whatever it represents as income is eligible to be sheltered as "housing allowance" and therefore isn't taxed. (To understand this more clearly, cross-reference the list of what is included as housing allowance with the list of limits on housing allowance.)

This is important when considering the common question, "which is better: a parsonage/manse or a larger salary package?" because in most cases the decrease in salary correlates to the value of the provided housing. In the immediate value, then, choosing whether to accept a manse or parsonage (if one is offered) or to buy or rent housing is a material wash.

One important factor, though, is the availability of housing in the area of your church. You will want to live relatively nearby to your church's property; there are a dozen reasons for this, which I won't go into here.[4] If houses are for sale in an established area, however, they may be more expensive than what you can afford. If your church is in an expensive neighborhood and they have a parsonage available, you should seriously consider using it.

There is also the intangible relational capital that you'll spend if you refuse a manse or parsonage. By turning down the offer of housing, you are suggesting that it is in some way inadequate or no good. You may be rejecting a treasured piece of property with a significant history for your new congregation. And you may be putting the church in a difficult financial position, since they will have to maintain a property they own whether you occupy it or not. While you may have good reasons for wanting to live elsewhere— you're afraid of being "too available", for example, or you like doing renovations and you doubt the congregation will allow it— you should rethink these in light of the message you're sending by refusing such an offer.

Another consideration with regard to a parsonage is its long-term effect. The real advantage of owning your home instead of renting (or living in a parsonage) is that you build equity as you pay off the mortgage. The longer you own your own home, the more of it you own— and eventually you will have paid it off. Traditionally, this has coincided roughly with retirement: you finish college or graduate school in your early to mid-twenties, then get married; after struggling through the early years of work for low pay, you finally begin to save up enough to buy a home in your late twenties or early thirties, taking out a 30-year mortgage to do so; perhaps a move to

---

4   I will discuss it briefly in the next chapter, called "A Sea of Cardboard".

a larger home happens once or twice, and you eventually pay off your home in your mid-sixties, just in time to retire.

When you rent, you lose all sense of equity. And when you live in a manse, you also lose any equity that you might otherwise gain. So one of the things you should include in your negotiations, if you will be living in a church-provided home, is an increase in contribution to your retirement savings. (I'll be talking about retirement savings in broader terms at a later point.) I would recommend calculating— or having someone else calculate— the per-year equity value of the housing provided and ask for that (after all, your church is gaining that amount, or already has, so they should be in a position to afford it).

In other words, if you were taking the cash instead of provided housing, and investing it into a mortgage, how much equity would you be accumulating? That is what you should work toward in your negotiation of the housing allowance portion of your salary package.

How Great Is the Tax Benefit of a Housing Allowance?

I asked my friend Maria (who is a CPA) a few questions about the housing allowance. Her answers are quite informative.

> *Me:* Does the portion of the pay package designated as "housing allowance" affect the Adjusted Gross Income (AGI)?
>
> *Maria:* Yes it does— it is not included as a part of the AGI.

This is huge; the AGI is the primary determinant of the tax owed for Federal Income Tax. Since the housing allowance is not factored into the AGI, the AGI necessarily remains a lot lower than the total salary package. This, by the way, is THE way that the housing allowance is a tax benefit to ordained pastors.

> *Me:* Is the AGI the primary determinant for tax brackets?
>
> *Maria:* Yes. The amount you are taxed is based on your AGI.
>
> *Me:* So a pastor's salary package will have to be pretty high to move him out of the 15% tax bracket?
>
> *Maria:* Yes.

This is also huge. For a typical pastor's family (married filing jointly), the AGI must be $61,300 or higher to shift up to the next tax bracket (the 25% bracket).[5] But assuming that the housing allowance represents 1/4 to 1/3 of the total pay package, a pastor's housing + cash salary would have to total $76,000 (or more, depending on the amount of the housing allowance) to exceed this.

Depending on the circumstances (for example, in an area where housing costs are exceptionally high), it's possible for the package to be well over $100,000 and the pastor to remain in the 15% tax bracket.

Maria's comment sums it up well: "It's a really big benefit."

Typical "Benefits"

In addition to cash salary and a housing allowance, many (if not most) congregations will provide at least some benefits for their pastor(s). Normally, this will begin with

---

5   By the time of this printing, these will surely be old numbers; the tax code changes frequently to adjust where the ceiling is for a given tax bracket, so the number of $61,300 is best taken as a ballpark-figure.

some sort of medical care coverage, and will expand from there. I won't go into great details about these benefits, because they vary so greatly— but I will say a few words about each.

One vital thing to understand up-front is that there are many great professionals who can help you understand a lot of this. A good insurance agent will guide you through much of the (often-confusing) information I'm about to summarize. Likewise, there are great agents and others who can help you navigate the esoteric world of retirement planning. If you read through the next few pages and feel like your head is swimming, don't despair! Find someone locally who can work with you on it; the odds are good that there is someone in your local church who does this for a living.

Traditional Health Insurance: the idea behind health insurance is pretty simple. You (and thousands of other people) pay regularly into a pool of money, and when you (or any of the thousands) have a medical need, that pool is available to pay for it. In practice, it's not nearly so simple: the emergence of ideas like "preferred providers" and "pre-existing conditions" can turn health insurance into a complicated and frustrating mess.

Here are a few very basic guidelines for looking into health insurance:

- Generally, a group insurance plan is better than an individual policy; costs may be lower (possibly substantially lower), and the coverage might be better. If a group policy is available to you, seriously consider it before passing it over for an individual policy (and have a definite reason for passing it up).
- Your "deductible" is how much you have to pay out of your pocketbook before the insurance company will chip in for costs; your "premium" is the amount you pay monthly to have access to your insurance. Lower deductibles mean higher monthly premiums, and higher deductibles can be an effective way to reduce premiums— but be careful about going so high that the insurance represents no value (except in a catastrophe).
- Make sure that the coverage you need is included. Take note of whether things like prenatal, labor and delivery, and "well baby" visits are covered under your policy; if you have children, and/or if you plan on having any (or any more), you will severely regret these if they aren't in your coverage! There may be other things that are included or excluded; read through your policy and do your best to decipher whether important things are left out. Ask lots of questions of your agent about coverage, too.
- Before you commit to a health care plan, make sure there are providers of health care in your area that are covered under your insurance. If there are few or no providers, it doesn't really matter how low your premium is; you won't be able to make adequate use of the insurance plan! (Be prepared to wade through long lists of providers who are "in-network" or "out-of-network" for an insurer.)
- Take note of the ratings for insurance companies through services like A.M. Best. This is not unlike doing a credit-check on the insurer: how quickly they pay their bills, how often they are late or delinquent in payment, etc. They grade their scores from A++ down to D (poor), E (under regulatory suspension), F (in liquidation!), and S (rating suspended). My wife, who worked in the insurance industry for a while, tells me that an A.M. Best

rating below A- should raise concerns. Also take time to do an internet search for reviews, ratings, and other feedback about an insurance company— especially if it is one that is very small or that you haven't heard of before. We have had insurance with a company that was very slow to make payments on bills, sometimes taking a year or more to pay our medical expenses; more than once, we had our providers threaten to submit us to credit collection agencies. Don't let that happen to you, if you can avoid it!
- Recent (as of 2010) laws are bringing a lot of changes to health care and insurance. In a few years, you will be required to have some sort of health care coverage, or you will pay a fee for not being covered. There are also changes that will be of great benefit to you. Ask your insurance agent to explain how your health care coverage may change in the next few years based on new laws.

Alternative Plans for Health Coverage

There are some ways to obtain health care coverage without going with a straight-up traditional health insurance policy. Here are a couple of options that I am aware of:
- *Health Savings Account*— an HSA is an account that you pay into regularly, and you may withdraw funds to cover your medical expenses. If that sounds a lot like health insurance, you're right— except that an HSA is only **your** money, so when you have higher costs than money available, you lack adequate coverage. A typical solution, therefore, is to secure a high-deductible insurance plan ($1000 individual/$2000 family is the legal minimum) to cover catastrophic events and pay the difference in premium costs into an HSA. What's the benefit, then, if you're paying the same amount? HSAs don't expire; your contributed dollars "roll over" year after year, accruing over time. After a few years, often HSAs become a way to lower premiums, and they can become a key part of retirement planning as well.
- *Medical Cost-Sharing options*— there are some groups/companies that function in a very similar capacity to insurance companies, but instead offer "cost-sharing" as their benefit. Depending on who you ask, the differences between insurance and "cost-sharing" are either wonderful or frightening. Like insurance, you pay monthly toward a "pool" of money that covers the costs of collective health care; you have a certain amount that you must pay out-of-pocket before collecting from the cost-sharing group or company; and many pre-existing conditions may have limited or no coverage. Unlike insurance, your monthly premium may actually go down if you are paying more out-of-pocket; there aren't profits or shareholders that syphon dollars away from health care costs; and you may actually learn whose medical bills your monthly payment helped to cover (so that you might pray for them). Also unlike insurance, these groups are not regulated at all, and payments for your medical bills aren't guaranteed.[6] However, a cost-sharing group or

---

6 My sister used one of these cost-sharing companies for a number of years, and never encountered any problems with her bills being paid eventually— and, as I mentioned above, this problem can arise in traditional insurance, too.

company may reduce your monthly obligation by as much as a third— not insubstantial, given that insurance can cost hundreds of dollars a month.

Vision & Dental Insurance. These are often overlooked, but can be vital when they are needed, and usually add only a nominal cost to an existing health insurance plan. If you wear glasses or contacts, vision insurance can reduce your costs significantly; our has reimbursed us most of our costs for Optometry appointments over the last few years, as well as for glasses.[7] Dental insurance, while typically not as generous as vision, will still represent a substantial savings if you encounter a larger procedure like a crown or a root canal. It's worth asking what the additional cost might be to include one or both of these on your policy.

Life Insurance. Most health insurance plans will include a very basic life insurance policy; these will offer something like $10,000 (or maybe less) on the event of your death. This may be enough to cover the substantial costs of a funeral and burial, but it will offer nothing for your family to help them through what will be an already difficult time. You will want to secure life insurance, and it is not uncommon for this to be included in your benefits package.

There are different ways to determine what sort of life insurance coverage you may need. If you are single, there may be no need for any further coverage beyond what your health insurance provides. If you are married with no children, you and your wife (or husband) may determine that a minimal additional policy will be sufficient— perhaps $100,000, which would allow your spouse to take a good bit of time to grieve and spend time with family before they would be required to work.

If you have children, however, that changes things substantially. When your children are younger, you may choose to secure enough insurance to allow your spouse to stay at home with them until they begin school. As they get older, you might amend your coverage to pay enough to cover the high costs of education (possibly both in college as well as before). You should take into account the fact that your earning capacity may not be at the same level as your spouse's, and thus you may need more (or less!) life insurance to accommodate that.

There are plenty of good insurance agents who can counsel you through securing an adequate amount of coverage. Once you have a good coverage amount set, negotiate for whether you will pay for it out of your salary, whether it will be covered as part of your benefits, or whether you will split the costs with the church.

Retirement Savings. Right now, you may feel like you will gladly serve God in ministry until the day you die! Lord willing, you will be right about that— but any number of things may prevent that. You may grow ill or feeble in body. You might become so tired in mind and spirit that you can't continue as you planned. You may need to retire from full-time ministry to care for an ailing spouse. Or you might simply decide to retire and rest from your many years of labor! Retirement savings is an important solution in such cases.

Some Christians will argue that we ought not save for retirement— this, they claim, is failure to trust in God for His provision through life. There are biblical arguments for and against this, and other practical arguments as well. I won't go into great

---

[7] A quick note here: we began buying our prescription glasses online a few years ago, and regularly pay around $50 for a pair; this makes reimbursement easy.

detail on this here,[8] but there are some reasonable questions to ask if you start down that path. If I shouldn't save for retirement, should I save for a car? Should I save up to pay my bills at the beginning of next month? Should I even question the need for a checking account?

I'm firmly convinced that saving for retirement is good stewardship. Even if you don't intend to "retire" in the typical American manner today (somewhere between age 62 and 67, you simply quit working), you will need to consider strongly whether retirement savings isn't prudent at least for the possible situations I posited above (and others like them).

Assuming you determine that you do wish to begin saving for retirement, you should be at least vaguely aware of your options. Here is a thumbnail sketch of some of them:

- *Traditional IRA*— an IRA, or Individual Retirement Account, is essentially what it sounds like: an account that is set up for retirement accounts on an individual basis (instead of through an organization or work arrangement). You deposit or contribute your money into this account, and it accrues interest over time. Contributions made to a traditional IRA are tax-deductibe, so the funds you contribute are deducted from your income when you file your returns. Most traditional IRAs are based on some sort of investment strategy; you can set up an IRA that invests wholly into a single mutual fund, an account that invests in multiple mutual funds, or even into individual stocks, bonds, and other securities. Any dividends from these investments are re-invested as well, which can result in a substantial cumulative gain over time. Your contributions, plus the reinvested dividends, compound along with the growth of investment.[9] Ordinarily, you cannot withdraw funds from an IRA prematurely— that is, before 59 ½— without some sort of penalty in the form of fees. (There are exceptions to this, such as withdrawal to pay for education expenses.)
- *Roth IRA*— much the same as a traditional IRA in terms of structure— these are usually investment-based retirement savings that cannot be withdrawn prematurely without penalty. Unlike traditional IRAs, though, you pay taxes on contributions in the year that you make them; however, any withdrawals (after reaching retirement age) are tax-free, regardless of whether those funds came from your contributions, re-invested dividends, or gains on the securities. Consequently, these often represent the better long-term strategy for IRA investment.
- *403b Retirement Plan*— this is the nonprofit organization's equivalent to the 401k, which most people have heard of as a retirement instrument common in the corporate world. With a 403b, your employer (in this case, the church or ministry you serve) sets up the plan, and you make deposits, or contributions, to it. Your employer may also make contributions on

---

8 I discussed this subject at length on my blog, Pastoral Transition and Placement Reflections, which can be found at the Doulos Resources website or at www.pastoraltransition.com.

9 Historically, no single 10-year period of investments in securities has lost money— even during the Great Depression— and therefore long-term investments like this often yield substantial returns.

your behalf, up to a point. Like the others, such plans are typically based on some sort of investment portfolio; most are set up as tax-deferred (wherein you pay taxes upon withdrawal after retirement), but Roth-style options are available too. If you are in a situation where the church you serve is willing to match your contributions to retirement (or make contributions outright, regardless of any "matching" requirements) then a 403b may be a good choice. In fact, it may be that your church already has such a plan in place. If not, however, a friend tells me that these are not as attractive an option as they once were, and that many organizations are moving to a SIMPLE 401k (or even a regular 401k). Some pastors are eligible for a SEP IRA, which employers may also contribute to. The bottom line here: bring in professional help for any of these options if you move in this direction and your congregation doesn't already have something in place.

Retirement savings is not an uncommon part of the benefits package for a pastor or ministry worker. When discussing your terms of call, don't hesitate to ask about retirement savings options that they may be willing to discuss. Their response may vary: some may be willing to simply offer you a set amount every year, while others will be familiar with different instruments and will encourage you to explore one or more of those that they know about (or already have in place). Some may indicate that there is no money available for such a plan, but may be supportive of you designating a portion of your cash salary for one on a pre-tax basis.[10]

Long-Term Disability. Many people are increasingly aware of the need for disability insurance. This coverage would handle most (if not all) of the financial burden in the event of some type of disabling accident or illness. For example, if you were to become injured in such a manner that you were unable to work, long-term disability insurance would provide for your lack of income as well as for incurred medical and care costs.

In the United States, laws are in effect that require that any employee of any organization or corporation who is injured while working is entitled to medical care and, in many cases, some form of compensation for financial loss due to temporary or permanent disabilities as a result of that injury. This is commonly known as "worker's compensation" and your new church should already have some sort of liability insurance in place to cover such a circumstance.

However, there are obviously ample occasions wherein you may be injured when not "on the job," and also those cases where you may become ill for an extended period of time or permanently. Disability insurance would cover these needs. Short-term disability insurance is becoming more common and mainstream, which would cover temporary loss— Aflac and other similar companies have done a good job of promoting themselves in this field.

Where you ought to be more concerned, however, is with long-term disability. These policies cover care required at home, in nursing homes, or some sort of assisted-living facility. While different kinds of policies are available, if you are interested in

---

10 In other words, technically you will be accepting less outright cash salary in exchange for a pre-tax retirement arrangement, such as a 403b.

securing this kind of insurance you will want to look for those which offer payout until age 65, and which are "non-cancelable" (or at least "guaranteed-renewable").

It isn't typical for a church to include disability insurance in a benefits package; like many of the other benefits options, you might consider requesting that the church provide such a policy at your expense. In essence, you will forfeit a part of your cash salary for it, but it will be provided for you in a pre-tax arrangement.

Allotted Time Away

Some of your terms of call will deal with the aspect of time rather than money. What follows is a summary of most of the items that might ordinarily (or at least occasionally) be included in a pastor's terms of call related to time.

Vacation. You will certainly need time off; every congregation should recognize this and offer it by default.[11] One of the big questions will be, how much time off is reasonable for vacation?

In my experience, about four weeks is considered "normal" for most pastors today. Those four weeks include Sundays, because that is one of the most heavy "work days" for a pastor— excluding them would not allow the vacation time to be very restful! Some congregations will stipulate adjustments to this; for example, one survey respondent who I interviewed mentioned that his congregation gave him four weeks, but only after the first six months of his service there. Another received two weeks the first year, which was increased to four in the second year he was there (and he was told the increase would come at the outset).

This may vary, of course. In one case, a pastor who also served as an officer in the Army Reserve received no Sundays off in his terms of call, because it was understood that he would be absent for one weekend a month already for his Reserve duties. (In practice, however, the congregation made sure that he and his family were allowed a weekend or two each year to get a true vacation.) Other factors may apply in like manner.

In general, though, be sure that vacation time is stated in your terms of call, and ask for a reasonable and normal amount of time off.[12]

Education Leave. You may already be thinking about pursuing further academic education while serving as a pastor. Or perhaps you have plans to regularly attend a conference or some other form of ongoing training. Maybe you simply want to take part in a retreat of some sort. If any of these are part of your plans, you might ask for some type of "Education Leave" on a regular basis as a part of your terms of call.

It's not uncommon for this category to be excluded, and in many (if not most) churches, it may be asking too much for this to be designated on the outset. Education Leave can usually be negotiated on a more ad-hoc basis with the other leadership of the church, and it may be prudent to leave this out of your request at the outset

---

11 If your congregation does not, consider this an important "yellow light" (harkening back to my suggested rubric for evaluation) and begin to dialog with them immediately about why not.

12 My experience as a Presbyterian has shown me that this, and other similar aspects of the terms of call, are one of the great benefits to being in a denominational structure of some kind: it is not uncommon for my presbytery (the body of regional churches and pastors) to ask that terms be amended if, for example, the allotted vacation time is considered insufficient.

(especially if you get the feeling that you are already asking for more than they intended to offer).

But there are times when it is important that you state your need for this time. If you are already in the process of completing a degree— perhaps a counseling degree, another Master's, or a doctoral-level program— then you must make the requirements known to your congregation in advance.

"Sabbaticals". Many pastors have found that an occasional longer break from ministry— perhaps a month, or even as long as six months— are beneficial to them, both personally and professionally. Often, sabbaticals are combined with some form of intensive study. One pastor I spoke with took two months to visit many of his living "heroes" and spend a day or two with each, inviting advice and learning from their lives. Another took six weeks to visit and worship with other congregations in the metropolitan area of his large city, later visiting with the pastors of those congregations and interviewing them about their worship services; he later reported back to his board about what he had learned about effective ministry in their area from this experiment.

Again, this may be an area wherein you deem it imprudent to pursue this with your congregation on the outset. However, those congregations where a previous pastor's sabbatical had proven profitable for both the pastor and the congregation may find this a natural request.

Sick-Leave. In my experience— and that of those I have interviewed about this— most congregations do not require any stated sick-leave to be included in the terms of call. The congregations I have worked with have seen it as both expected and as their duty as fellow Christians to allow their pastor(s) time to rest and heal when he falls ill.

In certain circumstances, however, sick-leave is stipulated in a pastor's terms of call. Some larger congregations, for example, will allot a few days each year where a pastor may take leave unexpectedly for illness. My advice would be to ask other pastors on the staff of the church you will serve— or previous pastors who have served there— if sick-leave was an issue, and discuss it openly if so. If it has not been a factor before, don't bother bringing it up.

"Outside Ministry". Anytime you serve in ministry outside of your congregation's community, it may be considered "outside ministry". This may include involvement with other churches in the region[13], or at the denominational level. It might be speaking at conferences, preaching at other churches, or serving on boards of other ministries.

You probably discussed your existing involvement, or your desire for it, at some point during the interview process. If so, exploring time allotted for it during the negotiation of your terms of call will be a natural extension of those discussions. If not, you should definitely bring this up during your dialogue regarding what time you will be given leave for; otherwise, you will risk unhealthy perceptions about your commitment to local ministry when they come up.

---

13 Such as in a presbytery or district.

Other Benefits

A pastor sometimes receives other monetary benefits as a part of his terms of call. These are a matter of course for some congregations, and extraordinary measures in others! It will require some discretion and care for you to discern which group your congregation falls into. Here are some of the items that I have seen as fairly common inclusions in the terms of call.[14]

Book Allowance. Pastors need books as the tools for their ministry. Many congregations, recognizing this, will budget an allowance for their pastor to continue to update, refresh, and add to his ministry "toolbox".

Subscriptions. Similarly, a pastor may be given some funds for maintaining subscriptions to scholarly journals and ministry-related magazines. (It's not uncommon for these to be expensed out of an existing Book Allowance.)

Organizational Memberships. If you must pay dues or fees to maintain membership in a network or some other organization related to your ministry, your congregation may be willing to pay it. One pastor I interviewed mentioned that his Session paid for his membership in a local Rotary Club, so that he could be active in that part of the community.

Costs for church/denominational activities. Denominations usually have regular meetings, and these frequently require registration fees for attendance. (They are usually out-of-town trips, as well, and therefore include food, travel, and housing costs for the the duration of the meeting.) Many (most?) congregations are willing to at least share in the burden of these expenses.

Continuing Education. Many pastors will prioritize the attendance of one or two conferences or seminars each year, in order to continue to hone their ministry skills and abilities. In such cases, churches may designate a certain amount for covering the cost of registration and other related costs.

Ministry-related Expense Accounts. It's natural for a pastor to incur expenses during the regular course of daily ministry. Breakfast and lunchtime visits with members, admission to attend a sports or cultural event that a member is involved with, and gas and wear on a vehicle for driving around all add up. Many congregations compensate for this by providing and expense account or reimbursement.[15]

A Final Note on Benefits

Many churches that are affiliated with denominations will have access to collective benefits resources. Some will utilize a denominational health insurance plan, retirement and annuities plans, and others. If you are accepting a call to a denominationally-affiliated church, be sure to look into the offices that your denomination has for this. The chances are good that there will be full-time professionals who can advise

---

14 One point that is important to bring out here: all of the following are legitimate items that qualify for tax-deductions as "work-related expenses"— so if you don't receive any of these, you will at least find some relief when you pay for them out of your own pocket.

15 If given the choice, opt for reimbursement of actual expenses. There are two reasons for this: first, there may be times when your expenses become excessive, and a designated amount per month may not cover it; second (and more importantly), reimbursement represents non-taxable income for you, whereas an expense account must be declared as taxable revenue.

you about the options before you, and help you make wise choices as you navigate these (often-unfamiliar) waters.

Thoughts On Opting Out Of Social Security

You may or may not be aware of the option available to you for "opting out" of Social Security, Medicare, and other like "taxes."[16] But if you are going into ordained ministry, this is an option that the law allows you to apply for a permanent exemption for! Before you jump up and down, however, it is vital that you understand the parameters and requirements for such an exemption.

Social Security, and other programs covered under the Federal Insurance Contributions Act (FICA), are normally divided in cost between employer and employee. In other words, if you are a standard employee working for any company or institution, your employer is required to pay half of your portion of this "tax". Ordained ministers, however, are considered self-employed when it comes to their status under tax law, and therefore aren't covered under FICA— instead, they are under the Self-Employment Contributions Act, or SECA.

This means that they pay the full amount of their contribution to these federal assistance programs. For instance, at the school where I worked during seminary, 7.65% was deducted from my paycheck to cover my FICA contribution; another 7.65% was paid on my behalf by the school. The same rate, however, applied to an ordained pastor (or anyone else who was considered self-employed under tax code) would be twice that: 15.3%.

Because of this, many pastors consider it a strong financial move to opt out of their SECA contribution— something that is allowed to ordained clergy almost exclusively (a few federal positions are afforded the same benefit). Many others choose to do so because they believe that the Social Security system is a "bad investment"— in other words, they think the system will go bankrupt before they themselves are able to reap any benefit for it, and therefore prefer not to participate.

In order to apply for exemption from SECA contributions, ordained pastors must complete IRS form 4361, entitled Application for Exemption from Self-Employment Tax for Use by Ministers, Members of Religious Orders and Christian Science Practitioners. This application must accompany tax returns no later than the second year in which you earned income under that status; if it is not received by then, you cannot apply for exemption. Also, the application is exactly that: as an application, it will be reviewed by the IRS and can be approved or rejected at their discretion. In other words, you aren't exempt simply because you filed an application. (Find out more about the IRS regulations concerning Social Security and other SECA constituencies through IRS Publication 517.[17])

The title of the application, however, should suggest to you that those who opt out of SECA contributions for purely financial reasons may be amiss in their decision. This option is provided to clergy for a very specific purpose: it acknowledges that

---

16 In point of fact, it is not actually a "tax" but is technically considered a "contribution;" this, I assume, is because it is for services that you may expect to draw from at a later point, such as retirement (Social Security) or healthcare (Medicare, Medicaid).

17 Links to IRS Publication 517 information and Form 5361 can be found on the Doulos Resources website— www.doulosresources.org— in the "Transition" section.

some may have particular religious convictions that governmental financial assistance is wrong in all cases. It must be a conscientious objection to the very concept of governmental aid, not unlike conscientious objection to military service.

Thus, while it may certainly be the case that you object to governmentally-controlled healthcare, or that you think that a government-run retirement program is probably a bad idea, you must go further than that. Can you, in good conscience, claim that your conscience would be violated if you participate in any of these:

- Social Security assistance
- Medicare
- Medicaid
- Welfare
- Disaster relief
- Government-guaranteed student loans
- Government-funded student grants (such as the PELL Grant)
- Food stamps
- Low-interest natural disaster-relief loans
- FHA or HUD housing loans

If you can claim violation of conscience to all of the above, *and* you are ordained, then you can and probably *should* apply for exemption from SECA contribution.

If, however, your opposition to these programs is not rooted in your faith-informed conscience, you are not being honest if you apply for exemption. In this case, you should not apply; if you do, you should be brought up on charges before the body that ordained you.

I'll go one step further: if you have received the benefit of any of these programs, I would challenge your decision to apply. Why? Because your receipt of benefit through a program that you now claim you have a conscientious objection to constitutes, if not hypocrisy, then at least an inconsistency that may hinder your credibility. It also suggests that your mindset is not the community-mindedness that Scripture requires of us.

Here's an example: while in seminary, Marcie and our children qualified for a program called WIC (Women, Infants, and Children) through which we received a lot of free food. The program was designed to ensure that those under a certain income level could provide their children with a healthy diet. We were one family of literally dozens in seminary with us who qualified for, and accepted, aid through this program. (By the way, we've also benefited from student loans, student grants, FHA housing loans, and Medicaid at various times since we've been married.) If I were to now claim a conscientious objection, at very least I would be suggesting that other seminary families should not receive the same assistance that I received, even though they may have the same or greater need for assistance.

Opting out of the Social Security program is a good option for those who qualify. If, like me, you don't qualify, please don't taint your ministry or the option for future pastors by applying. In truth, very few will qualify, if we take seriously the legal implications (penalty of perjury) and ethical implications (deserves to be defrocked) of the restrictions stated on the application.

The Nuances of Public Aid

My wife asked me an astute question about this: if the application form 4361 only requires a conscientious or religious objection to public insurance, why do I include things like student and housing loans in my list?

This is such a good question that it may account for why many have opted out even though they are not opposed to loan or disaster relief programs. My guess is that, when most people read the description on IRS form 4361, the government-guaranteed student loan that they are still paying off never enters their minds— so naturally they don't think that such loans have direct impact on this decision.

In fact, however, it is helpful to understand what it means for a loan to be "government-guaranteed". This doesn't mean that they actually make the loans; this is done through a state-run or private organization such as Sallie Mae (private) or, in the case of my student loans from seminary, Mohela (Missouri Higher Education Loan Authority). Instead, a government-guaranteed loan is actually insured by the federal government; in the event of default on the loan, the government would pay the balance.

This is a benefit to borrowers, because the lenders do not have to increase interest rates to account for defaulters. Thus, students can borrow at very low interest rates because the government will guarantee repayment. But it also fits under that category of "public insurance". If I were disabled and therefore unable to pay my credit card payments, I would have to declare bankruptcy unless I had taken out private insurance for my debts. If, on the other hand, I were unable to pay my student loans due to disability, the tax-payers (through federal taxes) would pay them for me.

The same applies to housing and disaster relief. And, while food stamps, welfare, and the WIC program I mentioned before are not exactly in the same category as loans, they are in the category of "public insurance" in the sense that the tax-paying public collectively insures against any individual member of the public not being able to provide for their own food and shelter.

Thus, the list I provided above is perhaps more comprehensive than what is immediately suggested by the term "public insurance" on IRS form 4361, but it is nevertheless an accurate list.

With all of that said: if you do believe that you may apply in good conscience, and choose to do so, please be aware of two factors. First, my understanding is that you have six months from the time of your ordination trials to make application for the exemption. (Note that this is from the time of your ordination trials, not the actual date of ordination; insofar as I understand the process, the clock starts ticking when the ordaining body approves you for ordination.) So if you intend to apply, don't delay! Second, remember that this is an application for exemption, and it is up to the authorities of the IRS to decide to approve— or not approve— your exemption. You should therefore continue to make regular contributions according to the law until you receive notice of your application's approval.

Some Salary Data

A 2007 survey by the National Association of Colleges and Employers showed that 2007 college graduates would likely fare better than in previous recent years. CNN provided a summary of the results in an article. The reported that even the lowly liberal arts folks (like myself!) showed improvement: starting salaries were just below

$31,000, which was a 2% increase from last year. Naturally, the hot careers were in media, technology, and engineering.[18]

What did this imply for ministry professionals? Probably not much: sadly, too few churches base their salary packages on the averages of other fields, or even on the average income for the same age, life-stage, or other similar data.

Where do churches get their starting points? My experience is that they find out what other churches are paying for the same type of ministry professional. Under normal circumstances, this would be a reasonable method. But ministry salaries have languished in the bottom tiers of the income bracket for so long that I fear this is a self-feeding cycle of mediocrity.[19]

Candidates, Don't Wimp Out!

At the risk of becoming cynical, let me say a word or two in their defense.

I think a large part of the reason for churches underpaying their ministry professionals is the ministry professionals themselves! After all, we're the ones accepting what they offer. I have to admit that I've felt it, and you've probably felt it, too: we're called to be servants of the Church, to suffer on behalf of Christ. Maybe a constant struggle to make ends meet is our cross to bear, right?

WRONG.

Time for a few disclaimers. Here's what I'm *not* saying: that you should take as much as you can niggle out of them, refuse to accept less than your "standard," or play a negotiation game until your wealth is growing through the roof. (Don't worry about the last one ever happening, by the way.)

But neither should you accept a salary that puts your family in financial jeopardy simply because the church you're negotiating with makes an offer. There is a big difference between giving of yourself and being used— between being a servant and being a doormat. In most cases, ANY employer will pay as little as they can get away with; it should not come as a surprise, therefore, that very few churches will **over**-pay. You must negotiate a salary that is fair, and that pays your bills. Too many of us will accept whatever is offered because we're afraid of losing an opportunity. "If I ask for more," we think, "they might not hire me."

Are you that uncertain that the Lord has led the hearts of those extending you this call? Then maybe you shouldn't be taking it— even if they double the amount they offer.

If they say, "we believe God has led us to call you— let's don't make this about money" then you should say, "I agree; if it's not about money, then you should be able to pay me what I need." You must help them understand that part of your calling as a ministry professional— a major part, in fact— is to take care of yourself and those in your family. If they don't get this, you don't want to work with for them.

Let me say that again: *if they don't get this, you don't want to work for them.*

---

18 Of course, that data was compiled in the months prior to one of the largest economic recessions in U.S. history, and a similar survey conducted a year later— in the thick of that recession— would almost certainly have reported very different results.

19 Sometimes churches dare to look outside for information: one church I interviewed with years ago told me they based their Youth Minister's package on the average starting salary for teachers in the local schools, as if I should be relieved, or even impressed. After all, we know that teachers are so well-paid!

There will always be a church that simply can't afford to pay you what you need. If you're equally convinced that God has called you there, then it comes back to you to figure it out. When you're satisfied that they have offered you as much as they can afford (or as much as you need, whichever is less), then it's time to find another source to supplement.

But if you're not negotiating with one of these churches, then you should expect more. Realize that this will help set a pattern of precedent for how the leadership will treat you. So many pastors who complain that their leaders give them as little investment in ministry as they can get away with could. I wonder how many could trace this problem back to the salary negotiations?

Consider this one of your first official acts as their pastor.

A Sea of Cardboard

Moving day is coming soon. Now that you have a sense of where you will be moving, you need to consider a few things about how you will be moving.

Moves are stressful. Part of the stress of moving comes from second-guessing whether or not you made the right decisions. Since getting married in 1998, my wife and I have moved nine times! I've also helped my sister move about a dozen times, so I've learned some things about moving along the way. In this chapter, I'll share what little bit I've learned, and offer guidance that, hopefully, will encourage and prepare you for your upcoming move.

Buy? Rent? None Of The Above?

One of the first questions you must answer is whether you will buy a home or rent one. (In some cases, a third option will be present: the manse or parsonage. I'll discuss this more in a moment.)

The conventional wisdom for most of the past century or more has said that buying is the better option, by far. It represented an investment that grew and built equity, and over time you would have greater buying-power as a homeowner. Even after just a few years, most homes sold for a higher price than they were purchased for— and combined with the principle paid toward the mortgage, homeowners gained significantly. For first-time buyers (which includes most recent seminary graduates), there were further incentives and more affordable mortgages available also. As recently as 2007, the best advice to a transitioning seminary grad would be to buy a home if you possibly could.

All of this has changed, and maybe permanently. Shifts in the U.S. and global economies have made home-buying a different exercise than it was. While the "Great Recession" technically ended in 2009,[1] Its effects continue to make circumstances difficult when it comes to home ownership. A 2010 article by Collin Hansen highlighted one such difficulty: some pastors in the process of transition are unable to sell their homes, and must reconsider their transition options accordingly.[2] Other pastors are finding that selling existing homes is simply not an option; whereas a home was once an investment that was all but guaranteed to hold its value (and probably increase in it), these homes are now burdensome obstacles toward transition in ministry. One pastor I know is renting his current home, because the house he left when he moved to his present ministry call appraises for $30,000 less than what he owes on it.

---

[1] The "rule of thumb" definition of a recession is two consecutive quarters of falling Gross Domestic Product (GDP).

[2] "Pastors Search for Churches, Home Buyers" by Collin Hansen, published on October 10, 2010 by the Gospel Coalition (http://thegospelcoalition.org/blogs/tgc/2010/10/10/pastors-search-for-churches-home-buyers/), accessed Oct. 25, 2010.

Another fellow pastor is almost $100,000 "underwater" on his mortgage. Owning a home may have become a detriment to the long-term ministry of a pastor.

However, there are advantages in home ownership to a transitioning seminarian. When the housing market declines, prices for existing homes drop significantly, making it much easier to afford to buy a home (when otherwise you might not be able to do so)— or to buy a larger home than you could otherwise afford. Typically, these circumstances bring lending rates down as well, which further reduces the month-to-month cost of owning a home and allows a homeowner to make greater progress on paying down the principle of a mortgage. In some ways, therefore, a stressed economic climate may be a great opportunity to take on home ownership.

In the end, the decision is much more difficult than it once was— and it is one that you must weigh carefully.

None Of The Above

Some will have an option that was once much more common that it is today: to move into a home that is owned by the church, commonly called a parsonage or manse.

I discussed manses in some detail in a previous chapter, so I won't re-cover the same ground. But I would point out this already-obvious aspect of the manse: it allows a pastor to totally avoid the conundrum of whether he should buy or rent. A manse is owned by the congregation, and even if they do not own it outright (if they have mortgaged the property, or they are still paying the original mortgage) then the financial obligation is not the pastor's to bear. Therefore, they are not encumbered by that burden when and if they decide to transition again.

This is not necessarily the end of the decision; you certainly have the option to pursue other housing arrangements. However, this may not be a financially-viable choice from the congregation's vantage-point, as they may not be able to afford to pay you a housing allowance and also maintain the cost of owning their pre-existing manse (and it is an unfair position to put them in to ask them to sell the manse to afford your housing allowance). Even if they can afford it, you should also consider the relational consequences of refusing their manse: they may be offended, assuming that you consider their manse an inadequate home for your family. But you may feel threatened by the issues of proximity and the "fishbowl" factor (where you and your family always feel like you are being watched). Either way, this is why considering whether a manse is the right choice for your housing arrangement is better-suited for the negotiation of terms of call.

Cautious Advice

I'm hesitant to offer advice, given the volatility of the market and the ever-changing nature of the factors involved. A few suggestions come to mind, which you must take with a grain of salt:

- If you are moving into a ministry that may have a shorter term, it seems prudent to seriously consider renting your home at the outset. This might include church planting, campus ministry, or a pastoral role that you don't envision becoming a permanent focus for your ministry career. In a call that has a relatively short life-cycle, it may be worthwhile to remain flexible in your housing arrangements.

- If you are beginning a ministry with some unknown quantities, you may be wise to rent first, and consider buying later. This may be a call to a church with a congregation spread over a wide area, and you don't know where to settle in yet. Or it might include ministries where the local community is very expensive and affordable housing is harder to come by. You might try to negotiate a lease that is month-to-month, or that only lasts six months; that will keep your options open should you find a good opportunity to buy down the line.
- If your call is to a congregation where you can foresee a longer-term ministry being likely, you may find it beneficial to go ahead and buy a home. You shouldn't base your decision entirely on the state of the housing market at the time you make your transition; for all you know, the market may shift substantially between now and when you eventually move.
- If you will be serving a church that needs a re-affirmation of stability in ministry, you may discern that it is prudent to buy a home. In the church I presently serve, a leader commented to me that, had I rented a home in the area, he would have wondered if I was earnest in my words of commitment; since we bought our house, that had sent an unspoken message affirming that we were serious about settling in for a longer ministry.
- If you are uncomfortable with the financial burden that will be placed on you through buying a home, you should probably rent. Whether it is because your terms of call are not adequate to sustain it, you have student loans or other debt to mitigate, or some other factor, you should not feel forced to commit to a mortgage that will place an undue burden on you and your family.[3]

The Move

When it comes to the move itself, you'll have several options. Depending on whether there are funds available to help you move (and how much is available), some of these options may be eliminated by default. Assuming that they are all open to you, however, you may choose between using professional movers, doing the move yourself, or some combination of the two.

Working with Pros

An option called "self-service moving" has become a popular alternative to hiring full-service movers (who pack your things and load the truck). With it, you pack your stuff in a provided cargo container or onto a 60-ft trailer, paying by the linear-foot of floor space you consume. They load the rest with standard freight, so you share the cost with shippers, and your trailer arrives at your new home in 2-3 days. You don't have to drive a truck, but you save by not paying movers to load and unload. The most well-known company that does this is ABF. One alternative is Help U Move; I'm sure there are a few others.

For local moves, if you can't (or don't want to) load the truck yourself you may find that companies like Two Men and a Truck has a location in your town; as of

---

3   In rare cases, the inverse may be true: it might be more expensive to rent a home than to buy one. However, even in these cases then the long-term commitment is not the same as it is with a mortgage.

2011, they are in 29 states and growing fast. They have earned a solid reputation of being reliable, careful movers. (They also have a great list of moving tips on their website.) They do both "self-service" and "full-service" moves. There are other similar services available for local moving options. This won't apply to most readers, but even churches in seminary towns have pastoral transition!

Check in with MoversWeb, Moving.com, Movers.com, JustMovers, 123Movers, "My Moving Quote" and/or Movers Directory to get quotes about your move. Some of them will contact you by phone or e-mail; depending on the type of move you're considering, some will do a free in-home examination and quote. Be judicious in how many of these services you use—your information will be shared with several moving companies, and some will flood your e-mail inbox with communication about your estimates.

You may find it helpful to check up on consumer complaints, scams and protection about moving and movers. Some helpful pages to read are Moving Scam.com, ConsumerAffairs.com's Good Guys, Epinions.com: Moving Companies and the American Moving and Storage Association to find out about the service you are considering. You can also check with the Better Business Bureau to get a reliability report on companies, including moving companies.

Quotes from moving companies (such as North American or Allied) or for self-service moving are based on two variables: how much stuff you have, and how far you need to take it. Thus, you can begin gathering quotes before you have a firm destination by using the location you might be that is furthest from where you are now. Once the final location is known, they can run a new quote based on that location—and since they will already have the estimated weight of your stuff, this will be a fast process (little more than entering a Zip Code into a field and clicking a button).

If you get a quote, be sure to ask for a copy of the "Cube Sheet." This is the document used to calculate the quote and lists all of the estimated weights and quantities that the quote is based upon. If you have a copy of this, you can compare it to other quotes' Cube Sheets. You should ask about any significant variance in weight estimation—they should all show about the same weight (give or take 300-500 pounds).

Make sure that quotes you receive are "Not To Exceed" quotes. This means that the amount quoted is the most you will spend, assuming the distance listed. Once your stuff is loaded, the actual weight will be determined and the cost re-calculated. You should also ask about fee rates and when they are changing. Moving companies pay tariffs, and these can change by several percentage points. Ask when the next change will be, and how much—and be sure to verify whether your quote will be good after that change. Be sure to ask, at the time of the quote, about any undisclosed fees. Also, ask for a discount. They are able to discount your fees significantly. (One quoter told me that they had a discount for everyone. He gave me a 69% discount on our quote!)

Inquire about the cost difference for packing your own stuff vs. having a moving service pack for you. This can sometimes be several thousand dollars in difference, which is a compelling case for packing yourself. If you are packing yourself and you are using a moving company, ask about whether you can get boxes through them. Some will offer heavily discounted or even free boxes (although they may be used ones) to those using their services. My wife and I used the same boxes to move us four different times, then we gave them to someone else—so used boxes can be a good deal. (I'm not talking about grocery and liquor store boxes either, but good-quality moving boxes.)

Finally, if you have a lot of books, you might consider shipping these bulk or media rate through UPS or the postal service. In one of our quotes, I asked for a calculation of what part of the total quote was books—it was almost $1000 (of an approximately $7000 quote). It may be much less expensive to ship them than pack them in your moving truck—unless the final cost is not based on weight. Do some checking to discover if you could save a lot of money shipping your books.

Do It Yourself Moves

If you want to rent a truck and drive it yourself (or you can't afford to do more than this), use one of the major rental companies: U-Haul, Budget, Penske and Ryder. These companies have adequate fleet sizes to accommodate your reservation. I've heard too many stories of moves that didn't happen on the scheduled day because the (small local) truck company rented the truck to an earlier customer. If you're not moving very much stuff—or if your move is local—you might consider looking at Enterprise's truck rental for a cargo van or pickup truck. (You may find ABF U-Pack's comparison/sales pitch about U-Pack vs. Rental — which is prominently available on the ABF website[4] — to be a helpful read.) The website Mover Max[5] has a helpful checklist about renting a truck.

I like U-Haul's low truck beds, which make loading and unloading a lot easier on the back; but there are lots of folks who urge against U-Haul based on mixed or negative experiences. For a while I would only use Ryder trucks for non-local moves, because I found their trucks to be very reliable; Ryder has since been sold, and while they still rent trucks I cannot speak to the quality or reliability of their fleet.

For All Moves

Once you know your move date, begin making plans immediately. Better yet, begin making plans before you know the date; as I mentioned before, you can begin gathering quotes and other information without a firm date or location. Just be sure to make reservations well in advance. If possible, avoid moving at the same time that "everyone else" is: weekdays are better than weekends, and seasonal moves (such as the beginning and end of college semesters) are almost always busy. If you have control over the dates of your move, plan them carefully. (Be sure to clear your plans with anyone who will be helping you move; it's a tough scramble to plan a mid-week move and learn that all of your friends are working.)

You will find help on changing addresses, forwarding mail, etc. at the Postal Service's Moving page. Be sure to let your employer(s) know your new address, so that they can send your paychecks directly to you; forwarded mail can be delayed as much as 10 days. If you're like me, details like this easily slip through the cracks, so find a moving checklist online or create your own so that you don't forget these before it is too late.

---

4   http://www.upack.com/
5   http://www.movermax.com/

ULine Shipping Supply[6] sells high-quality, affordable moving kits and supplies that are a great deal if you are packing yourself. A ULine rep told me that it's never a bad idea to ask the sales representative for a discount—they are authorized to grant discounts on-the-fly. Whether you buy from ULine or from somewhere else (U-Haul's local branches also sell good-quality moving boxes), it is worth it to get some of the specialized boxes for your move: divided crates with foam sleeves for glassware and dishes make a big difference, and the "wardrobe" boxes will save you hours of folding and ironing.

Finally, you should check with your city or town hall to discover whether you will need a permit to park a truck, trailer or pod in front of your house. (Oddly enough, some cities won't let you park a 75-foot trailer just anywhere.) If you cannot get a permit, it can cost you thousands of dollars to arrange a shuttle service through your moving company. Be sure to ask about this when you are getting quotes; movers are supposed to disclose "hidden fees" like this, but if they don't you can be subject to full-price (as opposed to a discounted price at the time of the quote).

Other Factors

As you go through the act of moving from one home and location to another, there is another factor that is a matter of great stress and anxiety, in addition to the questions of housing options and how you should physically get your stuff from one place to the other. That factor is what I call the "home" factor: the difficulty of pulling up roots from one place and trying to get re-rooted in a new place.

Sometimes this is a non-starter; perhaps your seminary experience was brief enough (or perhaps relationally and emotionally difficult enough) that you don't feel like you have many roots down there anyway— and the ones that are down are not deep. Maybe you are moving from a town or city that is far from your family, and into an area that already seems like home. It might be that you have few ties to place, and therefore feel freed to transition to wherever God leads you.

In most cases this will not be so. You probably will be moving from a place that is familiar to one that is unfamiliar, and from where you have friends and acquaintances to where you know few people. You must make adjustments to routines, meet new people, and work with new service providers. It will be difficult for you— but it will be even harder for your family.

In addition to learning a few things along the way from my own experience, I received some helpful comments in my placement survey. I also asked a number of fellow pastors what they did to ease the difficulty of the move for themselves and their family, and I asked them if their new congregation did anything in particular to help them. What follows is a conglomeration of brief suggestions and ideas.

What You/Your Family Can Do

- "I planned well in advance for what I would be doing with work, which made my schedule more flexible to help the family get settled. I got a head start on the first sermon series and Bible studies that I would be leading so

---

[6] http://www.uline.com/

A Sea Of Cardboard

that I I could spend time helping at the house and we were flexible to get out in the community and find our place."
- "We tried to get info about the area and visit a few times before moving; going fun places and eating at some restaurants; looking around, exploring. it helped to give us vision for what life might be like there and to look forward to it, instead of anticipating so much unknown."
- "We included them in important choices and prayers. For instance, we included their desires as well as needs when looking for a house. First, we asked them to identify our basic needs as a family (number of bedrooms, baths, location, etc.) and pray for those. Then we asked them to identify their desires (woods, friends their age, playroom, etc.) and pray for those. The Lord answered not only their needs but their (reasonable!) desires. It greatly helped their transition."
- "This won't always be possible for every situation, but I think we benefited from having 2+ months between the end of seminary and the move to our new call. This allowed for a less hurried transition time and ample opportunity to visit with family and friends (who we see less of post-move)."
- "We took our time . . . got from the church a start date that was reasonable and allowed me to help my family between the move and starting at the church. It was a period of about 1 month where I could focus on them, moving and settling in without new responsibilities."
- "We stayed in a nice hotel the first two nights we were in town and moving into our house. There was a pool for the kids to play in, free breakfast and a tidy place to sleep after long days. We used vacation money to do it, but it was worth it. Every time the kids see the hotel, they want to go back. It made them like something about our new hometown immediately, and that was really helpful for the transition."
- "I'd say the number one priority should be finding one or two good female friends for your wife. Not sure of the best way to facilitate that, but I'd recommend trying to figure out some ways! The transition was easier for me because I was out meeting new people all the time with the job (and being a guy, doing something carried me a good bit), but my wife's felt need for close relationships was greater and with other family stuff, it was just logistically harder for her to meet new people and find new close friendships."
- " If you treat it as an adventure and get the family involved, it changes the whole atmosphere."

What Your New Congregation Can Do

It may come across as demanding were you to provide this list with your new congregation— or even one or two items from it. But should they ask how they might help you or get things prepared, these are some ideas that may prove useful.
- "The leaders urged families to reach out to our children before we moved. So every other day our kids received a little gift or note or picture from a different family."
- "They provided meals and assistance (child care, unloading moving truck, etc.) with all that is involved with moving."

- "The congregation was very thoughtful. I am not sure we could have asked for more. Given that we moved internationally, there was lots of 'paperwork' attached to our move. I was given sufficient time to complete the basics— change over driver's licenses, set up bank accounts, establish identity, etc.— prior to being asked to come in to the office. This was a huge help. Also, congregation members helped clean up our rental, donated furniture, and were even thoughtful about lending toys so that our kids would have something to play with while we waited for all our goods to transport and come through customs. Bottom line, we were wonderfully cared for and I can only hope others in similar circumstance receive this level of practical care."
- "They gave us a 'pounding party': each family gave us something practical to set up our house (a pound of sugar or flour, laundry detergent, etc.). We didn't have to buy ketchup, barbecue sauce or cleaning supplies for over a year! They asked for preferred brands before hand, and that helped a lot too. We also can't stress enough the importance of bringing meals – it helps us get to know the cook and it is such a huge relief to not have to cook while moving in."
- "One of the things the secretary in my office did when we moved here: she put together a welcome packet with a phone book, congregational directory, coupons, a city map, and menus for local restaurants. That made us feel welcome and helped us adjust to the new city."
- "One thing my leadership did was to pass out a sheet to the whole congregation, giving them the opportunity to write down for us the local things we might need. The list had local doctors, local favorite pizza places, suggestions of things to do in free times, local businesses that were trusted, mechanics, dentists, etc. Then it had gift cards to the grocery store, restaurants, etc. included."
- "The thing we appreciated most was connected with those members of the church when we pulled up in the moving van… men, women, and children all showed up to welcome us and help us with the move in… the move itself became a fellowship event. I have strengthened relationships with many of those same people *because* of that first contact."
- "Assuming the wife is being moved further away from family and friends, they can acknowledge that this is hard, and be sensitive to this. They might find out her personality and what it will mean to make her feel welcome, also what will be 'too much' for her."
- "I think the best thing a congregation can do for a pastor when new is hammer them relationally. Invite them to things, feed them, have them in their home, make them part of the community as soon as possible. Ministry will move as fast as there trust and that will not come without high touch, relational connectivity with the place you are called to ply your craft."

Moving is always difficult. Even a move across town can consume time, energy, and attention, and leave you frustrated and weary. But with forethought and planning, a bit of intentional preparation, and the support of a new congregation, your move can go smoothly.

Not Done Yet

Candidacy is over, terms of call have been negotiated, the moving truck loaded and unloaded, and you're living in a sea of cardboard. The first day of ministry is approaching! Where do you begin?

It is impossible for me to counsel you on what your first priorities should be in your new ministry. The people and their personalities, demographics, and the history of those who came before you— not to mention the nature of the ministry position itself— all dictate how you should begin your ministry far more reliably than I ever could.

Nevertheless, there are some things to keep in mind as you begin your ministry. Whatever your first priorities are, you need to start them right. Your personal life, family life, and ministry life need to be healthy— and what you do (or don't do) will make or break the healthiness. The following eight principles will set you on a path toward all-around healthy ministry.

#1: Relationships

Start your ministry by stacking your boxes of books by the door of your office. Now leave them there for the next two weeks.

It should be no surprise that, if I am convinced that the key to placement is relationships, I am also sure that relationships are the key to good transition. And if one of the key questions for placement is, "Who do you love?" then surely one of the key questions for transition is, "How do you love?"

Forget the boxes of books, the adjustment to the new places, and the sermon you have to preach next Sunday. (No, not completely; but don't you have a few sermons you could re-work and save some prep time?) Begin your new ministry strong with a heavy focus on relationship-building. Let the logistics of the new position take care of themselves— or at least wait a while.

In one of the positions I served, I went the other way: I jumped into the logistical details during the first weeks of ministry. I was a Youth Minister starting on January 2, and Christmas break wasn't over yet; plus, it was wet, icy, and all of the students were just sleeping late and watching TV. So I spent my first days setting up my office, unpacking books, organizing my schedule, and establishing mobile phone service.

Looking back, it was a big mistake that hurt my ministry for the long-term: I was perceived by some as more concerned about my mobile phone than about ministry— that my computer was a higher priority than students. This wasn't true, and the way I spent my time after those first few weeks should have proven it. But the fact that I focused on getting books unpacked first was a precedent-setter for some in that church.

After all, ministry is not about those things. It's not about cell phones, bookshelves, or offices. It's not about the contents of the books on the shelves or the appointments on the schedule. It's not even about the sermons you preach— not essentially. If no one is listening, it won't matter how good you preach, how many appointments you make, or how many books you read. And once they decide that you're interested in things other than relationships with them (whether that is the truth or not), they stop listening.

Jump into your new ministry with both feet by building relationships. That doesn't mean you can't do anything else; obviously you must have something to preach or teach on Sunday, and you should take some time to prepare for that. But spend the bulk of your time in the first few weeks with people. And make sure they can see that this is your priority; if you can, see to it that everyone in the church knows that they'll get time with you soon. Maybe not this week, but based on how much time you're spending with others, they'll know it is coming.

#2: Who Are The People In Your Neighborhood?

Sing along if you know it:

Oh the postman always brings the mail, in rain or snow or sleet or hail...

The senior pastor I worked with in at one church I served had an interesting experiment going on when I started: he would stop for gas at the station less than two blocks from the church property and would routinely ask the attendant for directions to our church!

When he first started this practice, the response was usually something vague, at best. "I've never heard of that place," "Isn't that on ___ street [on the other side of town]?" and, "Sure— it's a half-mile south of here [exactly the opposite direction]" were some of the answers he received. In time, it became a joke— and not a very funny one.

Our church was fairly active in local issues, and though it would have been easy for my pastor just to explain who he was to the attendants, he wanted to see if they knew about the church by its reputation. I appreciate this desire, but I think that a new pastor can do great things for his ministry if he is attentive to intentionally building relationships with his neighbors, as well.

One of the aspects of transition that is probably overlooked more than any other is this sort of relationship-building outside of the congregation. Getting to know the physical neighbors around the church property (and around the pastor's home, as well) is definitely a ministry-builder, and an invaluable part of settling into ministry.

Here are a few things that such relationship-building accomplishes:
- It allows genuine fulfillment of the command to "Love your neighbor as yourself."
- It heals past hurts— particularly those inflicted by other Christians— by showing true care and concern.
- It is itself an exercise in hospitality, and it opens up further opportunities for hospitality.
- It creates a venue for the Gospel to be shown and told.
- It helps in future circumstances when civil and political difficulty may arise.

That pastor I worked with would agree with this: when Planned Parenthood erected a clinic directly across the street from our church property, he was the first one to extend a hand of hospitality (but not a hand of welcome, exactly, though the distinction is a fine one; make no mistake, he is strongly "pro-life" and was not supportive of what the clinic was built to do) and worked hard to build a friendship with the clinic's director. Rather than only showing opposition to the clinic's purposes (which he did in a loving way), he also led the charge to long for, pray for, and work for the salvation and redemption of those who work there. Those workers, it seems, are people too— in need of a Savior, just like me.

Who are the people in your neighborhood? You don't have to try to meet them all in the first week or even the first months, but set some goals— maybe you can get to know every merchant, businessperson, or resident on your block by name by the end of the first year of ministry. One new introduction a week would be fairly ambitious. Do you know your regular mail carrier's name, or the folks that make deliveries to your offices? How about the pastors of other nearby churches (more on this in a future post)?

Eventually, those station attendants did get to know us, and where we were. Not long before I left, my pastor came in from lunch beaming. "I stopped at the station like always," he reported, "But when I asked if they knew where the church was, the guy said, 'You're there! It's just in the middle of the next block on the left!'"

They're the people that you meet each day...

#3: The Pastor's Study

Anytime I'm left waiting in someone's office, I look at what is on the shelves: usually, the books capture my interest the most, though I was once fascinated to find a clean, yet broken, inner-race of a automotive constant-velocity (CV) joint on the shelf of a philosophy professor! (The CV joint is the amazing piece of a car's axle that allows the wheels to spin at different speeds around turns.)

You can learn a lot about a person from what is on the shelves in their office. In fact, you can learn a lot about them from the whole office. Now, this isn't *"feng shui* for the pastor." But there is a psychology to the arrangement of a pastor's study that those beginning a new ministry ought to pay attention to.

Take, for example, the shelves of books. Nearly every pastor or seminarian I know is a bibliophile, and most of us are somewhat proud of our book collections. Is my study the best place to store all of my books? Inevitably, there will be those in a congregation who are intimidated by the scholarly nature of their pastor, and the fact that his study is entirely lined with books will not help the intimidation. Perhaps the avenues of ministry would be less congested if some of the books were housed elsewhere.

Obviously, there will be some books that are essential, or nearly so, to a pastor's ministry and therefore have a proper place in his study. But many will not: in my office at the last church I served, I had an entire shelf unit filled with my philosophy books, though— surprisingly enough!— I never used them for youth ministry. They were a nice testimony to the degree I completed in that field, but probably hindered my ministry (and obviously didn't help it, since I never used them). At present, I would guess that 1/4 to 1/3 of my 2500+ books have no direct value to ministry whatsoever, and therefore are shelved at home instead of in my study.

Another aspect to consider is the desk and work space. It may take a while for a working system to emerge as the most efficient way of using the space you have, but let me make a few recommendations based on experience and/or reflection:

Don't bother with the "In-box/Out-box" sort of arrangement unless you will actually use it. Since I never did in one of my ministries, mine were always overflowing, which gave the impression that I was either overworked or never did anything!

Keep file storage close-at-hand. If you have ready access to your filing cabinets, you are more likely to actually file things regularly. Filing is usually tedious anyway, so any excuse (e.g., "I don't want to bother getting out of the chair to walk across the room") will be enough to prevent regular filing.[1]

If possible, place your desk so that it is visible from the doorway. When others walk by and see you working, it will affirm their sense of your work-ethic. Stated negatively, some congregants already suspect that a pastor loafs and slacks all week ("Pretty good pay for two hours a week..."), so if they can't see you working (or see the evidence of your work from the stuff on your desk), they may assume the worst. Obviously this only applies if you actually do work...

An ancillary point to the last one: *set up your computer so that the monitor can be seen from the doorway.* Hopefully you're not tempted by pornography on the Internet, but if you are (or is anyone suspects that you are), this setup will provide accountability and dispel suspicion. Also, if the door to your study doesn't have a window in it, insist that one be installed, or the door be replaced with a windowed one. This is for your protection, as well as for the peace of mind of those you counsel. Otherwise, your alternatives are three:

- leave the door wide open (which means anyone can hear you and your visitor);
- close the door but always have someone else sit in with you (which is not always possible, nor does it avail the privacy that counseling often requires);
- or close the door and be alone with them (which, at best, invites speculation...).

Of course, a fourth alternative is that you could simply refuse to do any counseling (but in that case don't bother unpacking the books).

The size, shape, and kind of furnishings in a pastor's study vary so greatly from one church to another that it is difficult to offer any concrete suggestions about how a study might be arranged. Here are a few thoughts. Make the space as inviting as possible. Have comfortable seating available apart from your desk chair (one pastor I visited kept metal folding chairs behind the door for guests— no wonder he seldom had them!). Light it well, but not harshly; indirect, incandescent light has been shown to be both soothing and restful, while fluorescent lights can make the eyes tired. The

---

1 N.B.: for a good system to get this under control, I recommend *Getting Things Done: The Art of Stress-Free Productivity* by David Allen.

perfectly arranged study is one that is comfortable and functional for long periods of time, both when you are alone and when others are with you.

A friend of mine suggested that the desk can become an unintended divider between the pastor and his people. I've seen a variety of arrangements that accommodate this, with one thing in common: all of them had a part of the study that was structured for sitting with others— almost an ante-room of sorts in some cases, while others were just chairs or a loveseat placed behind the desk, so that the pastor could turn around and face his visitors.

Finally, acknowledge the impact of nomenclature. What is the difference between a "pastor's office" and a "pastor's study?" Psychologically and semantically, there is a world of difference. An office is used mainly for administration, meetings, and business. A study, on the other hand, is a place for reading, reflection, contemplation (in other words, for studying). Which of those two best describes your calling?

#4: It's A Family Affair

You think the transition will be hard on you? Wait until you see the fallout for your family.

Any transition is difficult— not just for a pastor, but for his wife, children, parents, siblings, former friends... no one is left unscathed. Some friends of mine recently felt the force of this as they moved to seminary. They were doing pretty well with it, until it finally caught up to them. They fought, they cried, and then they crashed. Like the rest of us, they were hit with the troubles that transition brings.

I can remember how it was. Going to seminary was difficult enough: selling our home, leaving my ministry job, moving all of our stuff, settling into a new home, meeting new people, looking for/starting new jobs, finding a new church, and undertaking a new degree program. While we didn't have any children at the time, I can only imagine that those who do find the difficulty to be increased exponentially. The seminary transition, as you too will surely recall, is beastly.

Yet, it was also wonderful in its own way. The anticipation helped a lot. I also remember all that we hoped for: learning new things, meeting those who will become life-long friends, interacting with professors, getting training and experience for the fulfillment of our callings...

No, wait. That was just me who would be doing all of that. Marcie, on the other hand, would be working to put me through that. (Or working at home to raise our children.) She wouldn't really get to experience very much of that at all, would she?

Well, yes and no. Marcie had a great seminary experience too. But if you're married and in seminary (or if you were in seminary at some point), hopefully your wife has communicated to you some of the differences between what you are experiencing and what she is. Sometimes it is like night and day.

Don't forget this.

Keen awareness of this point will be essential information during the transition into pastoral ministry— because often, in ministry, the situation is surprisingly the same: you, the pastor, come in with great anticipation of all that will happen. You'll meet many wonderful new people who you'll call your flock and co-laborers. You'll be able to jump right into the hands-on work of ministry. You'll become familiar with the community, the town, and the places that will become your regular haunts. You'll begin to catch a vision for what the Lord may do with you there, and the excitement will be nearly overwhelming.

Meanwhile, your wife will be at home with the kids. Or starting a new job. Or looking for work. She'll be lonely, stressed-out, and tired. She'll feel the pressure to get the boxes unpacked while you're writing a sermon or visiting the home-bound. She'll be the one worrying about the family budget— after all, she still hasn't found a job and you've already been there four weeks!— while you're going out to lunch with an elder (on your dime).

Sunday will come, and you'll go in early, teach Sunday School, chat with the members you met earlier in the week, lead worship, preach your sermon, and accept an invitation to lunch with your new friends. What a wonderful Sabbath!

She'll wander into church uncertain of what class to attend, stand to the side and talk politely with folks she doesn't know, sit alone with the children during worship, and quietly eat her lunch while you talk and laugh, all the while worrying about getting the kids down for a nap. Was that even a Sabbath?

Brothers, as you're settling in to your new position, making new friends, and getting a vision for the ministry God has brought you to do, don't forget the co-laborer that He gave to you for life— the one who knows you the best. Share her concerns and burdens. Pay attention to what she is struggling with. Help with the boxes. Watch the kids so that she can get coffee with an elder's wife. Open your heart and mind to her by telling her about the vision God is giving you.

And take her out on a date very soon after the move— and regularly thereafter.

#5: Make New Friends

How long will you live in your new town, serving your new church, before you seek out and befriend other pastors in the area? Will you even refer to it as your "new church" by then?

My guess is that most pastors put this at the bottom of their priorities. After all, one group that every pastor can be certain will never join their church are other pastors in the area! And there are already so many things to do— and so many relationships to build— that getting to know other pastors seems like an unnecessary distraction. But in fact, it *is* necessary. And it is not a distraction, but a key part of your new ministry.

Let me insert a few disclaimers here. First, I am not a broad ecumenist who would insist that churches should be united and working to erase all denominational boundaries; as much as I value unity in the Kingdom, I recognize the importance of denominational distinctions and what the inherent variety offers the Church. And I am not suggesting that buddying up with other pastors is more important than shepherding the flock God has called you to serve, but I do believe that many pastors set themselves up for burnout, in part, because they fail to prioritize the fellowship, support, and accountability that can come from other local pastors.

"But," you counter, "I made some great friends in seminary who will be that for me!" Great, I say. (And I'll address that more fully later in this chapter.) I happen to believe, however, that there are benefits to deep friendships with local pastors that your friends from seminary can rarely fulfill. Some of them include:

- **They know the area.** Ministry occurs in a context; your fellow local pastors will know and understand that context in a way that your seminary friends won't (unless they happen to also be local)— and you won't either, at first. What are the difficult social and political issues that you need to have insight and answers about? Who are the locals— merchants, politicians, parachurch staff— that you will want to partner with? The other local pastors know. Early on, these friends can become a part of the process of integrating unto your community, learning how to minister within it.

- **They are easy (or easier) to meet with.** How will you keep up with those friends from seminary? However you do it, it won't be as simple as a lunch appointment across town. Your new friends are just around the corner compared to anyone else.
- **They are hard to avoid.** When I need accountability the most, I often also want to avoid it the most. Maybe you struggle in the same way. If so, local friends can get in your face, showing up at your office or home if necessary.
- **They present new ministry opportunities.** Whether it be a pulpit exchange, a regular joint worship service (holidays like Thanksgiving offer good opportunities here), or a collaborative effort at a regular ministry, having another pastor (and therefore his church) to try out these ideas is easier if you are already friends. Ending them if they don't work out is easier, too.

My first long-term, paid ministry job emerged out of a relationship just like what I am describing. Two pastors at different churches each needed development for their youth ministries, but neither could afford staff. Their good friendship with me and each other, and the familiar relationship between their churches, opened the door to a collaborative youth ministry that I oversaw.

In my own current position, I have two other area pastors— like-minded brothers— with whom I meet most weeks for coffee on Tuesday mornings. We enjoy lively and interesting discussions about ministry, theological topics, and denominational activity. We also share in one another's lives, rejoicing and mourning together. These meetings are often one of the high points of my week.

Befriending other pastors is the kind of thing that is easily put off indefinitely; then, when you really need that friend, you're all alone. Start now, and make it an essential part of your transition. You might even communicate this need/desire to your elders or deacons, so that they can support you in it— perhaps they'll even hold you accountable for getting started.

#6: Joining The Y

I don't know many seminarians who have lost weight or gotten in better shape during seminary.

Don't get me wrong— I do know a good handful of guys that found time to exercise. Even I found streaks of a few weeks— even a couple of months— where I was on the treadmill regularly. But my pitfall was, I would guess, the same as many of my fellow seminarians': some point in the semester (exam time, a major paper due, a break to travel home for a few weeks, etc.) interrupted my exercise patterns and the continuity was lost. Regaining it proved very difficult. Which is why the transition from seminary into a pastoral position is a great time to re-prioritize exercise for a pastor.

Once again, this can be difficult to rationalize; after all, when is it easy to find an hour (or more) to haul yourself over to the gym, get a full work out, then shower and change in order to get back to work? And doing this three to five times a week? Surely I'm kidding, right?

No... exercise has to fit in somewhere. If it means you have to rise early to get to it, then rise early. If it means you have to sacrifice your lunch break (though not your lunch) two or three times a week, so be it. If there is truly no time to exercise, then you're too busy. (This goes for seminarians, too!)

Studies have shown that the lack of regular exercise affects levels of stress, fatigue, energy, attention— all negatively. This is not to mention the increased strain your heart, lungs, and structural system endure when you gain weight, which is the result that most of us experience when we fail to exercise regularly. One doctor told a friend of mine that every pound of weight gained amounted to five additional pounds of pressure on the joints when walking or running. No wonder my knees hurt.

On the other hand, regular exercise is just short of magic in its effects on your body. As you exercise (over an extended period of time), your muscles grow and require more energy for even mundane tasks like getting out of a chair, walking across the room, or even typing; thus, your body loses weight more efficiently as your muscular system expands. Meanwhile, your metabolism increases due to the efficiency for burning carbs, proteins, and fats, so that you digest food more efficiently (leading to more weight loss). If you maintain a regular diet— even the same diet you've always had— your body will eventually balance out at a healthy weight. You rest more efficiently, you have more energy and endurance, and your overall health improves.

Amazingly, other things also seem to be "magically" handled through exercise: cholesterol issues, high triglycerides, and chronic conditions such as diabetes and asthma can be managed, if not overcome, through exercise. Even smokers and heavy drinkers who also exercise fair far better than their inactive counterparts. It is almost as if you can do just about anything you want— eat what you want, drink what you want— and, as long as you also exercise regularly, you'll be fine. (Almost... but not really.)

So you don't have to join the YMCA, or any other gym for that matter. If you'd rather jog around the neighborhood or swim laps in your next-door neighbor's pool, that's fine. Ride your bike to work on days when you'll be in the study all day anyway. Or get a treadmill and walk or run regardless of the weather. (Some people read on the treadmill, finishing dozens of books a year that way.) Joining an athletic club does have this draw: by shelling out money regularly to a gym, not exercising will weigh that much more heavily on your conscience.

President Bush exercised 6 days a week while he was in office; he said once that it never entered his mind that he wouldn't work out. If he could find the time, why can't you? Start tomorrow— or re-start tomorrow. Exercise is similar to your devotional life: re-starting regularly is better than the alternative.

#7: Keeping Up With Your Fellows

Most of the men I know who have remained in ministry for a number of years have done so in part through the friendships they made in seminary. In whatever way that it has materialized, these men (and often their families alongside them) have maintained friendships with a few very close friends from their seminary years. Those friendships have been a central factor in keeping them in ministry, stable, and focused on serving God.

I know few men who have been in ministry for more than ten years for whom this is not the case, and everyone I know who has been in ministry more than 20 years has done this. It doesn't always look the same, but some common factors arise among all of the people I've talked to about this:

- All of them are in contact regularly— usually by phone at least once a quarter, and visiting face-to-face at least once a year.
- All of the relationships have a component of basic accountability to them— checking in on the health of marriage and family life, personal spiritual growth, avoiding temptations, etc.
- All serve as a "dumping ground" for ministry problems and frustrations— allowing an outlet for all of the things that these men want and need to talk about, but feel they can't with anyone in their congregation (or even in their town).
- All eventually become a "true North-pointing compass" for the individuals— giving them a safe and trustworthy place to explore where the Lord may be leading them in the future.

What usually happens is that good friends in seminary become a committed group after graduation, and they agree to keep up with each other. They may try different models of how to do that, but they eventually settle into a routine that they repeat year after year.

One man I know has a week-long "vacation" with two other families, and they've been doing this for over 25 years. Another man meets twice a year for 48 hours with his two closest friends from seminary, and they call each other periodically. One friend gathers with a dozen others for three days, and they close up on a family farmhouse to play, talk, sing, pray, and laugh together. Another takes turns with a best friend, each visiting the other's house every six months— whoever is the visitor "dumps" everything while the other listens.

However it turns out, the constant among variables is this: having one or several close friends who can— over the years, through the moves and transitions, in spite of geographic differences— be the kind of peer and brother that every Christian needs has become one of the very few keys to long-term, Godly ministry for the men I know.

On the other hand, among any of the men I know who have been in ministry for 10 years or more and don't do this in some form, not one of them has the kind of ministry that I want to be a model for my future. I frankly don't have a lot of admiration for their ministries. I can't say for certain that this has been the deciding factor, but it certainly seems to have been a contributing one; it's at least a stark, consistent coincidence. (I should mention that I don't really know very many of these— which is probably also related to the absence of this factor; without this kind of support, you are almost certainly more likely to leave the ministry earlier.)

The lesson here for new graduates and new transitioners: get in touch with those few closest friends from seminary and work out how you will keep in touch. Then do it. Don't put this off.

#8: Exams For Ordination

If you are pursuing ordination in any denomination, you will almost certainly face a "floor exam" before some portion of your local church or of that denomination. This floor examination has a single, clear purpose: to test your readiness for ministry. Notice: I didn't say, "test your knowledge" or "test your theological acuity." This is a test of how ready you are for the day-to-day, hour-by-hour work of ministry.

A little background from my denomination— when a Candidate for Gospel Ministry pursues ordination in the Presbyterian Church in America (PCA), he will be examined orally at least twice: once by a committee of presbytery, and once on the floor of presbytery. The committee exam will be private and closed, generally speaking. No one else will be there but the committee and possibly a few other ordinands. This exam will also take longer than the other; the committee exams sometimes go for several hours.

The floor examination, in contrast, will be an open exam. Everyone in attendance who is a member of presbytery will be there, and any other visitors are welcome to attend. It is not uncommon, for example, for an ordinand's wife or parents to come and watch. In fact, visitors may even stay after the ordinand has been asked to leave so that the vote may be taken (although the presbyters do have the right to call for visitors to be excused as well).

The **committee** exam is essentially all about what you learned in seminary and in other preparation for ministry. They will grill you on church history, fine points of theology, your knowledge of the English Bible, your understanding of the sacraments, and so on. These questions can be as particular as, "what was the point of difference between Ratramnus and Radbertus?" or "explain the rationale for a supra-lapsarian position," or "give a detailed outline of the books of 2 Chronicles, Nahum, and 2 Thessalonians." They want to be sure that you have learned as much as you can learn.

The **floor** exam, on the other hand, is quite different. There will be a few obligatory questions from each major area, because the Book of Church Order of the PCA requires that the floor exam include them, but when the questioning is opened up to anyone at presbytery, most of the questions will not be so particular with regard to "book learnin'."

Instead, most will be directly related to the kind of issue or question that your ministry will put you in the line of fire for. One floor exam I sat in on included a question about how the ordinand (who had a call to an upper-middle class suburban church) would encourage racial and ethnic diversity in his congregation, and another about how he would support and advance that church's already active pro-life ministry.

Many of the questions in a floor examination will touch on things that the ordinand may never have considered before, and he will be forced to articulate an answer on the spot. A friend of mine told me about a question he received at his floor exam: must a person believe that the Bible is the Word of God in order to be a Christian? His answer: "No, one need not believe that the Bible is the Word of God to be a Christian, but I believe that if you are a Christian, you will believe that the Bible is the Word of God."

The best thing about this kind of examination is that it requires an ordinand to understand his Bible, his theology, his confession of faith, and even his church history in practical, tangible ways. How else should a man be examined for his preparation for ministry, after all?

Now, not every denomination does it this way— but there are still some essential take-aways here. Unless your experience is, sadly, like that of a friend of mine (in a different denomination) where his ordination involved no exams or serious consideration— merely the signing of paperwork by sympathetic and relatively unqualified parties— you should expect to be examined at some point. And that exam should be rigorous. It *should* be hard— this is, after all, an important work that you're being ordained to do.

BENEDICTION

Recent and soon-to-be graduates, I offer you my prayers and hopes that every letter of the Bible, every word of theology, and every moment of history that you were exposed to in seminary may become so real and useful, so life-changing and ministry-shaping, so Gospel-driven and Christ-centered that you will find your ordination exams and all of the ministry that follows a delight and a welcome challenge. I pray regularly for those who are transitioning in ministry, especially those transitioning from seminary. Though we may never meet, my prayers are for you also. May God bless your transition and your new ministry.

Appendix A:
Recommended Reading

You surely already have books a-plenty on your shelves, but perhaps you're like me in this way: I always appreciate another book recommendation. Here I'll provide a handful of books that I personally recommend for a variety of topics, many of which I've touched on through the book and referred to this section about. I've also included links to some websites which, hopefully, will not become outdated by the time of printing! I hope you will find some useful reading here.

On Your "Divine Design" & Sense Of Calling

Richard Nelson Bolles. *What Color Is Your Parachute?* (Berkely, CA: Ten Speed Press, 2011.) One of the "original" books to deal with calling and understanding yourself in relationship to work and career. Bolles was a pastor, too, before he was let go because of financial struggles; he has spent the rest of his career ministering to those who are wrestling with these questions.

Sinclair Ferguson. *Discovering God's Will.* (Carlyle, PA: Banner of Truth Trust, 1982.) Good wisdom from a great thinker and writer about having confidence in God's will and leading in your life.

David Keirsey. *Please Understand Me II.* (Del Mar, CA: Prometheus Book Company, 1998.) Very helpful insight into temperament and character, and thus quite useful for discerning matters of calling.

Jane A.G. Kise, David Stark, and Sandra Krebs Hirsh. *LifeKeys.* (Minneapolis, MN: Bethany House, 1996.) While not quite a workbook, still a highly-interactive book with great instructions for exercises to help you discern a greater sense of calling.

Florence Littauer. *Personality Plus.* (Tarrytown, NY: Fleming H. Revell Compnay, 1995.) Good insights here into matters of personality and temperament, and their effect on communication.

Os Guinness. *The Call: Finding and Fulfilling the Central Purpose of Your Life.* (Nashville, TN: Thomas Nelson, 2003.) Great content here from a man who is both scholarly and pastoral in his approach to thinking biblically about the call God gives to people.

Aubrey Malphurs. *Maximizing Your Effectiveness: How to Discover and Develop Your Divine Design.* (Grand Rapids, MI: Baker, 2003.) This one is the basis for the material I used in seminary, and is wonderful in both its comprehensive approach and its pastoral style.

Raph T. Mattson and Arthur F. Miller, Jr. *Finding a Job You Can Love.* (Phillipsburg, NJ: P&R, 1982.) Here is a fine book on understanding calling and its relationship to effectiveness and contentment. The authors have worked in recruiting for decades, and have great sensibility about their material.

On Candidacy, Placement, & Transition

Michael J. Anthony and Mick Boersma. *Moving On, Moving Forward.* (Grand Rapids, MI: Zondervan, 2007.) A solid guide to the process of pastoral transition. This book is geared toward the existing pastor moving from one call to another, and based largely on anecdotal experience and testimony.

Kennon L. Callahan. *A New Beginning for Pastors and Congregations.* (San Francisco, CA: Jossey-Bass, 1999.) This consultant compiles years of experience and many testimonies into a solid book on forging a strong beginning to a new pastoral ministry.

John R. Cionca. *Before You Move: A Guide to Making Transitions in Ministry.* (Grand Rapids, MI: Kregel Publications, 2004.) Previously published as *Red Light, Green Light*, this updated version offers one of the best rubrics for considering transition that I have encountered. Much of this content will be helpful to the seminary candidate in evaluating opportunities; the book will prove exponentially more valuable when he believes his first call is coming to a close.

Christopher C. Moore. *Opening the Clergy Parachute.* (Nashville, TN: Abingdon Press, 1995.) Another volume focused on pastors in existing calls shifting to a new ministry, but there is still insight to be gained from this helpful and pastoral book.

Roy M. Oswald, James M. Heath, and Ann W. Heath. *Beginning Ministry Together.* (Herndon, VA: The Alban Institute, 2003.) Good material here on beginning a new ministry well— and also on ending an existing ministry well. Both are important, and while you hope your predecessor will have left well, what will be valuable in this book is the material on making a strong start.

Roy M. Oswald. *New Beginnings: A Pastorate Start Up Workbook.* (Herndon, VA: The Alban Institute, 1989.) Another helpful guide from Oswald on how to begin a new ministry well.

Joseph L. Umidi. *Confirming the Pastoral Call.* (Grand Rapids, MI: Kregel Publications, 2000.) While a significant section of this book is aimed at search committees, even that content is helpful for insight into the work and process of the search committee. The remaining content, focusing on pastoral candidates, is great material.

On Pastoral Ministry

Richard Baxter. *The Reformed Pastor.* (Carlyle, PA: Banner of Truth Trust, 1997.) One of the classics from the puritans on pastoral ministry, there's much to be learned and found here.

Philip Douglass. *What Is Your Church's Personality?* (Phillipsburg, NJ: P&R Books, 2008). Here is wisdom rarely found, or even understood, elsewhere: how the dynamics of your congregation's temperament and personality affects their expectations, relationships, communication, and community life. This one is also great for candidates considering a call.

Appendix A: Recommended Reading

John F. Evans. *A Guide to Biblical Commentaries & Reference Works*. (Oakland, TN: Doulos Resources, 2010.) This one will save you a lot of time and money as you begin new studies and grow your library of commentaries.

D. Martyn Lloyd-Jones. *Preaching & Preachers*. (Grand Rapids, MI: Zondervan, 1972.) Considered by many to be the finest preacher of the 20th century, "the Doctor" is an authoritative voice on this topic and a great read.

Donald MacNair. *The Practices of a Healthy Church*. (Phillipsburg, NJ: P&R Books, 1999.) A masterful work on what healthy congregational life and ministry looks like, and how to achieve it. This should be a guidebook for every session, board, or classis in every congregation!

Aubrey Malphurs. *Values-Driven Leadership*. (Grand Rapids, MI: Baker, 1996.) Understanding core values (your own and those of your congregation) will go far to help your pastoral ministry thrive and keep a healthy focus.

Eugene Peterson. *Five Smooth Stones for Pastoral Work*. (Grand Rapids, MI: Baker, 1992.) Peterson's insights into the heart of pastoral ministry are profound and refreshing.

—. *Working the Angles*. (Grand Rapids, MI: Baker, 1987.) This book challenged and changed most of what I understood pastoral ministry to be about.

William Still. *The Work of the Pastor*. (London: Paternoster Publishing, 1996.) One of the finest (and shortest!) books on pastoral ministry that I've ever read.

Charles H. Spurgeon. *Lectures To My Students*. (Peabody, MA: Hendrickson, 2010.) Another classic, these lectures will enrich and delight you in your anticipation of your coming ministry.

On "Getting Things Done" (GTD) & Productivity

David Allen. *Getting Things Done: The Art of Stress-Free Productivity*. (New York: Viking, 2001.) This is the guide for Allen's system, which has a cult-like following all its own. There is much to glean here for managing time and tasks well for pastoral ministry.

—. *Ready For Anything: 52 Productivity Principles for Work & Life*. (New York: Penguin, 2003.) Allen's follow-up volume offering additional principles and tips for GTD and other general aspects of productivity.

Peter F. Drucker. *The Effective Executive: The Definitive Guide to Getting the Right Things Done*. (New York: Collins, 2006.) Drucker, a master at organizational management, and is definitely worth reading. This one is a great guide to prioritization.

Merlin Mann. Inbox Zero (website: http://inboxzero.com/). Merlin is a whiz at handling productivity from a digital angle. Every pastor should read his stuff on "Inbox Zero" as well as other great insight from Merlin.

On Pastor's Wives & Family Life

Lorna Dobson. *I'm More than a Pastor's Wife: Authentic Living in a Fishbowl World*. (Grand Rapids, MI: Zondervan, 2003.) Easy to read, with a realistic perspective and a good sense of humor about the struggle of pastor's wives.

Appendix A: Recommended Reading

Lynn Dugan. *Heart to Heart with Pastor's Wives: Twelve Women Share the Wisdom They've Gained as Partners in Ministry.* (Ventura, CA: Regal Books, 1994.) While out of print, this one is worth finding a used copy of.

Diane Langberg. *Counsel for Pastor's Wives.* (Grand Rapids, MI: Zondervan, 1988.) A licensed counselor, Langberg offers great words of healing for those who have been stung in the unique role of pastor's wife.

Lisa McKay. *You Can Still Wear Cute Shoes: And Other Great Advice from an Unlikely Preacher's Wife.* (Colorado Springs, CO: David C. Cook Publishing, 2010). I recommend this one especially for seminary wives who have never been ministry wives before. There's great advice here for getting started as a pastor's wife.

Clara E. Molina. *The Pastor's Wife, Missionary to the World: The Dos and Don'ts of a Pastor's Wife.* (Bloomington, IN: CrossBooks Publishing, 2009.) There's a lot of great content here, and it's a worthwhile guide for any pastor's wife, particularly those who are new to the ministry life. Good advice about parenting and ministering to children as well.

Just Between Us (Magazine; for more information, visit: http://www.justbetweenus.org/). From the wisdom and leadership of Jill Briscoe (herself a pastor's wife for decades), this magazine is a great bi-monthly resource for ministry wives.

Pastors' Wives.org (Website; see: http://www.pastorswives.org/). A good website dedicated to encouraging pastor's wives, including an active discussion forum.

Parakaleo (Ministry; for more information, visit: http://parakaleoministry.org/). This ministry is particularly focused on ministering to (coming alongside, which is what "parakaleo means in Greek) the wives of church planters.

Appendix B:
Questions & Answers

Over the years I have collected a number of questions that I was asked as a candidate; I have also developed many questions that I myself might ask. In this appendix I'll give you a healthy sampling of my collections, including those that I have been asked, those that I would ask myself, and some general advice about approach with regard to answering questions.

Questions I Have Been Asked[1]

Personal & Family
1. Tell us about yourself— who is Ed Eubanks?
2. How did you come to know Christ?
3. Please give a brief testimony of your Christian experience.
4. What are your hobbies and special interests?
5. What about our position description made you excited about considering our church?
6. What are your spiritual gifts?
7. There are two kinds of people— visionaries and task-oriented. Where do you place yourself?
8. Tell us about your personal organizational skills— how do you keep yourself organized?
9. What is your passion?
10. Tell us about your family.
11. What are some difficult issues your family faces?
12. Are your children be in public or Christian schools, or do you home-school them?
13. Is your wife persuaded of your call to pastoral ministry?
14. How do you anticipate her being involved in your ministry?
15. In what areas do you have particular weaknesses?
16. What are your greatest strengths personally?
17. What is your wife's role in the church?
18. Is she willing to teach a women's Bible study or take a position on the WIC Council?
19. Tell us about your current financial situation.
    i. Do you have significant debts?

---

[1] This is a compilation of questions I've been asked, and not a list from a single opportunity. Therefore, you may sometimes notice questions that are somewhat redundant, and others that are completely contradictory.

ii. What are your financial needs?
20. Have you ever been under church discipline and if so for what?
21. Have you ever been charged with or convicted of a felony? If yes, please explain.
22. Have you ever been accused of or disciplined for sexual misconduct, child or spousal abuse, or financial improprieties? If yes, from what congregation, presbytery, or classis? Please explain.

Spiritual Life & Growth
1. Regarding your personal devotional life, briefly describe your approach and practice.
2. Are you quick to admit when you are wrong and seek forgiveness? Do you quickly repent before your wife and children when you have wronged them? Is repentance a consistent part of your life?
    i. Would your wife and children agree with this answer?
    ii.. Give a recent example.
3. Define discipleship.
4. Are you being discipled now?
5. What makes you squirm? What questions (in discipleship) are the most difficult to answer?
6. What do you struggle with?
7. Are you currently discipling anyone?
8. On our scale for ministry skills (1-2=acquiring; 3-5=functional; 6=others come to you as a mentor; 7=expert, could teach on it) where do you rank yourself on discipleship?
9. Of those you have discipled, have they caught the vision for what discipleship is about and are they dscipling others too?

Candidacy & Placement
1. What kind of church are you looking for?
2. Have you thought about what goals you will have in a new call?
3. What have you done to prepare for this interview?
4. Why our church?
5. Why do you want to be an assistant pastor and not a senior or solo pastor?
6. Why do you want to be a solo pastor and not an assistant/associate pastor?
7. Are you pursuing other opportunities?
8. Have you ever been to this area (where the church is)?
9. What do you know about this area?
10. If you get the position, what is the most important thing you can do for the congregation?
11. Tell us about _____ (a person from my reference list).
12. Tell us about ___ (high-profile person I have known).
13. What would you like for us to know about you that the Ministerial Data Form doesn't tell?

Appendix B: Questions & Answers

Pastoral Ministry & Philosophy of Ministry
1. What are the core values that define your vision for ministry?
2. How do you handle conflict between people within the church?
3. What are the greatest strengths in your ministry?
4. What do you consider to be the primary areas for your own personal growth?
5. What aspects of the pastor's job do you like most?
    i. The least?
6. What has been the clearest evidence of God's blessing on your ministry?
7. What goals and objectives do you have for your ministry?
8. Detail your perfect job description.
9. Describe the type of person to whom you would be able to most effectively minister.
    i. Next, describe the type of person to whom you would find it most difficult to minister
10. Which churches/ministers in our denomination would you say have most influenced your philosophy of ministry (list at least three)?
11. Briefly describe your role and style as a leader.
12. How do people change and what would you do to promote sincere transformation among people in your church?
13. Please describe your approach to evangelism.
14. What is your present involvement in evangelism?
15. Describe your relationship with the officers in your church.
16. What do you do for leadership training for church officers or would do as a senior pastor?
17. What does leadership training mean to you, and where do you rank yourself (on our scale)?
18. What objectives do you have for your relationship to potential elders in a church?
19. Given your bent towards academia and writing, how would you marry that with your job?
20. What does Marcie bring to your ministry besides just being your helpmate? What is her passion?
21. Briefly describe your understanding of the nature and purpose of preaching and type of sermons you normally preach?
22. What does this statement mean: "Every good sermon should have both law and gospel?"
23. How does the "historic-redemptive unity" of the Bible bear on preaching an OT and a NT text?
24. Do you think it is possible and/or desirable to include Christ in every sermon? Explain.
25. What translation do you preach out of?
26. Who is the best preacher in [our denomination] right now?
27. Describe your philosophy of worship.

28. What style of worship do you favor? (traditional, liturgical, contemporary, blended, other)? List several churches that have shaped your perspective in this regard.
29. Describe how worship style reflects or forms our theology. In other words, does the way we worship effect, change or form our beliefs? If so, what does the above style [referring to another question] communicate?
30. What elements do you believe should be generally included in a worship service?
31. What type of music and instrumentation do you believe are acceptable or unacceptable for a morning worship service?
32. Are there any elements or activities that some include in a worship service that you believe should not be included?
33. We are trying to grow a Presbytery in this area, would you be supportive and active in this process?
34. What do you envision being your primary responsibilities as an assistant pastor?
35. What do you see as the greatest dangers for an assistant pastor? The greatest challenges?
36. Describe briefly how you would go about carrying out your responsibilities as an assistant pastor at our church?

Church Ministry
1. What does church administration mean to you?
2. What is your experience with men's ministry?
3. What is your experience with small groups?
4. Do you visit members of the church that are shut-in or in rest homes?
5. What is your ideal of ministering to young adults and singles?
6. How do you feel about small groups and prayer meetings in homes?
7. Using our scale, how would you rank yourself on teamwork?
8. How do you work with others during times of conflict? Give an example of when you have handled it well and when you haven't.
9. What is your experience with older members in the church?
10. What are your views on the church supporting missionaries?
11. What were or are the most effective programs in your church that you have been involved in?
12. What is your vision concerning world missions? Have you taken any trips personally? How do you see yourself helping our church get more involved in missions?
13. What is your understanding of the community in which our church is ministering?

Hot Topics & Issues
1. What do you believe the role of women in the church should be?
2. Please describe your view regarding ministry opportunities for women in the church. Specifically address what role a woman may have in the worship service and in what contexts and to whom she may teach.

3. What are your thoughts on the church, youth, or WIC having fund raiser for special projects?
4. What do consider profaning the Sabbath in relations to activities after church services? (examples: watching TV. playing sports, shopping or going out to eat).
5. How do you feel about women wearing slacks or capri pants to church?
6. What are your views concerning the so-called "charismatic gifts" of the Spirit including speaking in tongues, word of knowledge and healing?
7. How often do you believe the sacrament of Communion should be observed and why?

10 Questions I Would Ask A Search Committee...

...Or maybe sets of questions; this is a list of over 50 questions that I have tried to ask, grouped into categories to make it (a little) easier to try to get to real answers.

- **(Regarding church description)** Describe the church to us; if you were describing the church to an out-of-town visitor, what would be the key elements that you would include in your description? What are the various ministries of the church, and how would you characterize them? Is the church currently in a growth trend, and if so how is that growth affecting what goes on in the day-to-day ministries of the church? Has the church seen growth primarily by transfer of membership, or by conversion (and how many conversions has she seen in the last year)? Give a brief description of each of the following ministries in the church, and how they are overseen: small group ministry, women's ministry, evangelism ministry, discipleship ministry (if separate from small group).
- **(Regarding community)** How is this church engaged in encouraging fellowship through inter-generational relationships? How is she engaged in encouraging fellowship through cooperation and co-ministry with sister churches in the area?
- **(Regarding current/former pastor(s))** What strengths and values were sought in the calling of the current/former pastor? How does/did he relate to other staff members—as members of his flock, co-laborers/partners in ministry, etc.? How involved in leadership and activities is/was his wife? Does/did he and his family socialize generally within or outside the church?
- **(Regarding the Session and Diaconate)** What does the Session see as its primary duties? What does the Diaconate see as its primary duties? How often are ruling elders and deacons rotated, and how many terms are they expected to serve? What is the general attitude of ruling elders or deacons who are not active on the Session/Diaconate? What is the process for training and preparing new ruling elders and deacons?
- **(Regarding other leadership/administration)** Is there a committee system in place– if so, how does it work, what relationship does it have with the Session/Diaconate, what does it do that could not be done otherwise? What sort of support staff does the church have? How does the church budget work, and who develops it? How often are staff performance and salary evaluations done, and by whom?

- **(Regarding general philosophy of ministry)** What are the areas of ministry that have really shined in this church? What areas of ministry have had particular struggles? What are the areas of ministry that you believe should get the primary focus from the pastor? What areas of ministry should be handled by volunteer leadership?
- **(Regarding particular ministries)** What are the particulars of the focused ministries of this church (children's, youth, college, singles, women's, elderly, small groups, evangelism, other)? What are the histories of each of these ministries? What are the hopes and expectations that the congregation has for them? What consideration has been given for staffing of these ministries— are they typically staff-led or volunteer-led, and how might that change?
- **(Regarding church finances)** What is the annual budget of the church? Who makes the decisions for the budgeting process? How have budgeting trends changed over the past 5-20 years? How have the stayed the same? What are the church's policies/methods for major expenses, such as building projects? What significant expenses do you anticipate this church facing over the next five years?
- **(Regarding pay package)** What is the current or expected salary package for the pastor? How does it include or exclude the following: housing, health insurance, retirement savings, vacation, continuing education/study leave, sabbatical, ministry-related expense reimbursement? How often will consideration be given to raises and cost-of-living increases? Will some type of performance review be given on a regular basis?
- **(Regarding pastor's family matters)** What sort of housing would be appropriate for the pastor– what neighborhoods, proximity to the church, etc.? What sort of expectations are there for the pastor's wife? What roles have the wives of other pastors and staff members taken?

Always Be Prepared To Give An Answer

As an example of how to approach interview questions (either on the phone or in-person), I will provide you with three anticipated questions for your upcoming interview(s). Be assured of this: you will almost certainly be asked these questions directly (as in the case of #1) or others like them (#2 and #3).

In each case, I'll discuss my answers— why I answer the way that I do, and how you should think about your answers for similar questions.

Question #1:
"Tell us about your greatest weakness."
Here's a basic three-part answer to this question:[2]

---

[2] This advice is adapted from an audio podcast called "Manager Tools" (http://www.manager-tools.com). Mike and Mark offer a lot more insight into how to understand the question, identify a good weakness, and even things like presentation of the answer. I would encourage everyone to have a listen to their advice.

1. *Qualify your answer*— in other words, state outright that this is not your struggle in every moment. Say, "sometimes" or "in certain situations" or some other like qualification.
2. *State a real weakness.* Don't soft-pedal or understate, and don't find something utterly irrelevant to the job.
3. *Tell what you are doing to improve on it.* Notice the present active tense— this is not what you plan or hope to do, but the action you are in the process of taking to strengthen what is weak.

As for me, here's something akin to the answer I'll give:

In situations where I have a conflict with someone else, I sometimes have difficulty accepting my part of the responsibility for the conflict and responding appropriately. In those moments I become defensive, rather than apologizing for my errors and seeking repentance. In the past, this has caused tension in relationships, and has hindered me in ministry. I have learned a lot about dealing with my own pride and sin through studying Ken Sande's *Peacemaker*, and I've recently begun reading Miroslav Volf's *Free of Charge: Giving and Forgiving in a Culture Stripped of Grace* which is teaching me a lot about living relationships more graciously. I have also been dialoging about this problem with my friend Dan Zink, who is Professor of Christian Counseling at Covenant Seminary.

Question #2

Another question I anticipate getting, at least in some interviews, is regarding current "hot topic" issues. Every denomination has it's controversies and conflicts (if they aren't theological, as they often are in the PCA, they may be ecclesiological or even just matters of pragmatism). I've posted about how to understand the relative importance of these issues (see here and here), and early on I posted some thoughts about how to think about them (see here and here). Now I'll talk about how I would approach answering questions about them.

Honesty

First and foremost, candidates should deal with issues honestly. By this I mean two things: be honest about what you believe, and be honest about what you know.

Do you have a position on topic X? Then state it concisely. If you believe in the practice of paedo-communion, struggle with accepting infant baptism, or consider yourself a strict reconstructionist, say so. If you think that pastors must wear robes in the pulpit or that worship should include only Psalms in singing, be upfront about it. Don't try to hide or mask your beliefs in complex, esoteric, or misleading language, but put it in plain terms. Why would you want to imply that you don't believe what you do? If you've reached conclusions about these or other issues, you should see it as your obligation to profess those conclusions at this time.

On the other hand, if you haven't reached conclusions about an issue— or if you simply don't know enough about it to say— then admit this plainly, as well. It is perfectly acceptable to acknowledge that you are undecided or uninformed about them. No one can keep up with all of the issues and discussions and still be attentive to study, ministry, or family. If they happen to ask about something you know about, great— but if you don't know, just say, "I don't know."

Charity

The folks interviewing you are listening as much to how you answer as they are to what you answer. You may be utterly convinced that your position is true; thus, Ephesians 4 requires that you speak that truth "in love."

Said another way: when you are asked about a hot topic, the chances are that it is because the committee or even the whole church has encountered it in some way. Do you know what way that is? Are you confident that every member of the committee— and the church— will agree with your perspective on the matter? Would you be comfortable if the most outspoken opponent of your position were in the room? If you cannot answer these questions with a confident "yes" then you should re-think how you state your position.

The candidacy interview is not an inherent opportunity to instruct and correct the committee or team interviewing you. It is not your job (yet!) to shepherd them to a new level of understanding about difficult issues. You will demonstrate a respect for the dignity of their role as members of the search team if you deal with them charitably.

Humility

Even if you are convinced of your position, take care to hold loosely onto it loosely enough that you don't put ideas before people. (the singular exception is, of course, if you are asked about one of those "Primary Issues"— but of course that shouldn't fall under the category of "hot topics.")

I was recently confronted with the reality of this in my own life. A dear friend mentioned that, at times, it seems like I don't care about what other people think of me. This may be because I regard truth highly enough that I would rather be in accordance with the truth than compromise but keep the esteem of others. But my friend remarked how this sometimes made her feel rejected, as if I didn't appreciate being loved. When it comes to that, I've sinned pridefully, even though my intentions were the opposite.

Along similar lines, my friend and hero Joe Novenson commented about one of the current discussions in the PCA, sometimes known as Auburn Avenue Theology— so called because it centers around ideas first introduced at a theological conference held at Auburn Avenue Presbyterian Church. Joe reminded me of the humility needed when he said, "Before Auburn Avenue was a theology, it was a church." That church is not essentially the ideas behind that theology, but the people of her membership.

Approaching these questions with honesty, charity, and humility, here is how I might answer a difficult question:

Q: What is your perspective on Federal Vision?

I believe that the questions raised by the proponents of a Federal Vision view are important, valuable concerns about our understanding and practice of the sacraments. In some ways, I applaud the men who have raised these questions, and I do not believe that they have always been dealt with in a loving, brotherly manner— which has prevented fruitful, productive discussion from taking place. To be perfectly candid, I have not studied the writings of those who promote the Federal Vision view in depth, nor am I familiar with the historical writings that they appeal to with a level of confidence to comment. I have read several summaries of the issue, including some that are sympathetic, if not supportive, of Federal Vision theology, and from what I have read of these I cannot say that I fully agree with any of the main points of discussion. I am not comfortable claiming a decided position, however, nor am I convinced in any way that those who hold a Federal Vision perspective should be seen as unorthodox or unbiblical in their convictions.

Question #3

This may seem like a subject to fit under the category of "hot topics" but in reality, this topic has matured beyond that point.

While once a matter of debate similar to that of other theological controversy— which is to say, largely theoretical and abstract for most— the question of what role women have in the local congregation is now anything but abstract or theoretical. Indeed, one who cannot answer this question to the satisfaction of his constituents will find one portion or another quite concerned with what the future holds.

The reasoning behind this is several-fold, in my analysis:

We cannot begin anywhere except the fact that our forefathers in the Church have mishandled this question terribly. Accusations hurled at the Church of misogyny and male chauvinism in years past were not far off the mark, at least as far as the practice of the Church goes.

This poor practice in the past (and to a lesser degree in the present) has unfortunately been tied to the theological truths that were (mis)used to justify such action, so much that these truths have themselves become targets for skepticism. Coupled with a looser hold to the authority of the Scriptures, this is a treacherous association; however, even when the authority of Scripture is upheld, then the trustworthiness of the leadership that applies Scripture is weakened by poor practices.

None of this is helped in any way by the fact that mature, godly men serving in strong, careful leadership roles are more scarce today than ever. While refreshing, it is often a surprising exception to find a great elder who can lead women while esteeming their dignity. The absence of men who can handle this balance well is more the norm than the exception.

Meanwhile, a growing number of Christian women are becoming mature to the point of surpassing their male counterparts, and they take their mature faith seriously. Thus, when called upon to lead, they do not shy away. More women than ever are, for example, pursuing training in seminaries, which prepares them well for leadership in a local congregation.

The question then becomes: in what capacity should a woman have leadership in the local church?

Without going much further into the underpinnings of an answer, I'll simply offer what mine is— hoping that there is enough there for you to intuit some of the rationale. Here's how I would answer the question immediately above:

I think the first thing that must be said is that women have been dealt with poorly in the Church at large, and more particularly in the Presbyterian Church in America, and they have not been given the dignity and respect they deserve as sisters in Christ and co-laborers for the Kingdom. I believe that there is much repentance and reparation to be done in that area, and that it is only with the gracious forgiveness of the women in the church that we can even begin to move further in considering the question.

That said, I believe that there is much available to women as opportunities for service and leadership within the local congregation. Traditionally, women have been offered leadership opportunities in Children's Ministry, Youth Ministry, and Women's Ministry, and these remain wonderful opportunities for women who are called to them. However, there are many other areas of church life and ministry that the gifts and abilities that are unique to women, or at least stronger in them, are a good fit: mercy ministry, hospitality, lay leadership development, and congregational care are a few that come to mind.

Furthermore, many women have gifts and abilities that equal or surpass those of their male counterparts, and in the appropriate contexts they should be encouraged and empowered to exercise them. My understanding of the Scriptural teaching on what women can and cannot do tells me that, apart from leading and teaching in corporate worship, women are free to perform whatever tasks a non-ordained man may do. In other words, if a woman is gifted for teaching, she may teach— provided that the context is not teaching in worship.

One final distinction on the matter: concerning the question of women as deacons or elders, I believe it is Scripturally forbidden, and therefore prohibited for practice today, for women to be ordained as elders. I think that a reasonable case could be made from Scripture in favor of ordaining women to the office of deacon, which is defined by Scripture as essentially an office of service. However, the rules of government in the PCA outlined by the Book of Church Order forbid this, and unless this were to change I believe it would be unethical— given the vows that I am prepared to take for my own ordination— to go against these rules. I am, however, grateful that the Book of Church Order allows for the appointment of godly men and women to assist the Diaconate in their duties.

Appendix C:
Survey Instrument

The following survey was presented to Master of Divinity graduates of Covenant Theological Seminary (St. Louis, MO) in the summer and fall of 2004. The survey was sent to almost 350 graduates, spanning more than five years of graduating classes, in a variety of ministry contexts: some in active ministry (in the Presbyterian Church in America as well as over a dozen other denominations), some pursuing further education and training, and some who were not (or were no longer) in ministry. Note: because the survey was done in cooperation with the seminary, a few questions were specific to Covenant Seminary (abbreviated as "CTS") classes and education, and/or to those in a Presbyterian denomination; most, however, would be applicable to any seminary graduate from any institution.

Pastoral Candidacy Survey

This survey is primarily for graduates who accepted a call to vocational ministry upon graduation from Covenant Seminary. If you are unsure whether you fit into this category, please answer all questions which apply to you. If you know for certain that you did NOT transition into vocational ministry after graduation, please write your name at the end of this survey and leave the rest blank, then return it to us in the accompanying envelope.

Please write the letter for the <u>best</u> answer in the space provided for each of the multiple-choice questions. For some of the questions, a short answer is required; please provide one or two sentences for these.

General Information…
1. How long ago did you graduate from Covenant Seminary?
   — Less than 1 year
   — 1-2 years
   — 2-3 years
   — 3-4 years
   — 4-5 years
   — More than 5 years

Appendix C: Survey Instrument

Your Specific Call…

2. Which of the following best describes the vocational ministry position in which you served following graduation from Covenant Seminary?
   — Ordained church or Presbytery position (such as RUF or Church Planter)
   — Non-ordained church position
   — Non-ordained Presbytery/Synod or Denominational position
   — Parachurch position
   — Other (go to question #4)

3. If your answer to #2 was "A. Ordained Church or Presbytery position," which of the following best describes that position? (If your answer to #2 was anything other than "A," please go to question #4.)
   — Solo Pastor
   — Head Pastor of multiple-pastor church
   — Head Pastor over non-ordained ministerial (not administrative) staff
   — Associate/Assistant Pastor (general ministry)
   — Associate/Assistant Pastor (specific ministry; i.e., Youth, College, Small Groups, etc.—please specify:)
   — Campus Pastor (Reformed University Ministries, etc.)
   — Church Planter

4. If your answer to question #2 was any position not described in question #3, please give a brief description of that position below.

5. Are you still serving in that position? (If "no" then please state how long you served in that position.)
   — Yes
   — No (how long:)

6. If you replied "no" to question #5, are you still in a vocational ministry position?
   — Yes
   — No

7. If you replied "no" to question #5, would you still consider your first placement a "good" or "successful" placement? (That is, were the factors that led to your departure from that position things other than ministry-related factors?)
   — Yes
   — No

Candidacy Information…

8. Did you take Covenant Seminary's "Candidating & Transition into Ministry" class? (If "yes" then please indicate whether you took the class for credit.)
   — Yes (for credit? (yes or no)   )
   — No

9. If you took the "Candidating & Transition into Ministry" class, how important/helpful did you find the class in preparing for your candidacy process? Please use the following scale: 1= not important/helpful at all; 2= of very little

importance; 3= somewhat important/helpful; 4= important, but not essential; 5= essential to my candidacy.

10. When did you first begin the candidacy process in search of a ministry call? (E.g., when did you first send out a resume, Ministerial Data Form, make inquiry about a position, etc.?)
    — At or after graduation
    — 1-3 months before graduation
    — 4-6 months before graduation
    — 7-9 months before graduation
    — 10 months-1 year before graduation
    — more than 1 year before graduation

11. Approximately how long did your candidacy process take? (That is, how long after you began did you receive the call to the position which you eventually accepted?)
    — Less than one month
    — 1-3 months
    — 4-6 months
    — 7-9 months
    — 10 months – 1 year
    — more than 1 year

12. Approximately how many different opportunities did you contact during your candidacy efforts?
    — 1-2
    — 3-5
    — 6-10
    — 11-20
    — 20-35
    — more than 35

13. To what extent did you work with Covenant Seminary's Placement Office?
    — I did not know there was a placement office as CTS
    — I checked the "Hot List" occasionally
    — I checked the "Hot List" frequently
    — They occasionally sent out some resumes for me
    — I worked with them as closely and as often as possible

14. How early in the candidacy process did you begin working with the CTS Placement Office?
    — Not applicable
    — From the start
    — Near the start
    — About half-way through
    — Near the end

15. To what extent did you work with your denominational administrative or placement office?
    — I do not know if there is such an office for my denomination
    — I checked a "vacant pulpit/ministry opportunity" list occasionally
    — I checked a "vacant pulpit/ministry opportunity" list frequently
    — They occasionally sent out some resumes for me
    — I worked with them as closely and as often as possible
16. How early in the candidacy process did you begin working with your denominational placement office?
    — Not applicable
    — From the start
    — Near the start
    — About half-way through
    — Near the end
17. How did you first make contact with the church or organization with which you were eventually placed?
    — A friend or relative who was a part of that church or organization
    — A friend or relative who had some contact with that church or organization
    — Seminary placement service / "Hot List"
    — Home church / Presbytery (at the time of your candidacy)
    — Denominational administrative or placement office
    — Other (Please specify:)
18. What interaction, if any, did you have with that church or organization prior to pursuing the position you eventually accepted (e.g., pulpit supply, summer internship, etc.)? Please describe briefly.

People And Relationships…

19. Which of the following attitudes best describes your understanding of the concept of "networking"?
    — An unhealthy idea, common in the business world, in which every relationship is viewed from the perspective of personal gain.
    — A somewhat "professional" approach to relationships, in which some relationships are seen as beneficial beyond the normal extent of friendship and acquaintance.
    — A natural process of relating to others, sometimes benefiting from them and sometimes being of benefit to them.
    — A sense of community in which everyone serves one another toward the common benefit of all.
    — Other (please describe:)
20. To what extent did you utilize a "network" in your candidacy process?
    — This question is not applicable to me
    — I do not believe that "networking" is a biblical means of finding a ministry call.
    — I utilized a "network" but not to any great extent
    — I utilized a "network" to a great extent / to every extent

Appendix C: Survey Instrument

21. Who was included in the "network" that you utilized for placement? (Please indicate all that apply.)
    — My friends and former classmates
    — My home church pastor(s)
    — Other pastor(s) I knew in my home presbytery
    — Other pastor(s) I knew outside of my home presbytery
    — Others I knew who were staff of my denomination
    — Faculty and/or staff from the Seminary
    — Others not mentioned (please describe:)
    — All of the above
    — This question is not applicable to me
22. How did you first come to know the person(s) through which you first made contact with the church or organization with which you were eventually placed? Please describe briefly.

23. Please describe briefly what role your home church and/or presbytery (prior to/during seminary) played in your candidacy and placement.

24. Who was instrumental in the final placement decision? Please rank each of the following people or groups of people according to the scale given; also, please be sure to include at least one "5".
    1= not important; 2= of little importance; 3= somewhat important; 4= important, but not essential; 5=very important
    — Spouse
    — Friends/ former classmates
    — Home church pastor(s)
    — RUF pastor / college ministry staff
    — Members of the candidates/interns committee in my presbytery
    — Other pastor(s) in my home presbytery
    — Other pastor(s) outside of my home presbytery
    — Others who were staff of my denomination
    — Seminary faculty and/or staff
    — Other:
25. Please comment briefly on who the "5s" from question #24 were, and what role they played that was important.

Final Thoughts…
24. What one or two things would you do differently if you were facing graduation and candidacy again?

25. What was the best thing you did in your own candidacy? (That is, what one thing would you urge all who are currently involved in the candidacy process not to miss the opportunity to do?)

Optional Information...
Name:
Telephone #:
E-mail address:
Name of home church and/or Presbytery during seminary:
Are you willing to participate in a brief follow-up interview by telephone or e-mail, if necessary? (check one)
Yes
No

Appendix D:
Summary of Survey Results

The results for the survey (instrument provided in Appendix C) are below. Of the nearly 300 graduates queried, 170 (61%) responded to the survey. Of these, 37 responded that they were not in a ministry role, and therefore will factor out of many questions. Answer to the subjective questions are not provided in these results.

General Information...
1. How long ago did you graduate from Covenant Seminary?
   10 (7.5%)= Less than 1 year
   32 (24.1%)= 1-2 years
   25 (18.8%)= 2-3 years
   25 (18.8%)= 3-4 years
   22 (16.5%)= 4-5 years
   19 (14.3%)= More than 5 years

Your Specific Call...
2. Which of the following best describes the vocational ministry position in which you served following graduation from Covenant Seminary?
   102 (80.3%)= Ordained church or Presbytery position (such as RUF or Church Planter)
   13 (10.2%)= Non-ordained church position
   2 (1.6%)= Non-ordained Presbytery/Synod or Denominational position
   3 (2.4%)= Parachurch position
   7 (5.5%)= Other
3. If your answer to #2 was "A. Ordained Church or Presbytery position," which of the following best describes that position? (If your answer to #2 was anything other than "A," please go to question #4.)
   11 (10.9%)= Solo Pastor
   3 (3%)= Head Pastor of multiple-pastor church
   0= Head Pastor over non-ordained ministerial (not administrative) staff
   35 (34.7%)= Associate/Assistant Pastor (general ministry)
   29 28.6%)= Associate/Assistant Pastor (specific ministry; i.e., Youth, College, Small Groups, etc.—please specify)
   12 (11.9%)= Campus Pastor (Reformed University Ministries, etc.)
   11 (10.9%)= Church Planter

5. Are you still serving in that position? (If "no" then please state how long you served in that position.)
   93 (72%) Yes
   36 (28%) No (how long: average 28.4 months)
6. If you replied "no" to question #5, are you still in a vocational ministry position?
   32 (84.2%) Yes
   6 (15.8%) No
7. If you replied "no" to question #5, would you still consider your first placement a "good" or "successful" placement? (That is, were the factors that led to your departure from that position things other than ministry-related factors?)
   25 (71.4%) Yes
   10 (28.6%) No

Candidacy Information…
8. Did you take Covenant Seminary's "Candidating & Transition into Ministry" class? (If "yes" then please indicate whether you took the class for credit.)
   104 (80%) Yes (for credit? (yes or no) 61% YES)
   26 (20%) No
10. When did you first begin the candidacy process in search of a ministry call? (E.g., when did you first send out a resume, Ministerial Data Form, make inquiry about a position, etc.?)
    13 (11.6%)= At or after graduation
    4 (3.6%)= 1-3 months before graduation
    31 (27.7%)= 4-6 months before graduation
    32 (28.6%)= 7-9 months before graduation
    18 (16.1%)= 10 months-1 year before graduation
    14 (12.5%)= more than 1 year before graduation
11. Approximately how long did your candidacy process take? (That is, how long after you began did you receive the call to the position which you eventually accepted?)
    15 (12.3%)= Less than one month
    31 (25.4%)= 1-3 months
    33 (27%)= 4-6 months
    19 (15.6%)= 7-9 months
    15 (12.3%)= 10 months – 1 year
    9 (7.4%)= more than 1 year
12. Approximately how many different opportunities did you contact during your candidacy efforts?
    45 (36.6%)= 1-2
    24 (19.5%)= 3-5
    21 (17.1%)= 6-10
    19 (15.4%)= 11-20
    10 (8.1%)= 20-35
    4 (3.3%)= more than 35

13. To what extent did you work with Covenant Seminary's Placement Office?
    19 (16.5%)= I did not know there was a placement office as CTS
    32 (27.8%)= I checked the "Hot List" occasionally
    39 (33.9%)= I checked the "Hot List" frequently
    7 (6.1%)= They occasionally sent out some resumes for me
    18 (15.7%)= I worked with them as closely and as often as possible
14. How early in the candidacy process did you begin working with the CTS Placement Office?
    42 (34.1%)= Not applicable
    46 (37.4%)= From the start
    27 (22%)= Near the start
    5 (4.1%)= About half-way through
    3 (2.4%)= Near the end
15. To what extent did you work with your denominational administrative or placement office?
    47 (41.6%)= I do not know if there is such an office for my denomination
    22 (19.5%)= I checked a "vacant pulpit/ministry opportunity" list occasionally
    33 (29.2%)= I checked a "vacant pulpit/ministry opportunity" list frequently
    4 (3.5%)= They occasionally sent out some resumes for me
    7 (6.2%)= I worked with them as closely and as often as possible
16. How early in the candidacy process did you begin working with your denominational placement office?
    62 (52.1%)= Not applicable
    23 (19.3%)= From the start
    19 (16%)= Near the start
    10 (8.4%)= About half-way through
    5 (4.2%)= Near the end
17. How did you first make contact with the church or organization with which you were eventually placed?
    18 (16.1%)= A friend or relative who was a part of that church or organization
    15 (13.4%)= A friend or relative who had some contact with that church or organization
    25 (22.3%)= Seminary placement service / "Hot List"
    20 (17.9%)= Home church / Presbytery (at the time of your candidacy)
    9 (8%)= Denominational administrative or placement office
    25 (22.3%)= Other

People And Relationships...

19. Which of the following attitudes best describes your understanding of the concept of "networking"?

    2 (1.6%)= An unhealthy idea, common in the business world, in which every relationship is viewed from the perspective of personal gain.

    16 (12.9%)= A somewhat "professional" approach to relationships, in which some relationships are seen as beneficial beyond the normal extent of friendship and acquaintance.

    72 (58%)= A natural process of relating to others, sometimes benefiting from them and sometimes being of benefit to them.

    31 (25%)= A sense of community in which everyone serves one another toward the common benefit of all.

    0= Other

20. To what extent did you utilize a "network" in your candidacy process?

    23 (18.4%)= This question is not applicable to me

    1 (0.8%)= I do not believe that "networking" is a biblical means of finding a ministry call.

    41 (32.8%)= I utilized a "network" but not to any great extent

    60 (48%)= I utilized a "network" to a great extent / to every extent

21. Who was included in the "network" that you utilized for placement? (Please indicate all that apply.)

    11 (14.3%)= My friends and former classmates

    5 (6.5%)= My home church pastor(s)

    3 (3.9%)= Other pastor(s) I knew in my home presbytery

    2 (2.6%)= Other pastor(s) I knew outside of my home presbytery

    4 (5.2%)= Others I knew who were staff of my denomination

    2 (2.6%)= Faculty and/or staff from the Seminary

    6 (7.8%)= Others not mentioned

    30 (39%)= All of the above

    14 (18.2%)= This question is not applicable to me

24. Who was instrumental in the final placement decision? Please rank each of the following people or groups of people according to the scale given; also, please be sure to include at least one "5".

    1= not important; 2= of little importance; 3= somewhat important; 4= important, but not essential; 5=very important (results shown are averages of ratings)

    4.4= Spouse

    2.9= Friends/ former classmates

    3.1= Home church pastor(s)

    1.5= RUF pastor / college ministry staff

    1.4= Members of the candidates/interns committee in my presbytery

    1.9= Other pastor(s) in my home presbytery

    2.4= Other pastor(s) outside of my home presbytery

    1.9= Others who were staff of my denomination

    3.1= Seminary faculty and/or staff

    4.5= Other

Acknowledgements

Many thanks are in order, as this book has been a very long time in the making. Perhaps I should start by acknowledging, with much gratitude, the faculty and staff of Covenant Theological Seminary in St. Louis, especially for their cooperation in conducting the original survey that kicked off my research. Out of your kindness and gracious support, all of this has emerged. Thank you.

Several members of the Covenant Seminary faculty and administration were particularly helpful. Donald Guthrie served as a sounding board and mentor in the research process. Mark Dalbey opened doors to administrative resources, and later gave me a platform and voice to present early findings and reflections. Phil Douglass supervised my research project, and has continued to buttress my interest in pastoral transition. All of you have been such a great source of support, and you remain not only key men in the formation of my ministry but also good friends.

Likewise, there have been several friends whose feedback and frequent words of affirmation have been a shot in the arm along a sometimes-tedious path. Richard Burguet, Craig Dunham, Joel Hathaway, Michael MacCaughelty, David Stewart, and Adam Tisdale, I am so grateful for your brotherhood through all of this.

I would be remiss to overlook the many friends and fellow pastors who kindly responded to my e-mail requests for advice, case studies, and other information that eventually made this a better book. These friends include Rod Arters, Eric Ashley, Sara Bartley, Nick Batzig, Grant Beachy, Jeremy Bedenbaugh, Lou Best, Wade Bradshaw, Richard Burguet, Luke Calvin, Ray Cannada, John Carrico, Jim Codling, David Dennis, Lee Fletcher, Nick Gleason, Robbie Griggs, Matt Guzi, Pat Hickman, Jim Holland, Kris Holroyd, Jonathan Inman, Jeremy Jones, David Keithley, Jeffrey Lancaster, Tim LeCroy, Tim Lien, Michael MacCaughelty, Brian Martin, Tim Martin, Michael Mathews, James and Debbie McCormick, Dave McMurry, Jonathan Olsen, Kyle and Davina Perret, George Robertson, Mark Ryan, Matt Schilling, Ken Shomo, Nate Smith, Russell Smith, Brian Steadman, Mike and Susan Subracko, Kermit Summerall, Patrick Tebbano, Dave Thomas, Nathan Tircuit, Adam Tisdale, Seth Wallace, Michael Walters, Mark Warnock, Mark Weathers, Josh Willadsen, and Eric Zellner. I am certain that I have forgotten someone in this list; please know that you are not forgotten in my affections.

Thanks go out also to the men who offered words of endorsement to my work in this book: Rod Culbertson, Mark Dalbey, and Will Willimon have graciously lent me their names and reputations as well as the strength of their words. I am grateful, and pray that my work does not reflect poorly on any of these.

Of course, I cannot omit the acknowledgement due to my family: my mother, MaryAnn Crews, and my step-father, Jerry Frank Crews, have both been great supporters of my writing in general, and of this book in particular. My sister and brother-in-law, Ann Louise and Dave Schmitt, are constant source of support as well. Thanks is also due to my children, whose patience with my many hours holding a laptop instead of them, and whose curiosity and appreciation that "Daddy is making another book," have contributed to the completion of this work more than they can know. Most of all, my deep gratitude for the love, encouragement, and endurance of my beloved wife Marcie can never be expressed properly in words; Marcie, I am, as always, eternally thankful for your companionship and care, without which I would be barely half of the man I am.

Finally, I give thanks to my Lord and King, Who has called me into His service and granted me both the opportunities and experiences that gave way to this book's inception and completion. Praise God, from Whom all blessings flow!

About the Author

Rev. John Edgar Eubanks, Jr. was born in Columbia, South Carolina, in 1972. He received a Bachelor of Arts from the University of South Carolina, and a Master of Divinity from Covenant Theological Seminary. Ordained in the Presbyterian Church in America (PCA), Rev. Eubanks serves a congregation in Eads, Tennessee. Ed also serves as the Co-Director of Doulos Resources. Ed and his wife Marcie have four children.

Ed has been writing for publication since 1998, and has also published the *Covenant Discipleship Communicants' Curriculum*, which he co-authored with Richard L. Burguet; an updated edition of James M. Chaney's *William the Baptist* (of which Ed was the editor); *For All the Saints: praying for the church*; and *Grafted Into The Vine: rethinking biblical church membership* (part of the Strengthen The Church series of booklets). All of these titles are available through Doulos Resources. Ed has written numerous articles in print and online, as well. For more information about Ed, and to read more of his writing, visit his website: www.edeubanks.com.

About Doulos Resources

Our goal is to provide resources to support the church and kingdom, and to build up and encourage the pastors and leaders within the church. Our resources follow the model of Ephesians 4:12— "to prepare God's people for works of service, so that the body of Christ may be built up." We produce books, curricula, and other media resources; conduct research to advance our goals; and offer advice, counsel, and consultation. We are Reformed and Presbyterian, but not exclusively so; while we do not lay aside our theological convictions, we believe our resources may be useful across a broader theological and ecclesiastical spectrum.

Our goal with *From M.Div. to Rev.*, as with all of our resources, is to offer well-edited, high-quality, and useful materials at an affordable price that makes our resources accessible to congregations and members of the church.

If you are interested in ordering additional copies of *From M.Div. to Rev.*, or to order other materials that Doulos Resources offers, please visit our website: www.doulosresources.org. If you are ordering in quantity for a church or other ministry, contact us to inquire about a discount for quantity orders.

Doulos Resources Contact Information:
U.S. Mail:
195 Mack Edwards Drive
Oakland, TN 38060
USA
Telephone:
(901) 451-0356
Internet:
website: www.doulosresources.org
e-mail: info@doulosresources.org